Lessons in Liberty

Lessons in Liberty

Bob Barr

Published in Nashville, Tennessee, by TDG Media

Library of Congress Cataloging-in-Publication Data

ISBN 9780615226217

Printed in the United States of America

Dedication

This book is dedicated to my wife Jeri's and my
children, and our grandchildren–those born and yet to be
born–for they will have to live in the world we have wrought,
and for whom we have a sacred obligation to do all in our
power to bequeath to them a nation that not only preaches
Liberty but actually protects and furthers it.

Acknowledgements

This book would not have been possible without the help and able assistance of many people. My profound thanks to James Bovard for his meticulous research and excellent draftsmanship. To my campaign staff, led by my seasoned and capable campaign director, Russell Verney, go my deepest appreciation. And to the millions of my fellow Americans who share my frustration with the loss of personal Liberty at the hands of government leaders in both the Republican and Democratic parties, I urge them to keep the faith and keep working—change is coming and it will happen because of them.

Table of Contents

MY JOURNEY TO LIBERTY

I was born in Iowa City, Iowa, in 1948. My father, a West Point graduate, served with the Army Corps of Engineers and, after his retirement from the Army, he worked as a consulting engineer on projects in many states and countries around the world. From the time I was in the third grade until my graduation from high school in Tehran, Iran, in 1966, we lived in countries including Iraq, Canada, Peru, Panama, and Pakistan. Living in such diverse societies and under such different forms of governments (including military dictatorships) instilled in me from an early age a deep love for the freedom, individual liberty, and governance according to the rule of law we enjoy in the United States—an awareness that so many Americans fail to understand or simply take for granted.

I attended the University of Southern California from 1966 to 1970, receiving a bachelor's degree in international relations. During my early days at college, I was briefly a member of the Young Democrat Club at USC. Although my family was never especially politically active, between my sophomore and junior years in college, while I was visiting with my family in Malaysia (my father was working on a project in Saigon, South Vietnam, at the time), at my mother's suggestion I read Ayn Rand's seminal novel, *Atlas Shrugged*. Rand's brilliant work opened my eyes to the perils of Big Government and helped me understand why a nation cannot turn businessmen into serfs or bureaucrats without making almost everyone poor. Based in large measure on the excitement for the philosophy of objectivism that *Atlas Shrugged* ignited in me, I became active in USC's Young Republican Club and in the campus Objectivist Society chapter. I was also moved in this direction by Ronald Reagan, then in his first term as governor of California. His actions and public rhetoric in support of smaller government, individual responsibility and economic liberty, moved me deeply.

After I graduated from USC, I moved to Washington DC to study international affairs at George Washington University. After I was awarded my master's degree, I began working full-time for the Central Intelligence Agency, where I had served as an intern while in graduate school. During the nearly eight years I was with the CIA, I served as an analyst and then as assistant legislative counsel. The primary focus of the government's foreign intelligence operation during this period—in the 1970s—were the threats posed to America's interests by the Soviet Union and Communist China. Ayn Rand, who herself had fled from communist tyranny as a young woman in Soviet Russia, helped me recognize the grave peril the Soviet government posed to the world. I wanted to do whatever I could to make sure that "evil empire" could never extend its sway here. During these years, I also studied law at Georgetown University Law School, attending classes in the evening each night after a day's work at the Agency's headquarters in Langley, Virginia.

I obtained my Juris Doctor in 1977. The study of constitutional law and criminal law and procedure during my law school years, with their emphasis on individual liberty and the need to safeguard it, ultimately led me to focus my legal interests on criminal law. When I left the CIA in late 1978, I joined a small law firm in Atlanta, Georgia, where I was able to concentrate my practice in my chosen field. When I left the government, the Watergate scandals, which included serious allegations of abuse of the mechanisms of government (especially the foreign intelligence and federal law enforcement apparatus), impressed me with the inevitable drive by government to expand and ultimately abuse its powers, and therefore the need to constantly and proactively guard against such abuses. (While the abuses by the Nixon Administration in the late 1960s and early 1970s were serious, they merely foreshadowed the insidious, systemic abuses to follow in the years ahead by the administration of George W. Bush.)

In 1986, President Ronald Reagan appointed me to the United States Attorney for the Northern District of Georgia. following years (1986–1990), I led the prosecution of a number public corruption cases involving local, state, and federal officials including the prosecution of a sitting Republican member of the House of Representatives for obstruction of justice and perjury (coincidentally, the same charges that led to the impeachment of President Clinton in late 1998 and formed the basis for his trial in the Senate, for which I served as a manager). My office also led the prosecution of many high-level drug-trafficking and -laundering cases, including some involving Colombian drug cartels.

The case involving sitting Republican Congressman Pat Swindall, who at the time represented Georgia's Fourth District, was particularly interesting. The prosecution won me few friends within the Republican Party establishment in Georgia, leading even to then-Congressman Newt Gingrich denouncing me publicly as a "rogue US Attorney." Of course, when the jury in the case returned a guilty verdict, which was upheld on appeal, much of the criticism from Republicans quieted down. The entire process reinforced in my mind the principal that justice is—and must always be upheld to be—blind and that the American people's faith in the justice system was not misplaced.

Swindall had sought an $850,000 loan from an undercover IRS agent, who told him the cash was "probably drug money." The deal was structured to avoid triggering currency-reporting requirements designed to detect money laundering. (This was similar to provisions that tripped up New York governor Eliot Spitzer in 2008.) Swindall claimed he was not guilty because he was ignorant of the law. Interestingly, however, Swindall's colleague on the House Judiciary Committee (on which I was later to serve from 1995 to 2003), liberal Rep. Barney Frank (D-MA), came to Atlanta planning to testify on Swindall's behalf that it was understandable a congressman would be ignorant about amendments to federal money laundering statutes for which they voted, because members of Congress often paid little attention to what they were voting on. This was a most peculiar version of the Rule of Law: the people who make the law should be exempt from having any

: they voted for, because they didn't know
The trial judge did not allow Rep. Frank's
Swindall was convicted of lying to a grand
justice.

ed to the House of Representatives as part
ide that returned my then-party to majority
e first time in four decades; I proudly took
following January. The oath was clear and
straightforward (as was the similar oath I took when I was sworn in
as US Attorney in 1986), and stated in part: "I do solemnly swear
that I will support and defend the Constitution of the United States
against all enemies, foreign and domestic; that I will bear true faith
and allegiance to the same . . ." I took special satisfaction in the
oath because I believed our Constitution, including its first ten
amendments (the Bill of Rights), is probably the most magnificent
piece of writing set down by the hands of man.

I was one of seventy-three new Republican members of
Congress that took office in January 1995. I had high expectations
from the Republican leadership. I thought we had a historic, almost
divine opportunity to turn this nation around and once again make
government the people's servant instead of their master.

The Clinton administration had already gone on power-grabbing
rampages in his first two years in power—and I wanted to do what I
could to help restore government *under* the law, not *above* it.

I was disappointed when it became obvious that most of my
fellow Republican members of Congress were unwilling to use
much elbow grease to put federal agencies back on a leash. In the
summer of 1995, congressional committees finally looked into the
federal debacle at Waco, which began with an unjustified attack on
a private residence by the Bureau of Alcohol, Tobacco and
Firearms, and ended with the FBI sending in tanks and dousing the
residence with toxic gas while firing pyrotechnic grenades into the
building. It was no surprise that a fire burst out, leaving some
eighty men, women, and children dead at the end of that day.
Despite the stunning federal abuses, the Waco hearings were a
great disappointment, little better than those conducted in the

previous 103rd Congress under Democratic leadership. Under the Democrats, the Waco hearings were nothing more than a virtual lovefest, during which members of the Clinton administration responded to softball questions from their colleagues in the House with superficial answers, and Republican queries were ignored or glossed over with disdain, if not outright contempt.

The subsequent hearings conducted in the 104th Congress under GOP leadership, while replete with a much more extensive witness list, and with pointed, purposeful questions by me and other Republican interrogators, resulted in little of value at the end of the day. This was largely because neither of the two subcommittee chairmen heading the inquiry—Rep. Bill McCollum of Florida and Rep. Bill Zeliff of New Hampshire—were up to the job of conducting a tough, focused hearing, one they should have made clear from the outset that they—and not the Democrats—were in charge. For example, Rep. McCollum told us fellow Republicans that his top goal for the hearings was "to be remembered as a gentleman." Unfortunately, this meant he allowed federal agencies and the Clinton administration to keep the lid on some of the worst abuses they had committed. At the end of the hearings, it was clear the Republican House leadership had neither an understanding of nor a firm commitment to tough leadership through the powerful oversight responsibility of the Congress. The Waco hearings were followed a few months later by the similarly indecisive Whitewater hearings, led by then-chairman of the House Financial Services Committee, Iowa Rep. Jim Leach (on which committee I also served).

The Oklahoma City bombing in 1995 may have been the biggest event of my first year in Congress. The Clinton administration quickly sought to exploit the cold-blooded attack on a federal office building to squeeze Congress to reassert his position as a "relevant" president, and to capture a laundry list of new powers, primarily for the FBI. Because of my experience as a US Attorney and my role in the House Judiciary Committee, I ended up becoming the Republican point man for opposing the legislation. I worked with the American Civil Liberties Union, the National Rifle Association (to which I would be elected to the board of directors two years later in 1997), and several other organizations from across the ideological spectrum to help assure that any new legislation would not impale the Bill of Rights. The Anti-Terrorism and Death Penalty Enhancement Act entered the statute book in 1996 only after it had been stripped of its most dangerous provisions by an amendment I authored and shepherded on the floor of the House during debate.

As the 1990s proceeded, I was appalled at how Bill Clinton was turning the White House into an ethical wasteland. His 1996 reelection campaign violated numerous federal laws. He had taken campaign contributions from real or apparent agents of foreign governments and he gave at least one of them—John Huang—a top job at the Commerce Department. Huang, who delivered illegally laundered cash to the Clinton campaign, had access to top national security secrets at a time when he had close ties to a foreign corporation bound to the military and government of Communist China. On top of this, the Clinton administration had rushed a program to create more than a million new citizens prior to the 1996 elections—resulting in up to ten thousand foreign felons becoming US citizens without the appropriate background checks. Hillary Clinton said the purpose of the program was to "provide the Democrats with a strategic advantage."[1] Meanwhile, the Justice Department under Janet Reno was obstructing investigation of these abuses with every trick it could muster.

In November 1997, I shocked official Washington by filing impeachment inquiry papers in the House of Representatives. I sought to summon fellow members of Congress and the American people to recognize that Clinton, like Nixon, had committed crimes against the nation, and he deserved to be held accountable and punished for them.

Two months later, the Monica Lewinsky scandal erupted. I was the first member of Congress to call for Clinton to resign. The Lewinsky investigation and the impeachment process continued throughout 1998. The House voted to impeach Clinton on narrow grounds deriving solely from the Lewinsky scandal. Ken Starr was

1. Bob Barr, *The Meaning of Is* (Atlanta: Stroud and Hall, 2004), p. 27.

courageous and a brilliant lawyer, but his investigation focused only on the perjury and obstruction of justice obviously committed by President Clinton, and ignored the president's far more serious abuses. This was a strategic disaster. Still, even the grounds on which Clinton was charged should have been sufficient to turn him out of office. During the debate on the House floor, I pointed out that Clinton had violated "the unshakable right each one of us has to walk into a courtroom and demand the righting of a wrong."

The Senate had a failure of nerve when it came to—and during —the impeachment trial. Republicans were again more concerned with likeability and maintaining the decorum of their "gentlemen's club" than with upholding the rule of law and the standards set forth in our Constitution and its foundational documents, such as the Federalist Papers. As a result, Clinton escaped justice and Congress set a precedent of tolerating presidential lawlessness.

Even though Congress had successfully rebuffed most of the administration's earlier power grabs in the name of antiterrorism, the Justice Department never stopped trying to seize more prerogatives. In late 1998 or early 1999, an anonymous memo arrived in my congressional office. It originated at the top levels of the Justice Department—for discussion purposes only—and cataloged the authority the department hoped to wrangle from Congress should the agency ever declare a terrorism emergency. Most important, the agency wanted to expand the definition of terrorism to include practically any violent crime the government deemed politically motivated. Under existing law, more than fifty violations were considered terrorist acts. Not content with such already-broad powers, the Justice Department (especially the FBI) wanted the power to add crimes to this list without congressional approval. That would give the agency the ability to take over the investigation of any crime simply by reclassifying it as terrorism. The Justice Department also wanted to vastly expand its power to confiscate assets—without any criminal conviction—based almost solely on a mere accusation of terrorism. To make its job easier, the DOJ wanted ready access to any person's motel records, e-mail, bank account, travel records, and whereabouts. It wouldn't mind if each person's DNA could be collected and set aside. A genetic database certainly would be useful during a state of emergency.

In that era—pre-9/11, that is—we in the Congress rebuffed the Justice Department. The bureaucrats bided their time, waiting for the right hook to try again.

9/11, the Patriot Act, and Beyond

The terrorist attacks on 9/11 turned the political universe upside down. Within a matter of weeks, the number of Americans who trusted the government to do the right thing doubled. The Bush administration responded like politicians normally do—racing to seize as much power as it could, and clearly not stopping to admit error (going so far as to award former CIA Director George Tenet with the Medal of Freedom, apparently for *failing* to piece together the intelligence evidence of a likely terrorist attack).

In the immediate wake of the 9/11 attacks, the Bush administration submitted legislation to Congress that would have given federal agencies almost free rein to do as they pleased. To protect America against terrorism, the USA PATRIOT Act (Uniting and Strengthening America by Providing Appropriate Tools Required to Intercept and Obstruct Terrorism Act) empowered federal agencies to treat almost anyone suspected of violating any law like a terrorist. Constitutional rights would have been gutted, if not shredded.

The Bush administration permitted its top Justice Department officials to testify at only one hearing before each of the House and the Senate Judiciary Committee prior to a congressional vote on the legislation. At the House hearing, I challenged Assistant Attorney General Michael Chertoff over why the administration was exploiting the 9/11 attacks to snare so many new powers: "Why is it necessary to propose a laundry list of changes to criminal law generally and criminal procedure generally to cast such a wide net? And why is it necessary to rush this through? Does it have anything to do with the fact that the department has sought many of these authorities on numerous other occasions, has been unsuccessful in obtaining them, and now seeks to take advantage of what is obviously an emergency situation?"[2]

Chertoff replied: "I think the department was very careful when we put this together not to engage in the temptation to treat it as a laundry list of all the things we wished we could have."[3]

I was completely unsatisfied with his answer, but Judiciary Committee Chairman James Sensenbrenner announced that my time had expired.

Many liberals on the Judiciary Committee were as appalled as I was at the proposed legislation. The Committee worked through the administration's proposal in good faith and crafted a compromise bill, which passed by a vote of 36 to 0—a near-miracle, considering the committee was very ideologically polarized. Committee chairman Sensenbrenner commented: "This shows that with respect to conflicting viewpoints and a bipartisan approach, the legislative process works. We are all the winners. The terrorists are the losers."[4]

But the Bush administration considered itself a loser because it did not get all the power it wanted. The administration railroaded its wish-list bill through the Senate. Then the White House squeezed House leaders and got them to scuttle the Judiciary Committee compromise bill and replace it with the wish-list bill. House Speaker Dennis Hastert forced the House to vote on the bill on the same day it was submitted and prohibited any amendments on the floor.

The administration also undermined congressional deliberations by issuing an obviously bogus terror alert. On the day before the House voted on the Patriot Act, the FBI announced: "Certain information, while not specific as to target, gives the government reason to believe that there may be additional terrorist attacks within the United States and against US interests overseas

---

2 "Hearing of the House Judiciary Committee," Federal News Service, September 24, 2001.

3 Ibid.

4 Robert Pear and Neil Lewis, "House Panel Approves Bill Expanding Surveillance," *The New York Times*, October 4, 2001.

over the next several days."[5] Many federal terrorism experts opposed issuing the alert because there was no solid evidence to justify it. The FBI may have recognized the bogus nature of the threat, based on its official warning at a Web page titled www.fbi.gov/pressrel/pressrel01/*skyfall*.htm. Regardless, the headline on the front page of *The Washington Post* on the day the House voted on the Patriot Act proclaimed: "Terrorist Attacks Imminent, FBI Warns."[6]

My vote for the Patriot Act is the vote that I regret the most during all my eight years in Congress. I supported the bill in part because the administration did agree to some significant changes to the legislation, and had agreed to add sunset provisions assuring that some of the most dangerous provisions in the bill would expire unless Congress renewed them in 2005.

But there were many other assurances the Bush team made on which they double-crossed Congress and the American people.

We were assured by the administration that if the Patriot Act passed and we supported it, they would not seek to expand it. They immediately sought to expand it.

Secondly, they assured us that the powers they were granted would be used for serious terrorism investigations (which was, after all, the reason they said they needed the Patriot Act in the first place). They also said they would not abuse the provisions in it. Such clearly has not been the case. The administration, for example, has used National Security Letters—a provision that was intended to provide a *limited* authority for FBI agents in vital, time-sensitive terrorism investigations, and which allows agents to compel disclosure of personal information without a search warrant—about fifty thousand times a year since then. The use of so-called sneak-and-peek warrants—which allow the government to conduct searches and seizures without providing contemporaneous notice of such searches or seizures to the persons

---

5 Michael Beach, "New terror warnings; attacks likely in days - FBI," *Herald Sun* (Melbourne), October 13, 2001.

6 Dan Eggen and Bob Woodward, "Terrorist Attacks Imminent, FBI Warns," *The Washington Post*, October 12, 2001.

whose homes or offices have been thus violated—have, since the power was gained in the Patriot Act, used the power largely for investigations having nothing whatsoever to do with terrorism.

Finally, the administration had also promised to report fully, openly, and accurately to the Congress on a regular basis as to how the act was being used, so the Congress could evaluate properly whether or not it need to be continued, cut back, or expanded in some way. The Bush administration has never even pretended to honor this pledge.

In every one of the instances the administration betrayed members of Congress who trusted them enough to vote for the original bill.

Whenever any legislative body takes action based on fear, the results are generally deleterious. The Patriot Act was conceived in fear, its gestation infested with fear, fear was its midwife, and its infancy fed by fear. The act presented an invitation to abuse and, of course, government agencies have accepted the invitation wholeheartedly. The act has been used to target antiwar protesters, organized crime, pranksters, the homeless, and artists. It has been utilized to protect the intellectual property of big business.

A few weeks after Bush signed the Patriot Act, he announced that he was suspending *habeas corpus* and that he possessed the power to indefinitely detain anyone he labeled an enemy combatant. I was stunned at such brashness, and joined with several of my Democratic colleagues in a letter challenging the power grab. (This will be discussed in depth in chapter 17). At the end of November 2001, the Associated Press labeled me "the most outspoken Republican opponent of President Bush's efforts to expand law enforcement powers to combat terrorism."[7]

I was disappointed to see so many conservatives who fought alongside me on the barricades against Clinton power grabs suddenly act as if Uncle Sam had become a sacred cow simply because the D had changed to an R. Attorney General John

---

7 Jeffrey McMurray, "Republican Barr has become harsh critic of Bush administration on privacy issues," Associated Press, November 29, 2001.

Ashcroft told the Senate Judiciary Committee in December 2001: "To those who scare peace-loving people with phantoms of lost liberty . . . your tactics only aid terrorists for they erode our national unity and . . . give ammunition to America's enemies."[8] This truly was a harbinger of things to come, and reflected a breathtakingly sinister view of how imperious our federal government had become. At the time Ashcroft made this blatant attempt to intimidate critics, the administration had already approved pervasive violations of the law by the National Security Agency. But those who complained were apparently still traitors—at least in the eyes of the nation's top law enforcement official.

Unfortunately, the Bush administration went from bad to worse, as far as the Constitution went. They came up with one scheme after another to target innocent Americans—to recruit millions of informants (Operation TIPS)—and to create legal precedents that would make it almost impossible to check the government's power.

And all the while, President Bush never tired of invoking freedom to sanctify practically everything he did abroad and domestically. The administration's "freedom talk" soon degenerated into utter pap. On the first anniversary of 9/11, for example, at a time when critics were increasingly warning of the perils from the Patriot Act and other policies, Ashcroft declared on National Public Radio: "I believe when you go out to walk the dog—and I wish I had a dog to walk; that's one of the things in Washington I haven't been able to keep is a dog—you're safer, more secure and your liberties are intact, and we'll fight to make sure that that's so."[9] It was as if Ashcroft was offering "freedom to walk the dog" as a substitute for the Fourth Amendment and as justification for the suspension of *habeas corpus*. Even when the leaders in Washington promised that they would not let the terrorists change our way of life, they were busy implementing policies that did precisely that.

---

8 Federal News Service, "Senate Judiciary Committee Hearing on War on Terrorism," December 6, 2001.

9 "Attorney General John Ashcroft Speaks about the Challenges Since September 11th, 2001," National Public Radio (Morning Edition), September 11, 2002.

Redistricted Out of Office

In 2001, the Democratic-controlled Georgia legislature took advantage of redistricting to combine my congressional district with that of fellow Republican incumbent John Linder. Even though Georgia had gained two new seats in the House of Representatives as a result of the 2000 census, the Democrats wanted to squeeze out at least one Republican incumbent, and a leader of the Clinton impeachment made an obvious and tempting target. My outspoken comments on Bush's civil liberties abuses may have made the difference in my loss in the Republican primary in 2002.

After I left Congress, I continued serving on the board of directors of the National Rifle Association and began working as a consultant with the American Civil Liberties Union. I also helped found an organization called Patriots to Restore Checks and Balances, a bipartisan group dedicated to eliminating oppressive provisions of the Patriot Act and restoring traditional checks and balances on government power so the country could again effectively fight terror without sacrificing the rights of innocent Americans, rights that are guaranteed by the Constitution.

I was shocked when *The New York Times* revealed in December 2005 that the president had launched a massive program for warrantless wiretaps of Americans' phone calls and e-mail. Even more stunning, he then called a press conference and essentially bragged about what he was doing. It was as if the president stood up proudly, before the American people and said, *Yes, I violated the [FISA] law, but I violated it for you.* The president of the United States was proudly proclaiming he had ordered a massive program of surreptitiously listening in to US citizens' conversations without court order. When President Bush boasted about his illegal wiretaps—renamed the Terrorist Surveillance Program—in his State of the Union address the following month, he received a standing ovation from Republican congressmen.

This was the final straw for me. I quit the Republican Party in 2006 and joined the Libertarian Party. The Libertarians are the only party standing up for the Constitution and the rights of individual Americans. The consensus in Washington these days is that government power should always expand. The only question in the minds of most people in our nation's capital is who should exercise that power. Libertarians recognize that no one—and no party—has the right to unconstitutional power.

The two major political parties have dramatically and openly tortured and deformed the very meaning of liberty. These parties have transmogrified into devices to wrest liberty *from* the people. These parties do not merely squander liberty; they steal it. They are the new robber barons of freedom. They tax far beyond any measure reasonably required to meet the necessary functions of government. They invade the privacy of citizens despite laws expressly crafted to protect privacy. They regulate businesses, schools, and virtually every mode of private enterprise to the point no such activities may be undertaken save by the grace of government. They trample rights guaranteed by the very words of our magnificent Constitution. They squander the fruits of *our* labor and then brazenly demand more, under pain of prison.

And the Libertarians are the only party that bluntly admits that the greatest threats facing America in this post-9/11 world are not foreign terrorists or rogue regimes in foreign lands. Rather, the true danger to American civilization lies in the insidious power of the state to diminish and ultimately destroy the right to privacy that has heretofore been considered the hallmark and birthright of free men and women born under the Stars and Stripes. It is that right to privacy that lies—as Ayn Rand noted many decades ago—at the very heart of civilization. In that right to privacy beats the heart of the freedom to own and protect property; to espouse and work for religious, economic, or political ideas; to possess firearms; to remain free from government surveillance or the gathering of evidence against oneself absent a sound and articulated basis rooted in the Fourth Amendment to the Constitution; and so much more.

The cause of liberty in America is in grave danger today. And now, as well as in the past, we have no one to rely on but ourselves in making sure that the new era of terrorism does not steal from us our most precious freedoms. The Libertarian Party is ready to fight tooth and nail against the government theft of our freedom.

America has lost its way, and the drivers of our national vehicle are clueless how to find the way once more. They refuse to reach over and retrieve from the nation's glove box the map that remains as accurate today as when crafted more than two centuries ago. The Libertarian Party stands for the Constitution in a way that the other major parties have not done for decades. If we do not work actively and quickly to restore understanding of and adherence to the Constitution and its component Bill of Rights, then surely that Bill of Rights will become less than a mere shadow of what it was intended to be and for most of our history in fact was. It will change from this:

The Bill of Rights As Adopted in 1791

Amendment I
Congress shall make no law respecting an establishment of religion, or prohibiting the free exercise thereof; or abridging the freedom of speech, or of the press; or the right of the people peaceably to assemble, and to petition the Government for a redress of grievances.

Amendment II
A well regulated Militia, being necessary to the security of a free State, the right of the people to keep and bear Arms, shall not be infringed.

Amendment III
No Soldier shall, in time of peace be quartered in any house, without the consent of the Owner, nor in time of war, but in a manner to be prescribed by law.

Amendment IV

The right of the people to be secure in their persons, houses, papers, and effects, against unreasonable searches and seizures, shall not be violated, and no Warrants shall issue, but upon probable cause, supported by Oath or affirmation, and particularly describing the place to be searched, and the persons or things to be seized.

Amendment V

No person shall be held to answer for a capital, or otherwise infamous crime, unless on a presentment or indictment of a Grand Jury, except in cases arising in the land or naval forces, or in the Militia, when in actual service in time of War or public danger; nor shall any person be subject for the same offence to be twice put in jeopardy of life or limb; nor shall be compelled in any criminal case to be a witness against himself, nor be deprived of life, liberty, or property, without due process of law; nor shall private property be taken for public use, without just compensation.

Amendment VI

In all criminal prosecutions, the accused shall enjoy the right to a speedy and public trial, by an impartial jury of the State and district where in the crime shall have been committed, which district shall have been previously ascertained by law, and to be informed of the nature and cause of the accusation; to be confronted with the witnesses against him; to have compulsory process for obtaining witnesses in his favor, and to have the Assistance of Counsel for his defense.

Amendment VII

In suits at common law, where the value in controversy shall exceed twenty dollars, the right of trial by jury shall be preserved, and no fact tried by a jury, shall be otherwise re-examined in any court of the United States, than according to the rules of the common law.

Amendment VIII

Excessive bail shall not be required, nor excessive fines imposed, nor cruel and unusual punishments inflicted.

Amendment IX

The enumeration in the Constitution, of certain rights, shall not be construed to deny or disparage others retained by the people.

Amendment X

The powers not delegated to the United States by the Constitution, nor prohibited by it to the states, are reserved to the states respectively, or to the people.

to this:

The Bill of Rights

As Envisioned by the Government in 2008

Amendment I

Congress shall make no law respecting an establishment of religion, or prohibiting the free exercise thereof; or abridging the freedom of speech, or of the press; or the right of the people peaceably to assemble, and to petition the government for a redress of grievances.

Amendment II

A well regulated militia, being necessary to the security of a free state, the right of the people to keep and bear arms, shall not be infringed.

Amendment III

No soldier shall, in time of peace be quartered in any house, without the consent of the owner, nor in time of war, but in a manner to be prescribed by law.

Amendment IV

The right of the people to be secure in their persons, houses, papers, and effects, against unreasonable searches and seizures, shall not be violated, and no warrants shall issue, but upon probable cause, supported by oath or affirmation, and particularly describing the place to be searched, and the persons or things to be seized.

Amendment V

No person shall be held to answer for a capital, or otherwise infamous crime, unless on a presentment or indictment of a grand jury, except in cases arising in the land or naval forces, or in the militia, when in actual service in time of war or public danger; nor shall any person be subject for the same offense to be twice put in jeopardy of life or limb; nor shall be compelled in any criminal case to be a witness against himself, nor be deprived of life, liberty, or property, without due process of law; nor shall private property be taken for public use, without just compensation.

Amendment VI

In all criminal prosecutions, the accused shall enjoy the right to a speedy and public trial, by an impartial jury of the state and district wherein the crime shall have been committed, which district shall have been previously ascertained by law, and to be informed of the nature and cause of the accusation; to be confronted with the witnesses against him; to have compulsory process for obtaining witnesses in his favor, and to have the assistance of counsel for his defense.

Amendment VII

In suits at common law, where the value in controversy shall exceed twenty dollars, the right of trial by jury shall be preserved, and no fact tried by a jury, shall be otherwise reexamined in any court of the United States, than according to the rules of the common law.

Amendment VIII

Excessive bail shall not be required, nor excessive fines imposed, nor cruel and unusual punishments inflicted.

Amendment IX

The enumeration in the Constitution, of certain rights, shall not be construed to deny or disparage others retained by the people.

Amendment X

The powers not delegated to the United States by the Constitution, nor prohibited by it to the states, are reserved to the states respectively, or to the people.

UNCLE SAM'S ENDLESS ABSURDITIES

Federal finances are in a catastrophic condition and are getting worse. The deficit in 2009 will run a half trillion dollars; the debt ceiling was just raised to $10.6 trillion. Still, Congress and presidents waste money on one harebrained scheme after another, laughing all the way to reelection.

There is no way to reform most federal programs; they are beyond salvation by tinkering. The only way to fix them is to abolish them. Following are but a few examples that illustrate how low the federal government has sunk in terms of absurd ways to spend taxpayers' money.

Looting the Treasury in the Name of Homeland Security

During the last seven years, politicians have missed few opportunities to invoke the 9/11 attacks to trumpet their devotion to protecting their fellow citizens. At the same time, those same politicians have hardly ever failed to pass up opportunities to squander money in the name of national security.

A congressional report last year revealed a few absurdities that are taking place with federal Homeland Security grants to local and state governments:

- The fishing village of Dillingham, Alaska (population 2,400) received a $202,000 Homeland Security grant to install seventy "downtown" surveillance cameras.
- Crawfordsville, Indiana, received a $55,000 Homeland Security grant to "to buy gym equipment, sponsor

puppet and clown shows, and turn first responders into fitness trainers."[10]

- Converse, Texas, received a $3,000 grant that was used to buy a trailer to "transport lawnmowers to lawnmower drag races."

- "The Department of Homeland Security gave more than $36,000 to the Kentucky Office of Charitable Gambling to prevent terrorists from trying to raise money for their plots at the state's bingo halls."[11]

- Columbus, Ohio, used $7,300 to buy bulletproof vests for police and fire department dogs.

- The Onalaska, Wisconsin, fire department spent $8,000 in Homeland Security grants to put on clown and puppet shows (congressional investigators did not reveal whether the clown shows had a 9/11 theme).

Unfortunately, the waste revealed in the congressional report represented only the tip of the Homeland Security abuse iceberg. In other reported scams, Newark, New Jersey, spent a quarter of a million dollars in 2005 on new, state-of-the-art, air-conditioned garbage trucks with its federal Homeland Security grant. Washington, DC received more than $100 million in Homeland Security grants and used its windfall to buy snazzy leather jackets for its police officers and to send sanitation workers to a Dale Carnegie course ($100,000 worth of making friends and influencing potential terrorist suspects).

Unfortunately, this type of waste is typical of how Congress, the president, and the bureaucracy blow through $3 trillion of your money every year. Congressmen view the US Treasury as their own play toy, their own ticket to perpetual reelection.

---

10 "Report on Security or Pork? A Review of National Homeland Security Funding Boondoggles," Rep. Anthony Weiner and Rep. Jeff Flake, March 1, 2007

11 There was no evidence that Al Qaeda or Hezbollah had infiltrated any of the state's bingo halls, but it is difficult to argue with free federal money.

Service Frauds from Uncle Sam

Over the last fifteen years, politicians have not been content to lecture Americans about their duty to serve their fellow citizens. Instead, they set up a program to get some people to volunteer—after which politicians brag to high heaven about all the good deeds they financed.

AmeriCorps, which currently has roughly seventy-five thousand paid recruits, was created by Bill Clinton and was widely seen as a monument to his idealism. In reality, AmeriCorps achieved little more than providing plenty of smiling faces with government uniforms to greet Clinton when he arrived on an airport tarmac.

As the Ripon Forum, the flagship of liberal Republicans, recently reported: "During the Clinton administration, AmeriCorps members helped run a program in Buffalo that gave children $5 for each toy gun they brought in—as well as a certificate praising their decision not to play with toy guns. In San Diego, AmeriCorps members busied themselves collecting used bras and panties for a homeless shelter. In Los Angeles, AmeriCorps members passed the time foisting unreliable, ultra-low-flush toilets on poor people. In New Jersey, AmeriCorps members enticed middle-class families to accept subsidized federal health insurance for their children."[12]

Unfortunately, AmeriCorps did not benefit from any managerial revolutions once the Bush team took office (despite widespread calls by conservatives to abolish AmeriCorps). Under Bush, AmeriCorps members have busied themselves passing out free gun locks in front of Wal-Marts, helping drum up support for a smoking ban in a Wisconsin county, hoeing at an Illinois farm museum, and lecturing high school students about "Super Bowl Surge" (when millions of football viewers hit the bathroom at the same time).

In his 2002 State of the Union address, President Bush announced the creation of USA Freedom Corps—a White House agency to oversee Americans' volunteer efforts and to supervise

---

12 James Bovard, "The National Service Illusion," Ripon Forum, April/May 2008.

AmeriCorps. One of the first things the Freedom Corps did was begin recruiting people for Operation TIPS (the Terrorist Information and Prevention System). TIPS aimed to sign up millions of informants—from truck drivers to letter carriers to cable television installers—who would report any out of the ordinary behavior of their fellow citizens to the feds. No clear guidelines were ever issued on what activities could be considered suspicious and therefore worthy of a secret federal dossier being created on a citizen.

As a congressman, I recognized that this was a Pandora's box; it was especially treacherous to the aura of volunteering's good deeds to subvert Americans' privacy. I denounced TIPS as a snitch system and warned: "A formal program, organized, paid for and maintained by our own federal government to recruit Americans to spy on fellow Americans, smacks of the very type of fascist or Communist government we fought so hard to eradicate in other countries in decades past."[13] The uproar on Capitol Hill and by outraged Americans helped deep-six Operation TIPS, at least in its original incarnation.

When Bush's first AmeriCorps chief, Leslie Lenkowsky, resigned in 2003, he admitted that AmeriCorps is just "another cumbersome, unpredictable government bureaucracy."[14] The Government Accountability Office (GAO) and Office of Management Budget have searched in vain for evidence that would redeem the $500+ million a year this program costs—but it continues on.

More than sixty million Americans serve as unpaid volunteers each year in counties across the country. Even if AmeriCorps was expanded to a quarter million recruits, as both Barak Obama and John McCain favor, it would amount to less than one half of one percent of the total number of people who donate their time for what they consider good causes. Americans can no

---

13 Adam Clymer, "Worker Corps To Be Formed To Report Odd Activity," *The New York Times,* July 26, 2002.

14 Editorial, "The AmeriCorps Follies," *The Wall Street Journal,* July 30, 2003."

longer afford the cost of bogus federally orchestrated good deeds. We simply do not need government-subsidized volunteers.

The Corporate Welfare Fraud

Government has no business doing much of what it does, and nowhere is this clearer than with business subsidies. Unfortunately, some of the most wasteful federal spending is among the most sacrosanct.

The federal government gave more than $100 billion in grants, loans, and loan guarantees to businesses in 2007.

The Small Business Administration makes almost $30 billion in subsidized, guaranteed loans each year; with less-than-stellar results. The agency provides handouts to less than 2 percent of the new businesses started each year, yet the failure rate for some SBA loan programs is far higher than that of business in general. *The Washington Post* rightfully called the SBA a petty-cash drawer for politicians. SBA loan files are full of intercessions by congressmen on behalf of their constituents—who kindly contribute to their patron after the federal money comes through. The SBA lends millions to CPAs, doctors, and lawyers—not exactly the hard-core needy. In 2002, The SBA made $12 million in loans to amusement parks and arcades, and another $85 million to bars and other alcohol-related venues. The SBA created a special loan program to help companies and individuals directly harmed by the 9/11 attacks. But the program spun out of control and shoveled money into such things as "a South Dakota radio station, a Virgin Islands perfume shop, a Utah dog boutique, and more than 100 Dunkin' Donuts and Subway sandwich shops"[15] around the nation. The SBA ruins the lives of many borrowers who are given far more capital than they can responsibly use—and end up in bankruptcy.

The Export-Import Bank shovels billions of dollars in loan guarantees to favored US businesses each year. The program is

---

15 Larry Margasak, "SBA Finds 9/11 Loan Recipients Ineligible," Associated Press, December 29, 2005.

unnecessary: the vast majority of American exports are unsubsidized by Uncle Sam. And it is often a question of political pull, rather than economic merit, that decides which companies received federal underwriting for their foreign sales. Ex-Im is a magnet for fraud. The notorious Enron corporation, for example, was a huge Ex-Im beneficiary, and American taxpayers got the shaft for its loan guarantees when Enron went belly-up. A Dallas TV station discovered in December 2007 that Ex-Im had guaranteed hundreds of loans to Mexican businesses that didn't even exist.[16]

Some of the most brazen federal business subsidies go to America's farmers. The farm bill that President Bush signed in 2008 will deliver more than $35 billion to farmers over the next five years. Even though the average farm household is worth almost a million dollars, Congress treats farmers as if they needed thousands of dollars to guarantee their next meal. Even though farm income was at very high levels, Congress sharply boosted subsidies. But there is a means test . . . sort of: farmers who earn more than $950,000 per year will suffer a slight reduction in their federal handouts, and those farmers who earn more than $2 million will receive nothing from the federal government. Still, most farm subsidies go to the wealthiest farmers—and the biggest political campaign contributors.

The 2008 farm bill was a budget train wreck full of the usual claptrap—including a tax break for racehorse breeders (inserted by Sen. Mitch McConnell, the senator from the Kentucky Derby state). The District of Columbia has zero farmers—but the University of the District of Columbia received $10 million in the farm bill. Congress added new crops to the list of subsidy recipients and boosted subsidies for perennially uncompetitive crops like sugar. The 2008 farm bill was a reminder that Congress has learned nothing—and forgotten nothing—concerning agricultural policy since the 1930s, when many of today's programs were first put in place.

---

16 Byron Harris, "Congressman calls for probe of bogus loans," WFAA-TV, December 22, 2007.

Politicians have no right to take any citizens' tax dollars and transfer them to some business trying to make a buck. It doesn't matter how worthy the business's product or how noble its mission. This type of preferential treatment has no place in a free society based on equal rights under the law.

Expelling Uncle Sam from the Neighborhood School

Government waste not only burns taxpayers; it also routinely blights lives. Nowhere is this clearer than in federal spending for education.

For example, Congress created a program to give money to low-income school districts in the 1960s. After forty years and countless billions of dollars ponied up, the program had expanded to cover almost half the school districts in the nation—even though there was no solid evidence that federal handouts boosted the quality of local education.

Cheap federal loans for college students have allowed colleges to boost tuition far faster than inflation, resulting in many young people having crushing debt loads at the age of twenty-two.

Federal subsidies for vocational education have been a con artist's best friend, with legions of shady operators getting fat off the federal till. *The New York Times* warned in 1994: "Instead of promoting education, some Federal student-aid programs have been used to victimize students."[17] But Congress did not fix the problem—in part, no doubt, because the victimizers make generous campaign contributions.

Presidents and Congress continually respond to the failure of old programs by creating new programs. That is why there are now more than seven hundred different federal education programs.

The Bush administration's contribution to the education boondoggle hall of fame is the No Child Left Behind Act (NCLB). Bush sold this legislation to Congress as a way to increase

---

17 Michael Winerip, "Billions for School Are Lost In Fraud, Waste and Abuse " *The New York Times*, February 2, 1994.

accountability and performance in education and thereby help boost local education. Instead, school districts across the country have been hammered by continually changing federal edicts and shifting federal standards of success.

The NCLB requires that all schools show "adequate year progress" for all groups of students. There is no national standard; instead, states can draw the starting line wherever they please.

And the lower the initial baseline, the easier it becomes for states and schools to avoid harsh federal sanctions and subsidy reductions. The Electronic Industries Alliance complained that NCLB "has the perverse effect of initiating a race to the bottom."[18] (The Alliance is concerned about how low education standards undermine American competitiveness.)

A report by the Hoover Institution found that NCLB has spurred sharp decreases in education standards in Arizona, Maryland, Ohio, North Dakota, and Idaho. The Bush administration has become a partner with state and local education bureaucrats who use statistical shenanigans to hide their failures from parents, taxpayers, and federal monitors.

The federal Department of Education is spending almost $70 billion in 2008 on a function neither mentioned nor implied in the Constitution. Since education is not a federal responsibility, a better way to promote educational opportunity is at the state and local level. There are now twenty-two different choice programs in fourteen states. Some of those initiatives provide vouchers; others create tax credits. Georgia Governor Sonny Perdue recently signed into law legislation creating a state income tax credit for individuals and companies that donate to groups that provide private scholarships for students.

In fact, private scholarships have become an increasingly important choice mechanism across the nation. Examples range from the District of Columbia's Washington Scholarship Fund to the Children's Scholarship Fund in Portland, Oregon. In this way,

---

18 Tam Harbert, "Why Johnny can't engineer," *Electronic Business*, July 1, 2004.

citizens who want to improve education can avoid the political obstacles to reforming the public schools.

Simply put, America's public educational monopoly is not working. The failure to adequately educate our children to compete in the international marketplace and to be good citizens in a free society is truly scandalous, and the answers certainly will not come from Washington.

Instead, answers and innovations will come from families across America as they educate their own children, put their children into private schools, and improve the local public systems. We expect choice and competition throughout the economy. It's time to return those same principles to education.

Parents have a duty to raise and educate their children, but without choice for alternatives to government schooling, the ability of parents to fulfill that role is severely limited. Education involves not just practical learning, but the transmission of moral values, making it even more important to return authority to parents for deciding their children's schooling without interference from government.

The free market naturally provides both choice and competition, providing goods and services of higher quality for less expense. These principles should be applied to education. Unfortunately, the government's near monopoly on education in the United States has seized control of our children's education from parents, and has trapped children in failing schools across the country.

A Commission to Cut Wasteful Government

If I am elected president, I will immediately freeze spending in the executive branch. I will send a message to the Congress that no piece of legislation will be signed that comes to President Barr's desk purporting to raise the ceiling on the national debt; it will be vetoed. Any appropriations bill that comes to President Barr that increases federal spending over the last fiscal year, which by that time would be 2009, will in fact be vetoed, and that will be the high water mark for such spending.

It isn't hard to identify individual programs that should be eliminated or whose budgets should be cut. However, salvaging the federal government's finances will require a systematic reevaluation of programs that are unconstitutional, unnecessary, wasteful, or sometimes all three at once. For this purpose, as president I will appoint the Commission to Cut Wasteful Government.

Modeled after the so-called Grace Commission, created by President Ronald Reagan in 1982—when federal outlays ran only $746 billion, compared to more than $3.1 trillion budgeted for 2009—the Commission to Cut Wasteful Government will be tasked with assessing every federal agency and program. The Grace Commission reported in 1984 and identified $424 billion in potential savings over the first three years alone. Unfortunately, Congress failed to act on the commission's recommendations, leaving expenditures and deficits to race ever upward. A decade later the new Republican Congress put a slight brake on government growth, but that slowdown proved to be only temporary. Despite his self-proclaimed title of conservative, outlays sharply accelerated under President George W. Bush and a Republican Congress, and continue to increase with Congress under Democratic control.

The Commission to Cut Wasteful Government will be instructed to be far tougher than the Grace Commission—rather like a Grace Commission on steroids. The panel will be directed to ask three questions of every federal program and agency:

First, is there constitutional authority for the expenditure, regulation, or agency? Most people in Washington have come to forget that the Constitution does not make the federal government a government of general jurisdiction. Rather, Article 1, Section 8 enumerates those powers possessed by Congress. The Constitution is best seen as establishing a few islands of government power in a sea of individual liberty and state of authority. Only those programs that fit on these islands of legitimate constitutional authority should be maintained.

Next, if the program has a constitutional basis, is that activity best conducted by the national government, or by states and localities? For instance, the Constitution does not authorize Congress to make laws regarding education. However, even if there were constitutional warrant for federal involvement in education, states and localities are far better able to design and manage educational programs to meet the needs of local communities and families. The federal government can legitimately promote interstate highways, but funding for and construction of intrastate transportation infrastructure should be left to states and localities.

Finally, assuming the program is constitutional and best provided at the federal level, is the specific initiative cost-effective —that is, do the benefits outweigh the costs? For instance, the national government has obvious authority to address pollution problems that extend beyond any single state, and a federal approach might offer the only feasible solution. However, many of the regulations promulgated by the Environmental Protection Agency impose far greater costs than the benefits achieved.

The Commission's report will become the basis on which my administration would identify and prioritize government programs, activities, outlays, offices, departments, and regulations to be eliminated or cut back. I would use this list as part of a concerted campaign to roll back federal spending and regulation, reduce outlays, reform regulations, and reshape the bureaucracy.

Controlling federal finances will not be easy. The primary problem is one of inadequate political will.

I would commit to working with Congress to bring spending under control and I would use my veto power, if necessary, to enforce fiscal discipline. I would make my case directly to the American people in order to win their support for the tough steps that are necessary if we are to put Washington's fiscal house in order, at long last.

Conclusion

It is not just a question of dollars; it is question of freedom. Slashing hundreds of billions of dollars of wasteful spending is not just a question of reducing government waste. It is also a question of safeguarding Americans' liberty. The bigger government becomes, the more it interferes in people's lives. Government generosity usually ends up hogtying its supposed beneficiaries.

In the next chapter, we will consider the Iron Fist used to finance all of politicians' good deeds.

TIME FOR A NEW
TAX REVOLT

Let's be clear: Americans are being brutalized by the IRS. The average family now pays more in taxes than it spends for housing, clothing, and food combined. In 2008, Tax Freedom Day didn't occur until April 23, which means the average American worked nearly four months simply to pay his or her taxes. That is longer than medieval serfs had to labor for their masters. And if you figure in the total cost of government, the average senior worked more than half a year ('til July 16 to be precise) to pay for all direct and indirect costs of government. People had to work 83.7 days to pay for federal spending, 62.6 days to cover the cost of regulation, and 50.5 days to underwrite state and local governments.

Politicians like to talk about how the government exists to serve the people. In reality, politicians have created laws and policies that turn the rulers into a parasite *on* the people.

Nowhere is this clearer than in taxation. Government officials like to brag about how Americans pay taxes voluntarily. But this is a *non sequitur*. As former IRS District Chief David Patnoe observed in 1998: "More tax is collected by fear and intimidation than by the law. People are afraid of the IRS."[19] An IRS instructor in the Arkansas-Oklahoma district was caught on videotape lecturing IRS collection agents in 1996 on how to treat taxpayers: "Make them cry. We don't give points around here for being good scouts. The word is enforced. If that's not tattooed on your forehead, or somewhere else, then you need to get it. Enforcement. Seizure and sales. That's our mind-set . . . You're not out there to take any prisoners. Prisoners are like an installment

---

19 William Roth and William Nixon, *The Power to Destroy,* (New York: Atlantic Monthly Press, 1999), p. 32.

agreement. They have to be fed and clothed and housed. All that stuff. They're expensive. We're not here to do that. If you've got an assessment, enforce collection until they come to their knees."[20]

At that time, the IRS was intentionally trying to whip up its agents' hostility to average Americans. This was epitomized by Culture Bingo—a game used to train agents and auditors to recognize "an IRS organizational culture regarding the audit process."[21] The game encouraged the use of summonses to obtain third-party records, to think of fraud referrals as a path to promotion, and to believe that most taxpayers deposit unreported receipts in their bank accounts. Culture Bingo included a lesson teaching IRS agents: "Taxpayers seem to live better than I do." The American Institute of Certified Public Accountants said of the course materials: "Every ethical issue presented finds the ethical result to be pro-IRS and anti-taxpayer. There is not one scenario where an IRS agent might act unethically against a taxpayer's interest."[22]

Congress made some reforms in 1998 to try to end such abuses. But the IRS continues browbeating innocent people and relying on pervasive fear to assure that people pay whatever the government demands. Congress has undertaken virtually no real oversight of the IRS since that dread agency was established in 1952.

The IRS Versus Political Freedom

James Madison, writing on the danger of taxation, observed in the Federalist Papers: "There is, perhaps, no legislative act in which greater opportunity and temptation are given to a predominant

---

20 William Roth and William Nixon, The Power to Destroy, (New York: Monthly Press, 1999), pp 76-77.

21 "AICPA says Financial Status Audit Techniques Undermine Taxpayers Right," *Tax Notes Today*, April 25, 1996.

22 Ibid.

party to trample on the rules of justice."[23] David Burnham, the author of *A Law Unto Itself* (an exposé of the IRS), noted, "In almost every administration since the IRS's inception the information and power of the tax agency have been mobilized for explicitly political purposes . . . Eleanor Roosevelt prompted Treasury Secretary Morgenthau to order a tax investigation of a conservative newspaper publisher who had become one of the Roosevelt administration's leading critics."[24]

Unfortunately, there is no reason to think that such abuses are confined to the history books. The IRS in 2005 collected information on the political party affiliation of taxpayers in twenty states. The data was gathered as part of an IRS quest to use voter registration rolls to find people who are not paying taxes. The IRS ceased the roundup after protests by the National Taxpayer Employees Union.

The IRS has abused its audit powers for political purposes in ways that strike at the heart of the First Amendment's guarantee of freedom of speech and press. A Senate investigation reported in 1976:

> Between 1969 and 1973, the Internal Revenue Service, through a secret "Special Service Staff" (SSS), targeted more than 10,000 individuals and groups for tax examinations because of their political activity. The FBI and the Internal Security Division of the Justice Department gave SSS lists of taxpayers deemed to be "activists" or "ideological organizations"; the FBI, in providing SSS with a list of over 2,000 groups and individuals classified as "Right Wing," "New Left," and "Old Left," expressed its hope that SSS tax examinations would "deal a blow to dissident elements." A smaller though more intensive selective enforcement program, the "Ideological Organization Project,"

---

[23] Federalist Paper Number 10, available at http://www.yale.edu/lawweb/avalon/federal/fed10.htm

[24] David Burnham, *A Law Unto Itself: The IRS and the Abuse of Power* (New York: Random House, 1989), p. 162.

was established in November 1961 in response to White House criticism of "right-wing extremist" groups. On the basis of such political criteria, 18 organizations were selected for special audit although there was no evidence of tax violation.[25]

Congress passed laws after this scandal surfaced that were supposed to permanently ban such abuses. However, the Associated Press confirmed that such machinations continued, revealing, for example, in late 1999 that "officials in the Democratic White House and members of both parties in Congress have prompted hundreds of audits of political opponents in the 1990s. The audit requests ranged from the forwarding of constituent letters and newspaper articles alleging wrongdoing to personal demands for audits from members of Congress."[26] The Associated Press noted, "Lawmakers' requests are stamped 'expedite' to remind IRS officials they must reply in writing within 15 days. A few requests reviewed by AP were marked with notations such as 'hot politically' or 'sensitive.'. . . The IRS computer tracking system in Washington denotes the name of a politician who refers a matter. The original letter from the White House or lawmaker is forwarded to the case agent."[27] For instance, Rep. David Skaggs (D-CO) asked the IRS to examine the Heritage Foundation and Citizens Against Government Waste. The IRS launched audits of those organizations within two months of Skaggs' request. Skaggs said that "of course" there is "a political dimension" to the IRS's decision to audit such groups. [28]

The IRS defended itself by claiming that "less than 1 percent of the six to ten thousand audits of tax-exempt groups each year

---

25 The Internal Revenue Service: An Intelligence Resource and Collector, Final Report of the Select Committee to Study Governmental Operations with Respect to Intelligence Activities, (The Church Committee), U.S. Senate, April 26, 1976.

26 John Solomon and Larry Margasak, "Documents Pinpoint Federal Audits," Associated Press, November 16, 1999.

27 Ibid.

28 "Politicians take aim at foes with IRS audits," Associated Press, November 16, 1999.

originate with complaints from lawmakers or the White House."[29] The IRS refused to disclose the documentation that would allow outsiders to verify this claim. But even if the IRS is launching *only* one hundred politically instigated audits per year of nonprofit groups, that is sufficient to sow fear and intimidate potential critics. The IRS knows that responding quickly to congressional audit requests will help assure the agency of getting a hefty budget from its Capitol Hill overseers. The fact that the IRS would kowtow to congressional requests symbolizes how the agency and the politicians conspire against average Americans.

The Internal Revenue Service is also reviving one of its old tricks of cracking down on churches that do not stay far enough away from politics as the IRS would like. The IRS launched an investigation of the All Saints Church, an Episcopal congregation, in Pasadena, California, after its minister criticized Bush in an antiwar sermon shortly before the 2004 presidential election. The IRS justified the investigation because the minister's criticism of Bush was supposedly an implicit endorsement of Democratic candidate John Kerry. But what is the world coming to when the IRS acts like it has a right to censor ministers who condemn war?

Internal Revenue Service chief Mark Everson announced in 2006, regarding the IRS crackdown on churches, "There are few bright lines for evaluating political intervention; our work requires a careful balancing of all the facts and circumstances."[30] But it is absurd to believe that IRS auditors could do a fairer job of sermon policing than they do in giving average Americans the third degree. The IRS for many years rewarded auditors for assessing additional taxes during audits, even when citizens did not legitimately owe taxes. Would "church speech" auditors get promotions based on how many guilty verdicts they reached?

Sen. Barack Obama's congregation, the United Church of Christ, came under IRS investigation after it permitted Obama to speak to church members. The IRS apparently believed that the

---

29 Ibid.

30 "Remarks of Commissioner of Internal Revenue Mark W. Everson at the City Club of Cleveland in Cleveland, Ohio," Internal Revenue Service Press Office, February 24, 2006.

fact that Obama had been a member of the church for many years was irrelevant to whether he should be able to speak to his fellow worshipers.

In late 2007, Iowa Republican Senator Charles "Chuck" Grassley launched an assault against several large churches whose congregations had authorized their pastors to spend money for purposes with which the parsimonious Senator Grassley disagreed. The Iowa Senator's efforts to enlist the IRS in his attacks on these churches continue.

The IRS Versus American Privacy

Americans are compelled to bare their financial soul to the government, but they have little or no reason to trust their rulers not to abuse the information thus captured.

The IRS has the power to smear taxpayers even without any proof of their wrongdoing. In July 2002, the IRS disclosed the names of hundreds of Americans who had contacted the accounting firm KPMG to inquire about tax planning. The IRS released the list at the time it was accusing KPMG of promoting a tax shelter that may—or may not—have been illegal. One of the people named was William Simon, Jr.—the son of the former Treasury Secretary Bill Simon and the Republican candidate for governor of California at the time of the disclosure. The IRS's revelations helped torpedo his election campaign. Another person tarred was Dale Earnhardt, the late NASCAR driver. The Treasury Department investigated the IRS and announced that the agency had done nothing wrong in releasing—and smearing—citizens who had done nothing more insidious than contact one of the nation's most respected accounting firms for advice.

Congress has such contempt for citizens' privacy that they passed a provision in a law in 2004 that entitled the chairmen of several congressional committees and their assistants and designees to access any American's tax return and use the personal data however they pleased. The provision effectively waived all the legal and privacy protections IRS Form 1040s supposedly receive. After a public uproar, Congress passed another law nullifying this prerogative. Congressional legislative staff tried to defend themselves by claiming that the intrusive provision was written by the IRS itself. However, the fact that Congress would even attempt to claim this power for committee chairmen and their designees, should be a clear warning about what to expect from Capitol Hill in the future. Apparently, the laws regarding citizens' privacy do not apply to congressmen any more than they apply to other federal officials in this day and age.

The government seems to have no sense of duty to insure that people are not victimized by the disclosures they make on their tax returns. The IRS recently proposed allowing tax preparers to sell the personal data from their customer's tax returns to third party businesses. This type of deal would be a windfall for data brokers that sell personal data to corporate marketers. Allowing the sale of all of a person's confidential financial information would have spurred even more identity theft than America is already suffering.

Subjugation via Mindless Complexity

Back in 1976, presidential candidate Jimmy Carter denounced the federal tax code as a "disgrace to the human race." His successor, President Ronald Reagan, took action—pushing through tax reform legislation in 1986 that slashed many of the tangles and snares of the tax code. But in the decades since Reagan's actions, Congress and subsequent presidents have rushed to turn the tax code back into the disgrace President Carter labeled it. The instruction manual for the IRS form 1040 is now more than twice as long as it was in 1987.

According to the Tax Foundation, the cost of complying with the federal income tax has soared from $79 billion in 1990 to $325 billion in 2008. This is another hidden tax that politicians hope Americans never recognize. In percentage terms, the compliance cost has increased from 14 percent of the total federal income tax collected in 1990 to 23 percent in 2008.

Federal tax law and regulations now amount to more than

nine million words. No wonder Americans must spend six billion hours a year simply to fill out their tax forms.

Our tax system is so tangled that even IRS employees are often clueless. A 2003 undercover test by the Treasury Department found that IRS employees give wrong tax advice almost half the time that citizens contact them at IRS centers. This was part of a hallowed tradition: another government audit found that the IRS gave nearly ten million wrong answers in 1999 to taxpayers who called its toll-free hotline.

Americans are at the mercy of the IRS in part because tax law is not actual law. Instead, it is simply the latest whim of the US Congress, or of the regulation writers of the Internal Revenue Service. There is no established law—because it is constantly being revised, reformed, and sometimes even retroactively changed. It takes the IRS several years to write the regulations for each change in tax law, and Congress routinely changes the law even before the regulations for the last legislative "fix" have been finalized.

Tax laws are drafted largely by lobbyists pulling strings in Washington. Congressional staffers then add provisions, not to aid the economy or achieve any notion of justice, but to meet political goals and the requests of lobbyists.

The only fixed rule for the tax code is that Congressmen will revise the law again if they can profit politically. (Members of Congress themselves can get free assistance from IRS officials who set up special desks and offices in the congressional office buildings at tax time.)

The "Tax Fairness" Fraud

Politicians and political appointees are continually trying to hornswoggle Americans with a deceptive notion of tax fairness. Pamela Olson, the Treasury Department's assistant secretary for tax policy, declared in 2003: "Americans' sense of fairness dictates that all Americans should pay their fair share."[31]

And just what is their fair share? In fact, a taxpayer's fair share is simply whatever politicians and bureaucrats demand.

Washington defines tax fairness as if it is solely a question of seizing the proper amounts from different income groups—not a question of how the government treats the individual citizen. (Incidentally, the 1 percent of households with the highest income paid more than 38 percent of all federal income taxes in 2005.)

President Grover Cleveland declared way back in 1886, "When more of the people's sustenance is exacted through the form of taxation than is necessary to meet the just obligations of government and expenses of its economical administration, such exaction becomes ruthless extortion and a violation of the principles of a free government."[32]

Taxes will be unjust as long as politicians can waste billions on whatever project or program their hearts desire. There can be no just taxes so long as Congress retains an unlimited right to waste citizens' tax dollars.

The IRS itself is often guilty of squandering the tax dollars it piously commandeers. At the same time the IRS is tightening the screws on working Americans, it is shoveling out money for ludicrous fraudulent tax refund claims. The Treasury Department admitted in 2002 that the IRS had paid more than $30 million for slavery reparation claims. The average payout was $43,000. This is part of a tax scam targeting African-Americans who are persuaded to file claims based on the notion that the government owes them the contemporary equivalent of "forty acres and a mule" for the time their ancestors were enslaved prior to the Civil War. A dozen current and former IRS employees were among those making the bogus claims.

---

31 Alan Fram, "Bush Budget to Up IRS Funding, Deficits," Associated Press, February 2, 2003.

32 Grover Cleveland's Second State of the Union Address, at http://en.wikisource.org/wiki/ Grover_Cleveland's_Second_State_of_the_Union_Address

Time for a New Tax Revolt

The fact that the IRS's power and abuses is not an issue in Washington shows that neither Republicans nor Democrats give a wooden nickel about average Americans. It doesn't matter how many citizens become impaled by wrongful or unjust bureaucratic decrees. So long as the money keeps coming in—as long as politicians have plenty of money to buy votes and reward their donors—then the system is considered to be working just fine for both parties.

The thirtieth anniversary of Proposition 13—the California tax revolt that sent a shudder of fear in politicians across the nation —occurred in 2008. Proposition 13 helped propel the Reagan revolution. The measure was a true people's revolt against the entire political establishment—politicians, lobbyists, interest groups, and unions.

It is time for another tax revolt—but this one must sweep across the entire nation. We must both reduce and simplify taxes. That could mean replacing the current income tax system with either a flat tax or a consumption tax.

A flat tax rate would assess all citizens at the same rate (after exempting a base income). A flat tax would have the advantage of treating all citizens equally—and therefore fairly. High tax rates punish high productivity and drive capital and talent to foreign lands with better tax systems. A flat tax would greatly reduce politicians' ability to demagogue over taxes, since they could not play one group off against another.

However, a flat tax would still leave much of the current tax system in place. There would still be a central tax agency charged with determining exactly how much each citizen allegedly earned.

Another alternative—more sweeping in its scope—is to replace the income tax with a consumption tax. This would be a federal sales tax added on to retail purchases throughout the economy. With a consumption tax, there would be no need for a massive federal bureaucracy to surveil the financial activity of every citizen. The government would no longer be treating prosperous individuals like suspected criminals.

It's time for Americans to say that they are mad and aren't going to take it anymore, just like they did in California three decades ago.

FIXING ENTITLEMENTS, SAVING FREEDOM

The cost of entitlement programs has put America on the fast track to financial ruin. Even though the traditional, bloated federal welfare system was reformed in the late 1990s, other programs like Medicaid, Medicare, and Social Security remain unreformed— even though they are unsustainable at their soaring spending rates. The latter two programs alone face estimated total unfunded liabilities topping $100 trillion. Uncle Sam will eventually face the choice of raising taxes by as much as 50 percent or slashing benefits in half. We have to take action right now to avoid careening off this fiscal cliff.

So-called entitlement programs are the largest and fastest growing part of the federal budget. Social Security and Medicare together account for almost $900 billion in federal spending each year.

There has been an entitlement program crisis in the United States off and on since the 1970s. In 1972, 1977, and 1983, Congress rushed through bailout packages to rescue a Social Security system that was in imminent danger of defaulting on benefit payments. Congress decided in 1983 to significantly increase taxes to the Social Security system's reserves over the next half century. The resulting tax hikes wiped out the 1981 Reagan "supply side" income-tax cuts for most wage-earning Americans.

But even though taxes have risen, the program is still shakier than a second-term congressman's campaign promise.

When I talk about the Second Amendment, I always stress that it is important not to get bogged down arguing about the pros and cons of specific gun control proposals. If you sink into the details, you will lose almost every time.

It is the same with entitlement reform. The details are often arcane, and are mind-numbing if one focuses on tables and figures in actuarial reports. We must keep our eyes on the goal. The most important entitlement reform is to reduce Americans' reliance on politicians. Self-help is far more reliable than pulling political strings. The goal is freedom—true individual independence—not simply better budgetary balance sheets.

The key for any reform is to recognize that politicians cannot be trusted. There is no superior wisdom in Washington waiting to finagle the system's rules to provide a perpetual shower of benefits to Americans. We have watched the brain trusts in Washington create programs that resulted in the crash and burning of the savings and loans in the 1980s. The 2008 bailout of Fannie Mae and Freddie Mac, with its potential exposure for the taxpayer of more than $100 billion, could make the S&L debacle of the 1980s seem like a good deal by comparison. Of course, there is no reason to expect that Social Security, if left unfixed, will not have a far more catastrophic demise; in fact, you can bet on it.

Social Security's Legacy of Defeat

Social Security was created in the midst of the Great Depression, purportedly to provide a retirement safety net for American workers. In reality, it has been a vote-buying con ever since Franklin Roosevelt signed the Social Security Act in August 1935.

From the start, the Roosevelt administration deceived Americans about the nature of the program. Americans were endlessly told that it was an insurance program that would give them vested rights akin to a private contract. But in a 1937 brief to the Supreme Court, the Roosevelt administration conceded that Social Security "cannot be said to constitute a plan for compulsory insurance within the accepted meaning of the term insurance"[33]

---

33 Friedrich Hayek, *The Constitution of Liberty* (Chicago: Regnery Gateway), 1972, p. 293.

and characterized Social Security as a public charity program under the general welfare clause of the Constitution. On the day in 1937 that the Supreme Court declared Social Security constitutional precisely because it was a welfare system and not an insurance system, the Social Security Administration changed the name of the program from "old age benefits" to "old age insurance." This political bait and switch should have set off alarm bells, but the news media back then deified FDR, so he got away with it.

Social Security has always relied on illusions. The Brooking Institution's Martha Derthick observed, "In the mythic construction begun in 1935 and elaborated thereafter on the basis of the payroll tax, Social Security was a vast enterprise of self-help in which government participation was almost incidental."[34] The government for decades assured workers that their contributions were being held for them in individual accounts. In reality, of course, there never were any such accounts. Social Security Commissioner Stanford Ross conceded in 1979 that, "the mythology of Social Security contributed greatly to its success . . . [s]trictly speaking, the system was never intended to return to individuals what they paid."[35]

If FDR and subsequent politicians had been forthright with Americans— informing them that they were becoming ensnared in a welfare system that quickly became a war chest for incumbents' vote buying—far more citizens would have opposed the system.

In 1935, congressmen blithely boasted that Social Security would encourage individual thrift and personal savings. But according to a study by Martin Feldstein of the National Bureau for Economic Research, having a guaranteed retirement income probably decreased personal savings by about 50 percent, thereby sharply reducing the rate of capital accumulation. Social Security

---

34 Martha Derthick, *Policymaking for Social Security* (Washington: Brookings Institution, 1979), p. 232.

35 "Outgoing Social Security Head Assails 'Myths' of System and Says It Favors the Poor," *The New York Times,* December 2, 1979.

has been a major factor in reducing saving, and in the sometimes subpar performance of the American economy.

But Social Security was a windfall for many retirees until recent times. As policy analyst James Wooton noted, Social Security takes money from the working poor and gives it to the retired rich. The income of the elderly rose nine times faster than the income for average Americans between 1971 and the late 1990s largely because Social Security benefits rose far faster than average wages.

Though some older Americans made out like bandits, many young Americans recognize that Social Security is a con that they expect will stick them with a large bill—and nothing else. A decade ago, a poll of eighteen-to thirty-four-year-olds found that only 9 percent believed Social Security would have the funds necessary to pay their benefits when they retired. More young people believed in UFOs than trusted that Social Security would be around when they retired. A recent survey by the National Bureau of Economic Research found that only 40 percent of thirty-year-olds believed they would receive their promised benefits.

The rate of return retirees receive on the Social Security taxes they paid is plummeting. While early retirees received far more than they paid in, workers born in the last fifty years are being shortchanged. Over the long term, the most the majority of people can hope for is to earn a return of one percent—far less than the average 5+ percent return on a mixture of stocks or bonds. The US government is literally stealing people's retirements from them.

The nation's roughly eighty million baby boomers, born between 1946 and 1964, are beginning to retire. The Social Security system will begin paying out more benefits than it collects in taxes as of 2017—radically changing the political dynamics of the program. The longer the wait to fix the problem, the bigger the almost certain train crash.

True reform of Social Security requires shifting control of retirement decisions to workers and their families, by changing Social Security from a government pay-as-you-go system to an honest, individualized system of private accounts. In the long term, this would expand freedom of choice, increase retiree returns, and reduce government expenditures. In the short term, some cuts in benefits and other government outlays, and possibly short-term federal borrowing, would be necessary in order to finance the transition, during which workers could increasingly shift their Social Security tax payments into private accounts while the government continued to pay current beneficiaries.

Unlike the current system, in which ownership plays no role whatsoever, the new private accounts would be citizens' own property, though they could not access their stash until age sixty-two. This would greatly reduce Social Security's drain on capital accumulation and stimulate the savings rate. Making the savings accounts mandatory, though against my grain as a Libertarian, would be necessary to satisfy frightened voters' belief that they need to be saved from themselves.

Private versions of Social Security are succeeding beautifully in other countries. Nearly thirty years ago, in 1981, Chile switched from a pay-as-you-go system to private investment accounts. Fully 95 percent of that country's workers chose to invest their tax contributions rather than to remain in the old system. The new program has been a great success, providing Chileans with higher returns, a large investment corpus as their personal property, and a more prosperous economy. A score of other countries across Asia, Europe, and Latin America have followed Chile's lead and created private, self-funding accounts. The programs vary in their details, but have delivered more retirement benefits at less cost—and without threatening to bankrupt their respective governments.

Other reforms are necessary to help the Social Security system survive the transition period to private accounts. At the time Social Security started, almost half of the people taxed for its benefits died before collecting a penny. Politicians could win votes by promising benefits, knowing that many people would pass on before collecting benefits. Advances in medicine and our general standard of living have thrown us a curve ball: life expectancy has increased from less than sixty years in 1935 to seventy-eight years in 2006. By 2040, beneficiaries are likely to live an extra eighteen years after starting to collect Social Security benefits. Under previous legislation, the retirement age will rise until it hits sixty-seven for those born after 1958. This needs to be accelerated and raised further. The early retirement age (sixty-two) should also be boosted. Both should then be indexed to longevity increases.

Another reason why Social Security's costs have risen out of control is because the Consumer Price Index exaggerates the impact of price changes on retirees. The cost of living adjustment (COLA) for Social Security retirees could be trimmed by either one-half-percent or 1 percent per year. The federal government has no obligation to overcompensate one group of citizens—federal entitlement recipients—at everyone else's expense.

The Social Security earnings test should be abolished. This penalizes people who retire at age sixty-two, slashing their benefits when they earn more than $13,560 a year. The current system's rules on earnings penalties are a tangled bureaucratic mess that does little more than confound retirees for no good reason.

Ending the earnings test and raising the retirement age would spur individuals to better prepare for retirement. Most baby boomers are not adequately preparing for the financial realities of retirement. Delaying the retirement age would give them more time to build up a financial stockpile. Discouraging early retirement would also spur economic growth because most people in their sixties still have valuable skills and talents that need not be mothballed.

Even if benefits are trimmed and retirement delayed, that will not be sufficient to balance the Social Security reform ledger during the transition from pay-as-you-go to private accounts. To make up the difference, it is vital to slash federal waste throughout the government and to abolish unnecessary programs. For a start, freezing domestic discretionary outlays could save nearly $200 billion a year. Eliminating corporate welfare could save another $100 billion a year. Military spending could easily be reduced $100 billion a year by refocusing to concentrate on America's defense, instead of protecting wealthy allies and engaging in nation building.

Fixing Medicare

Medicare suffers from the same flaws as Social Security. At the time that Medicare was created in 1965, a federal program already existed to aid the needy elderly who could not afford their own health care costs. But because this was means-tested, it prevented politicians from buying as many votes as they pleased. President Johnson railroaded Medicare into law as part of his Great Society.

Americans are increasingly losing their freedom because of Medicare. In 1982, the federal government imposed price controls on hospitals and doctors treating Medicare patients. The result was an explosion in paperwork and a decrease in health care quality, and endless changes in dictates and requirements. In 1997, Congress decreed that no doctor could accept direct payments from any elderly patient without permission from the federal government. Robert Moffit, a former deputy assistant secretary at the Department of Health and Human Services, observed, "This assault on the doctor-patient relationship is deliberately designed to make private contracts with Medicare patients all but impossible."[36] Also in 1997, the feds began paying hundreds of millions of dollars in what were essentially bribes to America's teaching hospitals, to slash the supply of doctors. This is typical of government bureaucrats: trying to make people better off by creating an artificial shortage of trained experts.

There is no easy solution for Medicare, but a huge step in the right direction would be to allow younger Americans to divert the Medicare tax portion of their Social Security (FICA) taxes to health savings accounts (HSAs). This would allow them to have a stockpile in case they are hit with a medical emergency. And, because it would be their own property, they would have a stronger incentive to safeguard their own health and to shop prudently for the cost of medical services.

Medicare has become a key cause of skyrocketing health care costs. The federal government must take its foot off the medical price accelerator.

---

36 Editorial, "Medicare Showstopper," *The Wall Street Journal*, August 22, 1997.

There are many causes of today's high health care cost crisis. Access to insurance is more limited by government than it should be; the practice of medicine is far more regulated and costly than it should be.

American health care policy must be reformed based on the principle of consumer-oriented health care. Regulations that mandate insurance coverage and inflate premiums should be eliminated. Controls that unduly restrict competition within the health care industry and that limit access to insurance across state lines should be ended. Current tax policy, which is biased towards employer-provided, comprehensive health insurance, should be reformed, and in so doing, encourage individual purchase of less costly catastrophic policies.

The solution is not socialized medicine in any form (referred to as a "single payer" health system). Countries that have nationalized their medical systems inevitably ration care through the political system; costs are driven down only by denying needed care and limiting facilities and technology. Politicians and bureaucrats commandeer the power to decide who lives or dies— and, far more often, who is forced to suffer along without treatment.

Federal health care programs have become financially unsustainable. These programs need to be transformed to emphasize patient choice, focus on the truly needy, and add cost-saving incentives. Here, too, market principles can bring better quality health care at less cost.

Safeguarding Democracy by Reducing
Political Dependency

Another reason to radically reform Social Security and Medicare is to safeguard American democracy. Self-government has continually been subverted by politicians demagoging about threats to people's benefits. For decades, Democratic candidates accused Republicans who opposed Social Security benefit hikes of favoring "throwing granny out into the street." In the 1996 presidential race, President Clinton and the Democratic Party went one step further. They used a "Mediscare" ad campaign that included one television spot showing "a steadily beeping EKG machine monitoring a patient's heartbeat. After a voice described how the GOP wanted to raise Medicare premiums and cut benefits, the machine stopped beeping and went into a monotone. Everyone who watches 'ER' knew what that meant—someone had died," the *Chicago Tribune* noted.[37] It was the entitlements program version of Lyndon Johnson's famous daisy nuclear bomb TV ad from 1964.

Entitlement programs have spurred the creation of senior citizen lobbies that have become perhaps the most vocal opponents of a constitutional amendment to require a balanced federal budget. These organized dependents often act as if taxpayers are their number one class enemy. And yet this type of predatory behavior was predictable once politicians created programs that give one group the right to everyone else's paychecks.

If we are to have cleaner elections, then they must not be referendums about who gets to plunder whom. Government entitlement programs divide the citizenry into those who work for a living and those who vote for a living, as H. L. Mencken quipped long ago.

---

37 Bruce Dold, "GOP Foolishness Overshadows Clinton's Errors," *Chicago Tribune*, July 25, 1997.

Charity Instead of Endless Aid Programs

One of America's great strengths has always been the willingness of Americans to organize to solve social problems. The great French classical liberal Alexis de Tocqueville commented on American social activism nearly two centuries ago in his classic work, *Democracy in America*. We see this same commitment today, with the news that Americans donated more than $300 billion to charity in 2007, a record level despite increased economic uncertainty. Most of this money came from individuals. Americans are the most generous people on earth. They even gave $13 billion to international organizations, a form of personal foreign aid.

Unfortunately, the Washington establishment remains mired in a government spending mindset. Indeed, the two major parties have even worked to hook private agencies on public funds. President George W. Bush initiated the so-called faith-based initiative to give federal grants to religious organizations. This is accustoming nonprofit groups to rattle their tin cup at politicians. These groups will spend their time writing grants applying for federal funding rather than helping people without the intervention of a government bagman. It would be far better for Americans to directly support such groups; then politics would not determine the choices of recipients or affect the organizations' operations. Moreover, getting more Americans involved would further invigorate the independent sector.

Instead of expanding government social spending, Washington should encourage Americans to take on greater responsibility in meeting charitable needs. The first step is to cut taxes. Government tax burdens are so heavy they leave far too little for the famous "little platoons" that do so much to improve American society.

Second, we should consider creating a special tax credit for charitable giving, to provide Americans with a dollar-for-dollar tax reduction for money contributed to social services. We could then deduct an equivalent amount from the federal welfare budget. This would enable Americans to shift welfare from the public to the private sectors. It would also avoid the inevitable politicization that accompanies government grant making.

Private charity is a better mechanism for helping people because it is more flexible and cost-effective. Government by its nature must be rule-bound and bureaucratic. But neighbors helping neighbors at the local level is the way Americans traditionally aided those around them in meeting difficult family circumstances and other social needs.

There are many costs to Big Government. One of the worst is creating a bureaucratic state that has absorbed functions once performed by individuals, groups, and communities. We must begin to reverse this process.

Conclusion

The current Social Security–Medicare regime relies on force and deceit. The IRS will seize your bank accounts or your other assets if you don't pay your Social Security taxes. Politicians will continually delude people about the soundness of the system and their own deserts to ever-higher benefits.

If people want to have secure futures, they need to build them on a foundation of voluntary agreements and honest dealing. This is why Americans must compel politicians to permit them to escape from Social Security's clutches. Just because some people might make bad investments is no reason to allow politicians to continue holding everyone captive.

Again, the goal is freedom. Dignity is the foundation of self-respect. If Americans are left in perpetual dependence on politicians—captive to the latest fear-mongering from Washington —their dignity will not survive.

THE FED, THE BAILOUTS, AND THE BETRAYAL OF THE FREE MARKET

The media and many politicians are telling us that one of the most important lessons of the last few years is that the free market cannot be trusted. Proponents of Big Government are weaving a fairy tale about how the profit motive led to the collapse of banks and housing values across the land.

This allegation itself is one of the great charades of our times. It is true that banks and housing are getting clobbered at the same time the US dollar is diving and inflation is soaring. The primary villain, however, is not the market but the Federal Reserve —along with federal monstrosities such as Fannie Mae and Freddie Mac, and federal bureaucrats and policies that rewarded and encouraged people to go on one borrowing binge after another.

The Federal Reserve: The High Price of Secret Power

It was only a few years ago that Federal Reserve boss Alan Greenspan was loudly congratulating himself for creating permanent prosperity, if not a permanent boom. Greenspan and other Fed masters of the universe were supposedly so wise that they could jiggle interest rates and rev up the money supply to create ever greater wealth for Americans. But Americans are learning again the hard way not to trust the money manipulators.

There is a myth that the Federal Reserve is independent of the government; thus wise financial overlords can do their magic without any political interference or repercussions. In reality, the Fed has usually been a political patsy.

The New York Times Magazine reported early in 2008 that President Lyndon Johnson persuaded then-Federal Reserve chief William McChesney Martin, Jr. to print more money to bankroll government deficit spending in the 1960s. According to Richard Fisher, the current president of the Dallas Federal Reserve, "Lyndon took Martin to his ranch and asked the Secret Service to leave the room. And he physically beat him, he slammed him against the wall, and said, 'Martin, my boys are dying in Vietnam, and you won't print the money I need.'"[38] Martin acceded to LBJ's demands before his skull was fractured. The surge of new money boosted the rate of inflation, but gave a very political president the political prize he wasted.

LBJ's abuse of the Federal Reserve was exceeded by his successor, Richard Nixon. In August 1971, Nixon imposed wage and price controls, purportedly to throttle inflationary pressures. At the same time, the Federal Reserve flooded the money supply with new dollars—creating the appearance of an economic boom while federal controls delayed the evidence of inflation. The Justice Department and federal regulators were harassing businesses that sought to adjust to market conditions by raising prices at the same time that the government was secretly destabilizing the market with a flood of freshly printed greenbacks. Nixon also closed the gold window—signaling that the US government was completely repudiating its prior promises to back up its paper dollars with precious metals. Nixon's policies helped cause international financial crises and the worst US recession since World War II.

Since 1913, when the Federal Reserve was created, the US dollar has lost more than 95 percent of its purchasing power. The US has suffered a net of more than 2100 percent inflation since the time the politicians and the bankers decided to "fix" the system.

In the first years after the Fed was founded, Americans had not become accustomed to the government covertly destroying the value of their money. Vice President Calvin Coolidge bluntly declared in 1922: "Inflation is repudiation." Nowadays, as long as

---

38 Roger Lowenstein, "The Education of Ben Bernanke," *The New York Times Magazine*, January 20, 2008.

the rate of inflation is not excessive—or as long as its effects are suppressed—there is little protest, at least by respectable experts, political appointees, members of the media, and bankers.

By generating free money for politicians, the Federal Reserve has allowed presidents to finance wars and other adventures and programs the American people would not have been willing to pay for directly out of their own pockets. The Federal Reserve's money-making machine is a charge card (with neither an expiration date nor a limit) that sets politicians free from being held accountable to the citizenry.

In the wake of the 9/11 attacks, the Federal Reserve made the Bush administration happy by slashing interest rates to levels that were below the inflation rate. The result was that government was forcing savers to subsidize borrowers, and encouraging everyone to borrow as much money as they could grab at fire sale rates. The new "free" money helped dramatically drive up housing prices, and also sharply inflated other commodity prices. But much of the new prosperity was an illusion.

The Fed's interest rate policy and the US printing presses' overdrive shredded the value of the dollar. Since 2000, the dollar has lost more than half of its value against the euro. In the ultimate disgrace, the value of the US dollar dipped below that of the Canadian dollar, the so-called Loonie. This debacle illustrates one of US Rep. Ron Paul's favorite sayings: "Every dollar created and spent by government makes the dollars in your pocket worth less and less."[39]

Independent experts warned that the Fed's policies would eventually derail the American economy, but politicians didn't care as long as the boom lasted until after the next election.

The Fed has resurrected the inflation monster that many Americans thought was slain once and for all in Ronald Reagan's first term. June 2008 saw the biggest monthly increase in the consumer price index in twenty-six years. The wholesale price index jumped in 2008 at the fastest rate in seventeen years.

---

39 Ron Paul, Faith-Based Currency, Texas Straight Talk, July 21, 2008

Inflation is an insidious tax on economic productivity and prosperity, as we learned nearly thirty years ago in the midst of Carter-era stagflation.

Yet in a sad but predictable Washington routine, the Federal Reserve is capturing ever more power as a result of its follies. The Fed's interest rate policies and flood of liquidity helped drive stock prices far higher than reality justified. Now that the market is floundering, the Fed has become directly involved in propping up stock prices.

At the same time the Justice Department vigorously prosecutes people corporate officials suspect of insider trading, the Fed is engaged in the biggest stock manipulation in recent American history. The FBI invested vast resources going after Martha Stewart based on an allegation that she relied on insider information when selling four thousand shares of stock in a friend's corporation. Yet, the Fed itself has loaned more than $100 billion to investment firms and banking firms in order to prop up the stock market; we don't know who is benefiting but you can bet someone in Washington, DC is.

In March 2008, the Federal Reserve made $30 billion in loan guarantees in order to persuade Wall Street bank J. P. Morgan Chase to take over the investment firm Bear Stearns, which was nearing bankruptcy because of its risky investment policies (such as heavy exposure to subprime mortgages). This was one of the biggest bailouts in American history, and yet it almost all happened behind closed doors. When Bear Stearns chief executive Alan Schwartz testified shortly afterwards before the Senate Banking Committee, he was treated like a martyr. In a statement bordering on surreal, committee chairman Chris Dodd (D-CT) told Schwartz: "On behalf of all of us here on this dais, our sympathies go out to your employees. There's no adequate way we can express our sorrow to them for what happened. Obviously, shareholders, same sort of feelings, but obviously the employees particularly. It's a particularly hard blow."[40] Senate Banking Committee members have received more than $20 million in contributions from the

---

40 Dana Milbank, "Buddy, Can You Spare a Billion?" *The Washington Post*, April 4, 2008.

securities and investment industry in recent years; Dodd alone received almost $6 million. Senators allowed the Bear Stearns chief to claim he was blameless for his firm's demise. Most senators exhibited no curiosity whatsoever at how the policies they and the Fed created bushwhacked shareholders and investors across the land. Schwartz's lenient, even deferential treatment on Capitol Hill is a reminder that politicians cannot be trusted to safeguard taxpayers when the government passes out billion dollar guarantees and other favors.

We are witnessing the corruption of financial markets by politicians and political appointees determined to spend any amount of other people's money to hide the damage from their own policies. The Fed depends on secrecy to work its wiles, but this is the same secrecy that has generated corruption in practically every other endeavor that combined vast arbitrary power and closed curtains. It is not in the national interest to artificially make stocks appear more valuable than they actually are—at least until the political insiders have a chance to sell and make their windfalls.

Stock prices have continued to sink regardless of the Fed heaving more billions of dollars onto the sacrificial altar. The Fed's actions are postponing adjustments, which will become more painful the longer they are artificially delayed.

The Fed, the Congress, and the Housing Bust

Nothing illustrates the folly of the Fed's inflationary policies better than what has happened to American homeowners in recent years.

The housing boom-bust has ravaged Americans far and wide. *Bloomberg News* reported in August 2008 that "almost one-third of US homeowners who bought in the last five years now owe more on their mortgages than their properties are worth."[41] The Federal Reserve reported earlier this year that, for the first time on record since 1945, Americans' debt on their homes exceeds their home equity; and housing prices continue falling.

---

41 Bob Ivry, "One Third of New Owners Owe More Than House Is Worth," *Bloomberg News*, August 12, 2008.

Not surprisingly, the stock prices of the two premier government-sponsored enterprises (GSEs) have largely collapsed. It was probably necessary to have a temporary stopgap propping up of Fannie Mae (Federal National Mortgage Association, created by Congress in 1938) and Freddie Mac (Federal Home Loan Mortgage Corporation, created by Congress in 1970) in order to prevent the crash of the entire economy. But Congress and President Bush betrayed taxpayers and homeowners by using the bailout legislation to expand political manipulation and control over the housing market.

The $300 billion bailout legislation is a shameless special interest Christmas tree: it bails out foolish homeowners and lenders, provides money for the irresponsible Fannie Mae and Freddie Mac, diverts taxpayer money to new home buyers, and takes more money from hard-pressed taxpayers for low-income housing. It also creates another piggy bank for activist groups at public expense, and forces responsible renters, homeowners, and taxpayers to bail out irresponsible investors, lenders, and buyers. The law includes almost $4 billion in grants to state and local governments to buy up foreclosed properties. Given the dismal record of public housing across the land, it is hard to understand why anyone would want politicians holding title to ever more homes.

The 630-page housing bailout bill was chock full of other mischief. For instance, it created a fingerprint registry for potentially thousands of employees in the real estate and mortgage industries: the Nationwide Mortgage Licensing System and Registry. This federal database will include the fingerprints of thousands of Americans (including real estate brokers) never suspected of misconduct, let alone of committing a crime.

The housing bailout legislation also included a new edict requiring credit card companies and online payment systems, such as Amazon and eBay, to turn customer financial data over to the IRS. The measure was justified as an aid to tax compliance, but there was no discussion, let alone public hearings, about the supposed problem being addressed. Instead, Congress rubber-stamped the trampling of scores of millions of Americans' privacy.

The data thus rounded up will be added to the mountains of personal data that is already helping the feds achieve total information awareness.

The fact of the matter is, the housing boom-bust was driven by Fannie Mae and Freddie Mac, two GSEs that are nominally private but which enjoy significant advantages over truly private companies, including cheaper borrowing, lower capital requirements, and an implicit federal guarantee.

Now, however, with the formal September 2008 takeover of Freddie and Fannie by the federal government, America's taxpayers are on the hook for incalculable billions in problematic mortgage guarantees. Yet, all the major Washington, DC players, including both major parties' presidential and vice presidential candidates, praised the move. Even Wall Street, which calls itself "free market," effused in praising the administration's actions.

Fannie and Freddie behaved irresponsibly in buying mountains of mortgages held by banks and mortgage companies, confident that they were too big to fail. They in fact own $5.1 trillion in mortgage debt, almost half of the nation's total. Yet their top executives continue to pay themselves salaries more akin to an oil magnate than an American public servant.

Treasury Secretary Henry Paulson commented in 2007: "If we knew then what we know now, we likely would not have designed entities like the GSEs that have private ownership but are required to undertake a public mission. These competing interests are too difficult to manage, and the potential long-term market distortions and public policy concerns are too significant."[42] However, as the Bush administration's front man, in announcing the government takeover of these two GSEs, Paulson shamelessly patted the administration on the back for having the courage to saddle the taxpayers with their bailout.

In reality, Fannie and Freddie have become American-style crony capitalism. Fannie and Freddie spent more than $200 million

---

42 "Testimony of Treasury Secretary Henry M. Paulson, Jr. Before the House Committee on Financial Services on the Legislative and Regulatory Options for Minimizing and Mitigating Mortgage Foreclosures," Treasury Department Press Room, September 20, 2007.

for lobbying and campaign contributions to Congress over the last decade, according to *The Politico* newspaper.[43]

Congress cannot be trusted to oversee these two entities. Senator Richard Shelby of Alabama is the ranking Republican on the Senate Banking Committee. *The New York Times* recently reported: "While on the Banking Committee, [Shelby] financed an apartment complex he owns in Tuscaloosa with a $5 million loan from Freddie Mac, the same government-sponsored mortgage company whose regulation his committee is reshaping."[44] Shelby has become very rich since being elected to Congress. His net worth is now between $9 million and $32 million, and the "single biggest source of his new wealth is the 124-unit apartment complex"[45] that Freddie Mac enabled him to buy. The *Times* noted that "Shelby has for years blocked legislation that would have restrained Freddie Mac and its sibling, Fannie Mae."[46] (Housing entities have been bipartisan in their distribution of favors. Countrywide Mortgage, one of the largest lenders, gave discount interest rates for a mortgage loan to Democratic senator Chris Dodd.)

Fannie and Freddie should be privatized *en toto*—no ifs, ands, or buts—and no strings remaining to once again rope innocent taxpayers to pay for their blunders. Taxpayers must never again be impaled for the follies of such government entities.

In 1979, when Chrysler received a $1.5 billion federal loan guarantee to keep afloat, there was an intense public debate over the wisdom of Uncle Sam bailing out a floundering corporation. Unfortunately, there has been no similar debate over the far greater bailouts of our times, including investment houses and mortgage guarantors. Instead, politicians and their friends in the media act like cops at the scene of a horrendous accident: "nothing to see here, folks—just move along now."

---

43 Lisa Lerer, "Fannie, Freddie spent $200M to buy influence," *The Politico*, July 16, 2008.

44 Eric Lipton and Eric Lichtblau,"Senator's Ties to Real Estate Draw Criticism," *The New York Times*, May 9, 2008.

45 Ibid.

46 Ibid.

Our free economy cannot survive if we allow politicians to continue picking winners and losers. We are creating a no-fault economy, in which the taxpayers bail out everyone for every mistake they make.

The Need for Honest Money

Putting limits on the government's right to artificially create money is as important as limiting its other powers. Economist Ludwig von Mises noted, "The idea of sound money . . . was devised as an instrument for the protection of civil liberties against despotic inroads on the part of governments. Ideologically it belongs in the same class with political constitutions and bills of rights."[47]

Americans should be wary because the Federal Reserve could commit far greater abuses against Americans' privacy and financial security in the future. In 1999, in what has to be one of the most bizarre proposals ever by a government official, Marvin Goodfriend, a senior vice president at the Federal Reserve Bank of Richmond, proposed that the government use new technology to penalize citizens who do not spend their cash as fast as the government wants. Goodfriend suggested the magnetic strip in our US currency could visibly record when a bill was last withdrawn from the banking system. A carry tax could be deducted from each bill deposited according to how long the bill was in circulation. The feds could effectively tax anyone who did not spend his earnings as quickly as politicians preferred. This bizarre proposal epitomizes how some Federal Reserve officials believe that Americans are obliged to live their lives for the convenience and profit of their rulers. With loony ideas like this floating around, is it any wonder why some Americans are paranoid about the Fed?

In the short run, Congress must begin limiting the Fed's power—prohibit it from bailing out private companies, and compel

---

47 Ludwig von Mises (1881–1973), *The Theory of Money and Credit*, first published 1912, available online at www.econlib.org/library/Mises/msTContents.html (Part IV, Chapter 21, paragraphs 3, 4), accessed 26 September 2008.

it to act with greater transparency. But we have to realize that congressional oversight of the Federal Reserve will probably not work any better than congressional oversight of Fannie and Freddie.

In the long run, America must find a way to return to an honest dollar. I don't know if this will mean the return to a gold standard, or to some other system of fixed values. But permitting politicians to arbitrarily manipulate the value of the currency upon which people depend has already created far too many costly disasters for Americans. Economist John Maynard Keynes warned long ago: "There is no subtler, no surer means of overturning the existing basis of society than to debauch the currency. The process engages all the hidden forces of economic law on the side of destruction, and does it in a manner which not one man in a million can diagnose."[48] Our freedom will not be safe as long as politicians can covertly destroy the value of citizens' savings and paychecks.

---

48 John Maynard Keynes, *The Economic Consequences of the Peace*, 1919, pp. 235-248. Accessed at www.pbs.org/wgbh/commandingheights/shared/minitext/ess_inflation.html.

IMMIGRATION AND TRADE POLICY

The United States government sets the policy for the entry of both people and goods into this nation. This has long been recognized as a uniquely federal responsibility. Unfortunately, it is another area in which the government has made a massive mess. Libertarians have far better solutions to both the immigration and trade challenges than do either the Republicans or Democrats.

Fixing Immigration

America is a nation of immigrants, but the process of assimilation has broken down. Although immigration provides economic benefits, it also affects America's cultural and national identity. Immigration reform must begin with securing the border. Our primary obligation is to protect American citizens.

Currently, America has too many illegal immigrants and too few legal ones, particularly those with entrepreneurial, professional, and scientific skills.

The United States has been enriched by immigrants from around the world. Free immigration remains an attractive ideal, but is impossible with the expensive and expansive nanny state we've created.

What made immigration work so well early in our history was America's famed melting pot and the absence of any welfare state. People came to America because they wanted to become Americans. Immigrants were expected to pay their own way and cover most of the costs of their own assimilation and adjustment to American society. People came for economic opportunities, not government benefits. The result was a strong and vibrant America —the world's first true superpower.

Today, however, the US government has lost control of its borders. Rather than consciously decide who should be welcomed as new citizens, citizenship is bestowed on anyone who happens to be born in the US. Current policy is a mess.

Step 1: Secure the Border

The US border can never be completely open or completely closed. But the starting point of any immigration policy is to secure the borders to the extent possible. America needs to be able to check potential immigrants for criminal background, communicable diseases, and possible terrorist activity. Only by deterring massive illegal border crossings can the US put in place a fair and enforceable legal immigration policy. Effective enforcement is more important than a physical fence.

Instead, the Bush administration has kowtowed in ways that make no sense. For instance, at the border checkpoint south of San Diego, at Tijuana, Mexico, US border agents are under orders, if the line of cars on the Mexican side gets too long, to just let people in. We care more about inconveniencing people from other countries than we are about upholding our own laws.

Even more bizarre, the Bush administration is encouraging US border agents to tromp off to Iraq. A 2007 memo from W. Ralph Basham, the head of Customs and Border Protection, to all Customs and Border Protection officers and border patrol agents solicited them to volunteer for service in Iraq. Actually, "volunteer" is not the correct verb here, since they would get almost double their current pay if they went overseas. The commissioner apparently concluded that it was more critical to help train members of the Iraqi Department of Border Enforcement than to do everything possible to stem the tide of illegals entering the United States from Mexico. The Bush administration intentionally reduced our own capacity to secure our borders in order to try and strengthen Iraq's.

Step 2: End Handouts for Illegals

Americans have always been a generous people, but we must recognize how government handouts can undermine the national character and endanger the republic. Handouts are subversive of a rational, responsible immigration policy.

As Nobel laureate economist Milton Friedman observed, "It's just obvious that you can't have free immigration and a welfare state."[49] Early immigrants to America never expected that governments would welcome them with an array of handouts and special treatment.

One of the biggest attractions for illegal immigrants was provided by a 1982 Supreme Court decision that mandates that Americans provide free education to the children of illegal immigrants. In the case of *Plyer v. Doe*, the Court held that state and local governments must pay to school the children of illegal residents. The court decreed that "no plausible distinction with respect to Fourteenth Amendment jurisdiction can be drawn between resident aliens whose entry into the United States was lawful, and resident aliens whose entry was unlawful."[50] The court declared that refusing to give free schooling to illegal children of illegal immigrants was illegal discrimination. Chief Justice Warren Burger, writing for three other dissenting justices, pointed out that "the Constitution does not provide a cure for every social ill, nor does it vest judges with a mandate to try to remedy every social problem."[51] Unfortunately, his sound arguments did not carry the day, and the results have been phenomenally costly.

The Fourteenth Amendment was put on the books after the Civil War to make it clear beyond dispute that freed slaves were American citizens. Unfortunately, liberal judges have stretched and contorted this amendment in ways that would have its original authors rolling in their graves. No one wants to punish children for

---

49 Steven Malanga, "The Right Immigration Policy," *City Journal*, Fall 2006.

50 Linda Greenouse, "Justices Rule States Must Pay to Educate Illegal Alien Pupils," *The New York Times*, June 16, 1982.

51 Ibid.

the sins of their parents, but the Supreme Court decision unfairly burdens American citizens and creates a powerful draw for illegal immigrants.

No foreigner should have the right to force Americans to pay for his kid's education. Our current policy makes as much sense as allowing Ciudad Juarez, Mexico, to levy a property tax on the homeowners of El Paso, Texas, to force them to pay for the Mexican schools on the other side of the Rio Grande.

And it is not simply a dollar cost we are talking about here. Deluging school systems with 15 percent, 25 percent, or an even higher percentage of children who speak almost no English creates a nightmare for teachers and American pupils. Naturally, the education bureaucrats have come up with a new euphemism for this group: English language learners. (One would hope that all elementary school children would be learning and improving their English.)

This tidal wave puts schools in a catch-22: if the schools try to mainstream illegal immigrants who can't speak English, instruction is often dumbed down for everybody. If they create a second tier solely for the children who speak no English, they risk being sued for discrimination or other legal challenges. American public schools have long at least aspired to the goal of equal treatment for all students. But that is almost impossible when so many students arrive without the foggiest notion of basic English.

The problems caused by this 1982 Supreme Court decision are compounded by recent federal legislation such as the No Child Left Behind Act. With that law, President Bush and Congress decreed that all children must be able to achieve literacy by the year 2014. Schools are judged as failures if any single classification of students fails to become competent at reading English. The combination of the red carpet for illegal immigrants and the federal law clobbering schools for any group of students not fluent in English results in diverting ever more resources to serve illegal aliens. In some cases, this can effectively put the children of American citizens at the back of the bus.

Unfortunately, honesty about this issue seems to be one of the remaining politically incorrect issues of our times. A 2008 *Las Vegas Review Journal* editorial challenged the government to honestly determine and reveal how many illegal alien school children are in Nevada schools:

> What, precisely, is it costing us? Without the influx of illegals, it's a good bet we wouldn't need to build any new school buildings for a while . . . Many school officials claim that to even bring this up would be discriminatory and racist. Nonsense. These educrats can tell you the percentage of African-American and Pacific Islander children in each school, down to a tenth of a percent. They know what percentage of kids in each school come from poor families and thus qualify for free meals. But they can't figure out how many children are here illegally? Taxpayers should be told the real cost of ignoring the illegal immigration problem. Count it, add it up and spell it out.[52]

The 1982 Supreme Court decision should be challenged and overturned. Or if the Court will not repent of its folly of a generation ago, Congress should pass a law curtailing the damage.

Health care is another area where the "rights" of illegal immigrants are increasingly adversely affecting American citizens.

The Emergency Medical Treatment and Active Labor Act (EMTALA) of 1985 compels any US hospital with an emergency room to treat virtually anyone who comes through its doors, regardless of his or her immigration status. This is an unfunded federal mandate that has helped bankrupt many hospitals, especially in California. Like most federal mandates, it is enforced by a federal iron fist: any doctor or hospital that refuses to treat an emergency case is subject to a $50,000 fine. The definition of

---

52 Editorial, "Counting illegals," *Las Vegas Review-Journal*, February 15, 2008.

emergency in the federal law is often vague, and doctors face legal perils if they ignore patients who claim dubious emergencies. According to Congressman Tom Tancredo (R-CO), some "illegal aliens specifically come to the United States to obtain health care. In fact, Mexican government documents provide details about this law and describe it as a benefit available to its citizens who travel illegally to the United States."[53]

President Bush declared last year that "people have access to health care in America. After all, you just go to an emergency room."[54] But the president has not visited a typical urban ER any time recently (apart from a controlled photo op). Almost 10 percent of hospital ER facilities have shut down since 1996. At the same time, the number of ER visits has skyrocketed, reaching almost 120 million in 2006.

The 1986 law is helping create long delays for many Americans going to the emergency room. If Congress wants to pass a law that openly specifies that Americans suffering medical emergencies must wait for many hours while doctors treat illegal immigrants using emergency rooms for free routine medical care, then members of Congress should be honest and responsible and take the heat. Instead, congressmen refuse to admit their responsibility for the national emergency room crisis.

Ordering hospitals and doctors to give freebies to one group means that other people will be hit with higher bills. The 1986 law also results in Americans paying much higher costs for ER visits, since almost half of the ER patients walk away without paying their bills (many, if not most, of such nonpayers are not illegal aliens). Compelling every hospital in the land to become a charity institution undermines the viability of the American health care system in order to cater to people who have no right to be in this country.

Both California and Texas spend substantially more than $1 billion a year to treat illegal aliens. Obviously, it is hard for a

---

54 http://weiwentg.blogspot.com/2008/08/should-emtala-be-reserved-for-legal-us.html

54 Paul Krugman, "Conservatives Are Such Jokers," *The New York Times*, October 5, 2007.

compassionate people to say no, but those who come illegally should not be allowed to abuse America's hospitality. If they still come, they should rely on charity care. The message would soon go forth that the free ride was over.

If a private charity wants to provide medical care for illegal immigrants, that is its right. In a free country, people should be permitted to donate their money for whatever peaceful cause they please. But it is outrageous that taxpayers are *compelled* to subsidize the health care for those who illegally enter America.

The free emergency medical care is often invoked by pregnant foreign women who come to have their children born in American hospitals. This is where the problem of birthright citizenship ties in. As the result of another flawed interpretation of the Fourteenth Amendment, citizenship is conferred upon anyone born in the US, even if the mother is here illegally. This peculiar policy demands no connection or commitment to America in exchange for citizenship. The members of Congress and state legislatures that approved the Fouteenth Amendment (in the late 1860s) never imagined that their work would turn the children of tourists, as well as illegal migrants, into citizens.

Some 400,000 babies are born each year to illegal aliens in the US; these children become "anchor babies"—not only do the babies qualify for various welfare benefits and other entitlements, but the illegal parents can use their newborns as anchors to stay in the United States. Having one legal citizen in a family can make it far more difficult to deport the rest of the family.

The administration should, as a policy and legal matter, reasonably interpret the Fourteenth Amendment as applying only to children born in the United States of parents *lawfully* in this country. Another remedy would be for Congress to enact legislation that would curtail the scope and damage from birthright citizenship claims. It is possible that a constitutional amendment will be necessary to correct this problem. America should join most of the countries of the world and require more than the location of birth to determine the privilege of citizenship.

Step 3: English as the Official Language

Another step that Congress should take to strengthen the forces of assimilation is to make English America's official language. It is none of the government's business what language people speak at home, but government business itself in this nation should be transacted in English. Congress should scrap bilingual ballots. If citizens do not learn enough English to read a simple ballot, then they should not be voting in American elections. A common language is an important national foundation. At the same time, federal agencies should stop punishing private businesses that require English as the language of the workplace. The Equal Employment Opportunity Commission has harassed numerous businesses for requiring English, as if it were a federal crime for a business to want its employees to speak the same language as its customers.

Step 4: More Legal Immigrants

At the same time that the United States must sharply reduce the number of people who enter the country illegally, we should expand legal immigration, especially of those who would contribute the most to America. The unskilled workers and their families coming from Mexico illegally assimilate more slowly and remain poorer and more dependent on government assistance than past immigrants.

In contrast, there is a perpetual shortage of H-1B visas for high-tech workers and other skilled professionals. These people create new businesses, generate patents, and strengthen leading firms. Current policy routinely prevents American corporations from hiring some of the smartest graduates of American universities. Microsoft chairman Bill Gates recently testified to Congress: "At a time when talent is the key to economic success, it makes no sense to educate people in our universities, often subsidized by US taxpayers, and then insist that they return home."[55] The National Foundation for American Policy recently

---

55 Jim Puzzanghera and Michelle Quinn, "Working Around Shortage of Visas," *The Los Angeles Times*, March 31, 2008.

estimated that "for each H-1B visa requested, technology firms hire five additional employees."[56]

We should expand the number of H-1B visas issued, and reverse the preference now granted to relatives of US citizens. The 1965 Immigration and Nationality Act, which has dominated US immigration policy for over forty years, resulted in legal immigration becoming dominated by the same country that provides the most illegal immigrants—Mexico. The 1965 Act is biased against Europeans, historically the source of many of our most creative and productive immigrants.

Finally, it is vital that neither the president nor Congress create any type of amnesty for current illegal immigrants. While there should be no intrusive effort to round up the millions of illegal immigrants already in the country, anyone hoping to get a green card or citizenship must be required to register and get in line with everyone else. To provide for citizenship without consequence for past lawbreaking would encourage continued illegal immigration, in the hopes of winning a similar, future amnesty. It also makes a mockery of the rule of law. I wonder if those who favor periodic amnesty for illegal aliens would also favor the IRS offering the same amnesty for delinquent taxpayers, erasing their taxes due simply because enough years had passed since the delinquency occurred.

Immigration policy helps determine what it means to be an American. We must control the nation's borders. Only then can we effectively address the question of immigration, and its impact on economics, culture, and nationhood.

There is no perfect immigration reform. The government must balance security and sovereignty concerns, which necessitate controlling the border, with the economic benefits of immigration. The best policy is to stop the flow of illegal immigrants while accepting more of the world's economically productive who want to come to America.

---

56 Jim Puzzanghera and Michelle Quinn, "Working Around Shortage of Visas," *The Los Angeles Times*, March 31, 2008.

Free Trade for a Free Nation

Trade policy is a much easier question than immigration policy. Trade policy is a question of whether politicians and bureaucrats will be able to make serfs of consumers. Will a small handful of Washington operatives have the power to decree what 300 million Americans will be able to purchase from the other 96 percent of the world's population?

Politicians and activists are increasingly demanding that the US achieve or impose fair trade on foreign trading partners. But no one offers a clear definition of the *fair* in fair trade. The theologians in the Middle Ages spent centuries splitting hairs to define the idea of a fair price and no one could come up with a sound formula. There is no reason to expect American politicians or federal bureaucrats to be any more profound than medieval theologians. We cannot trust government to set fair prices for imports any more than we could trust them to set fair prices for all the goods and services that Americans purchase.

Instead of creating new laws and restrictions designed to impose fairness, we should instead rely on the traditional standard used in contract law for fair prices: the voluntary consent of both the buyer and the seller to the deal. Many of the advocates of fair trade believe that the United States government should follow paternalist policies towards Third World farmers and craftsmen. But, aside from the insulting nature of such policies, it would be naive to expect that any such US policies would actually serve people beyond the US border. Low-income Guatemalan coffee growers do not have a strong lobby in Washington—thus practically assuring that they would be skewered if the US government intervened to take care of them.

While the average US tariff now is very low, the import tax on products purchased by low-income Americans is often very high. Edward Gresser of the Progressive Policy Institute pointed out that the tariff code has some of the highest tariffs on clothing, shoes, and other items far more likely to be sold at Wal-Mart than at Saks Fifth Avenue: "Young single mothers buying cheap clothes and shoes now pay tariff rates five to ten times higher than middle-class or rich families pay in elite stores . . . Cheap sneakers valued at $3 or less per pair carry tariffs of 48 percent."[57]

Some protectionists claim that the United States government must close American ports to foreign goods in order to protect American businesses. But this is not protection—this is using government force and threats against any American who would make a purchase that Washington does not approve.

Besides, protectionism is a nonstarter because the government cannot protect some businesses without sacrificing other businesses.

If the government imposes high tariffs on lumber imports (as it has on imports from Canada since the 1980s), it hammers our home building industry and home buyers across the nation. There are twenty-five times more workers in industries that use lumber than there are in logging and sawmills in this country. But that didn't matter as long as Washington politicians could get votes and campaign contributions from lumber producers by punishing lumber buyers.

The US government has imposed quotas on steel imports off and on since the late 1960s. When this happens, every industry that uses steel is sacrificed. The Center for the American Business estimated that import quotas on steel resulted in three jobs lost in steel-using industries for every job saved in the steel industry.[58] The Federal Trade Commission examined the impact of the quotas on the US economy in the 1980s and discovered that each dollar of additional steel producer profits cost the American economy twenty-five dollars.[59]

Another example of the folly of protectionism is our sugar import quotas. The US government has been directly subsidizing

57 Edward Gresser, "Toughest on the Poor: America's Flawed Tariff System," *Foreign Affairs*, November 2002.

58 Arthur Denzau, "How Import Restrictions Reduce Employment," Center for the Study of American Business, 1987.

59 David Tarr and Morris Morke, "Aggregate Costs to the United States of Tariffs and Quotas on Imports: General Tariff Cuts and Removal of Quotas. . . " U.S. Federal Trade Commission, 1984.

or heavily protecting US sugar growers for almost two hundred years. Yet American sugar cane producers are still hopelessly uncompetitive with farmers elsewhere in the world. Federal restrictions on imports and other measures assure that the US price of sugar is far above the world market price for sugar. The result has been an exodus of jobs in the candy and other food manufacturing industries. Federal sugar policy has destroyed more American jobs than the total number of employees in sugar producers in the US.

The US government not only restricts imports—it sometimes issues decrees prohibiting Americans from purchasing or dealing with foreign countries. For almost fifty years, the United States has maintained an embargo on trade with Cuba. The embargo is enforced by the Treasury Department's Office of Foreign Assets Control, the same agency charged with going after terrorist financing. As of 2004, that office had ten times more agents busily tracking violators of Cuban embargo than it had pursuing Osama bin Laden's money. Rep. William Delahunt (D-MA) complained: "We're chasing old ladies on bicycle trips in Cuba when we should be concentrating on using a significant tool against shadowy terrorist organizations."[60]

The embargo failed to topple Fidel Castro and actually provided him with a scapegoat to blame the failure of his socialist policies. We should end the Cuban embargo.

However, the US government should not accede to the demands of the US farm lobby and begin heavily subsidizing crop exports to Cuba. This would do little more than skewer US taxpayers and bankrupt Cuban farmers.

Some protectionists claim that the United States must impose tariffs and other import restrictions in order to retaliate against foreign government trade barriers against American exports. But this merely compounds the damage. If your neighbor kicks his dog, you don't teach him a lesson by kicking your dog. Washington politicians have no right to destroy the freedom of

60 Nancy San Martin, "More Focus on Cuba Embargo than Terror Trail Is Questioned," *Miami Herald,* April 30, 2004.

American consumers regardless of the actions of foreign governments. US farm subsidies have been justified for eighty years because of foreign government farm subsidies. Foreign follies provided the pretext for practically any unproductive or ill-advised agricultural policy presidents or Congress wanted to concoct. But farm trade continues to be tangled with quotas and restrictions in many countries, regardless of the hundreds of billions of dollars the US government wasted on farm subsidies in recent decades.

It makes as little sense to restrict imports to balance trade between the US and a foreign nation as it would to create trade barriers between individual American states. If the state of New York suddenly announced that it was closing its market to New Hampshire products because of a trade imbalance in granite, Americans would assume that the governor of New York had rocks in his head. But unfortunately, people don't reach the same conclusion when Washington politicians try to close the US border to foreign goods.

America is much less protectionist than it was half a century ago. But we should finish the work and abolish the remaining tariffs and end the remaining import quotas. Freedom is the best trade policy.

ENERGY/ENVIRONMENT/ GLOBAL WARMING

Americans can no longer afford to have an energy or environmental policy based on wishful thinking. With gasoline prices at the pump at all-time highs, we can no longer allow American drivers to be held hostage to political finagling or political posturing.

Since George W. Bush took office in early 2001, federal environmental policies have cost Americans more than a trillion dollars. This exceeds the total value of all the factories in most states. It exceeds the combined value of all the factories owned by Fortune 500 companies. The vast majority of these costs were shouldered by the private sector. Unfortunately, much, if not most, of these compliance costs were wasted—as far as making America a safer place for citizens. Political priorities mandated bottomless-pit spending in the name of environmental safety—protecting the environment by compelling people to burn money on the green altar of the month.

Republicans and Democrats alike have bought into the command-and-control model of environmental protection. It was Richard Nixon who created the Environmental Protection Agency in 1970. Both parties have repeatedly pandered to often bogus or overblown environmental fears that politicians exploited for their own profit. As a result, American industry and American entrepreneurs are increasingly hogtied when it comes to producing and innovating. We need risk-based environmental regulations—not government edicts based on the latest fad or aesthetics—creating the appearance of protection while doing little of real value.

How Government Protects the Environment

Private businesses are being decimated by federal regulatory mandates that the government itself is trampling underfoot. The Defense Department is by far the nation's biggest polluter. Especially in the last seven years, it has openly scorned EPA orders to clean up its hazardous waste sites—even when they pose "imminent and substantial" dangers to nearby communities. The Pentagon has ignored the fact that Fort Detrick, Maryland—the largest center for developing biological and chemical weapons (including anthrax)—may have leaked toxic chemicals into surrounding groundwater. When George W. Bush was campaigning for president back in 2000, he promised to make all federal facilities obey environmental laws and to "make them accountable."[61] Bush's pledge provides no consolation for citizens endangered by federal environmental abuses.

The Bush administration has perpetuated a trend that had grown worse under the Clinton administration. *The Boston Globe* reported in 1999: "Federal facilities are more likely to violate water standards than private companies, EPA records show. . . . Federal agencies are increasingly violating the law, with 27 percent of all government facilities out of compliance in 1996, the latest year figures were available, compared to 10 percent in 1992." One EPA official told *The Globe*: "The fact is the federal government is getting away with murder and the EPA is not legally or politically powerful enough to turn the tide."[62]

But, as with so many other areas nowadays, it is not a crime when the government violates the law.

Nothing symbolizes the folly of trusting the government to protect the environment better than the National Flood Insurance Program. This program, run by the brainiacs at the Federal Emergency Management Agency (FEMA), was created in 1968

---

62 Lyndsey Layton, Pentagon Fights EPA On Pollution Cleanup, *The Washington Post*, June 30, 2008.

62 David Armstrong, "Environmental Injustice: Government as Polluter," *The Boston Globe*, November 14, 1999.

purportedly to reduce the cost of disaster relief for the federal government. Instead, the lavish subsidies the program provides homeowners have swayed them to build—and rebuild—their homes in harm's way. Scott Faber of American Rivers, a conservation organization, observes, "Prior to the 1960s, you didn't have much development in flood-prone areas because you couldn't find any insurer crazy enough to underwrite it. But the federal government came along and said it is okay—we are going to make it financially possible for you to live in a flood plain. The effect of this has been much more dramatic in coastal areas, where we have seen a huge boom in coastal development in the last 30 years."[63]

There has been far more construction in "hurricane alleys" along the Atlantic and Gulf coasts than would have occurred without federal flood insurance, and the result is that taxpayers get skewered time and again to rebuild the same houses in the same areas.

The National Wildlife Foundation estimated that 2 percent of properties covered by federal flood insurance had "multiple losses accounting for 60 percent of the program's total claims." Almost $3 billion has been spent in the last two decades "repairing and rebuilding the same structures two, three and four times."

Professor Rob Young of Western Carolina University declared after Hurricane Katrina in 2005: "If coastal development is such an economic powerhouse that it is essential to the viability of a locality or a state, then let's let the free market decide. No more federal money for rebuilding infrastructure. No more federally subsidized flood insurance."[64] It is no loss to the United States if people choose to build their home in a danger zone. Yet because politicians enjoy playing Santa Claus, the federal flood insurance program continues encouraging and rewarding irresponsible behavior around the nation.

---

63 James Bovard, "Uncle Sam's Flood Machine," *The Freeman*, January 2006.

64 Ibid.

Global Warming Myths and Realities

As America confronts a variety of domestic and foreign challenges in the future, it is essential that we preserve our prosperous, productive, and innovative economy. Without a strong economic foundation, it will be impossible for our nation to deal with the many serious financial, social, and environmental problems facing us.

One of the most complicated and controversial issues facing America is global warming. There has been a warming of the atmosphere, but although temperatures have increased in recent decades, the scientific community has been unable to make definitive judgments as to the past cause or future course of climate change. Much more study is required.

Temperatures have shifted broadly over the centuries. Indeed, the models that predict problems in the future did not predict the lack of any temperature increase over the last decade. The United Nations Intergovernmental Panel on Climate Change concluded in 1999: "Overall, there is no evidence that extreme weather events, or climate variability, has increased, in a global sense, through the 20th century."[65] It is difficult to have confidence in long-range weather forecasts when the most sophisticated computer analyses routinely sometimes fail to predict next-day snowstorms.

Unfortunately, many climate processes are not yet clearly understood. While average temperatures may have increased slightly in the recent decades, there is no clear causal link between modern civilization and global warming. A report late last year by the minority staff of the Senate Environment and Public Works listed over four hundred prominent scientists from dozens of nations who had spoken out criticizing the prevailing view that global warming is a man-made problem. Many of these scientists are experts who currently or formerly participated in the United Nations Intergovernmental Panel on Climate Change.

We need to conduct more and better scientific research about

---

65 Quoted in Press Release, "U.S. PIRG Report Distorts Science of Global Warming," Competitive Enterprise Institute, April 6, 2000.

climate change to assess likely problems in the future and develop appropriate solutions. More dialogue is key to understanding global warming and developing the best means of dealing with the important questions surrounding the phenomenon. This dialogue must include scientists from all sides of the issue, including those who are skeptical of the assertion that humans are primarily responsible for global temperature changes and that those changes pose a substantial danger to humanity.

Moreover, we must develop cost-effective policies that will not undermine the US economy. There is a grave danger that concerns over climate change will become an excuse for imposing draconian new regulations. The most extreme proposals, rejected by the Senate, would cut American energy use by 70 percent by the year 2050. So-called cap and trade legislation, recently rejected by the US Senate—but supported by both Senators McCain and Obama—would do grievous damage to the American economy, threatening to create a permanent recession by reversing industrial growth and destroying millions of jobs.

We must address the issue of climate change, but do so *realistically*, recognizing the importance of simultaneously expanding energy supplies and maintaining economic growth. Our greatest strength in confronting the problems of the future is our free market economy. Only by reducing government barriers to private research and development are we going to achieve the innovative, even transformational, changes necessary in the years and decades ahead.

Many of the extremist complaints about global warming are not only mythical, they are profoundly mischievous. Global warming is being exploited by some environmentalists and those who favor vesting vast punitive power in international organizations. Much of the pressure on global warming is coming from the United Nations and other countries. China, of course, is pushing hard for the Kyoto Protocol. Why? Because the country is exempt! Kyoto would require us to shut down factories at the same time that China receives a blank check to increase its pollution as much as it pleased.

It makes far more sense to use American ingenuity and technology to adapt to future changes in the climate than to wreck the economy in order to prevent temperature increases that may never occur.

It would be folly to vest politicians with sweeping veto power over everyday life on the mere possibility that their decrees might generate environmental benefits in the distant future. One statesman and economist who has clearly recognized the broader context of the debate over global warming is Czech Prime Minister Vaclav Klaus, the author of the book, *Blue Planet in Green Shackles*. Klaus writes:

> "What is Endangered: Climate or Freedom?" My answer is: "it is our freedom." I may also add "and our prosperity. . . ."

> The real debate [about climate change] should be about costs and benefits of alternative human actions, about how to rationally deal with the unknown future, about what kind and size of solidarity with much wealthier future generations is justified, about the size of externalities and their eventual appropriate "internalization", about how much to trust the impersonal functioning of the markets in solving any human problem, including global warming and how much to distrust the very visible hand of very human politicians and bureaucrats. . . .

> . . . [T]he whole process [of global climate alarmism] is already in the hands of those who are not interested in rational ideas and arguments. It is in the hands of climatologists and other related scientists who are highly motivated to look in one direction only because a large number of academic careers has evolved around the idea of man-made global warming. It is, further, in the hands of politicians who maximize the number of votes they

seek to get from the electorate. It is also as a consequence of political decisions in the hands of bureaucrats of national and more often of international institutions who try to maximize their budgets and years of careers as well regardless the costs, truth and rationality . . . An entire industry has developed around the funds the firms are getting through the government. . . .[66]

Unfortunately, few American politicians have either the courage or the vision that Prime Minister Klaus brings to this subject.

Highway Robbery at the Gas Pump

Every American who drives an automobile knows that something needs to be done about the cost of energy in the United States. While Republicans are calling for more subsidies to oil companies and Democrats are seeking to micromanage energy companies with more regulations, laws, and taxes, Americans are left to watch helplessly as fuel prices go through the roof. Fuel costs have skyrocketed from $20 per barrel of oil in 2002 to $80 in the summer of 2007 to more than $140 in the summer of 2008.

Ironically, the invasion of Iraq was supposed to secure, among other goals, a long-term lower price of oil. Instead, the US government's Middle East policies have made energy more expensive than it would have been otherwise. As a July 2008 report by the National Security Network explained,

The invasion of Iraq, with its destruction of petroleum infrastructure, hundreds of uncontained attacks on production and transit facilities, and slowness to return production to pre-war levels has added a significant additional expense. So too has saber-rattling against Iran, which experts say has

---

66 Vaclav Klaus, *Blue Planet in Green Shackles*, Real Clear Politics, May 28, 2008. Accesed on www.realclearpolitics.com/articles/2008/05/blue_planet_in_green_shackles.html

affected the price of oil dramatically by as much as $11 in one day. Rising tensions in the world's oil producing hotspots contribute to an oil "security premium," increasing prices by as much as 30 percent.[67]

Threats of military action against Iran by the Bush administration have probably been a major factor in revving up the price of oil in the last year. If Iran is attacked by the US or Israel, it could relatively easily close the Strait of Hormuz, through which 40 percent of the world's oil supply passes. And an attack on Iran could spur a larger war in the Middle East that would devastate oil production facilities for years. While some people pretend the Bush administration's threats against Iran are zero-cost, they have already destroyed tens of thousands of American jobs by driving up the price of oil and undermining the viability of hundreds of thousands of domestic businesses. (The question of the best way to deal with Iran will be examined in depth in chapter 16.) It is dishonest for politicians to blame speculators for the price of oil when it is political policies that have caused the oil price to skyrocket.

There are many things the US government could do to reduce gas prices aside from ceasing its saber rattling:

Congress and federal bureaucrats have made it practically impossible to construct new oil and gasoline refineries. As Texas congressman Ron Paul recently observed: "Building a new refinery requires billions of dollars in capital investment. It can take several years just to obtain the necessary federal permits. Even after the permits are obtained, construction of a refinery may still be delayed or even halted by frivolous lawsuits. It is no wonder that there has not been a new refinery constructed in the United States since 1976."[68]

---

67 "Americans Are Paying at the Pump for the Failed Foreign Policies of the Bush Administration," National Security Network, July 1, 2008.

68 Ron Paul, "Big Government Responsible for High Energy Prices," Congressional Press Release, May 5, 2008.

Additionally, the Democrats have refused to permit drilling in Alaska's huge Arctic National Wildlife Refuge (ANWR), which is estimated to hold up to ten billion barrels of petroleum.

Congress has also severely limited drilling in the Outer Continental Shelf (OCS), which contains at least eighty-six billion barrels of oil. President George H. W. Bush issued the executive order prohibiting OCS development in 1990. Congress approved its ban in 1991. The result has been to leave Americans dependent on foreign oil producers, including countries like Saudi Arabia, Nigeria, Russia, and Venezuela, which increasingly are unstable, hostile, or both. President George W. Bush recently issued an executive order repealing his father's decree; welcome news, but about seven years too late.

Oil shale deposits in America's west could contain the equivalent of as much as one trillion or more barrels of petroleum.

The refusal to open up US lands is costing Americans at the pump. Politicians are offering a false choice of either protecting the environment or expanding energy production. Environmental groups have long balanced conservation and production on their own lands. They just don't want the Americans to have the same option.

The President and Congress also drove up the price of gasoline by mandating the use of ethanol as a fuel additive. Ethanol is one of the most popular boondoggles in Washington. The mandate for using ethanol as a fuel caused a huge surge in the amount of corn used for ethanol, resulting in domino-effect increases in other crop prices (which compete with or substitute for grain). The soaring price of feed grains clobbered cattle, chicken, and pork producers. The resulting boost in food prices is hammering Americans at the grocery checkout and causing severe misery in much of the Third World. The World Bank recently concluded that US and European biofuels policy (and derivative policies) helped drive world food prices up by 70 percent in recent years; and domestically, a 1986 Agriculture Department study concluded that increased production of ethanol costs consumers and taxpayers roughly $4 for each $1 of extra farm income.

Bush and Congress also justify the ethanol mandate for its environmental benefits, but ethanol is one of the biggest environmental frauds of modern times. In 1995, the Congressional Budget Office reported that ethanol "evaporates quickly, especially in hot weather, contributing to ozone pollution."[69] The same year, a federal appeals court decision noted that EPA "has even conceded that the use of ethanol might possibly make air quality worse."[70] Two studies reported on in *Scientific American* early in 2008 year warned that biofuels production results in a net increase in greenhouse gas emissions (caused in part by clearing new cropland, brought into the market by higher crop prices).[71] Scientists have long warned that using corn for ethanol results in a net energy loss, after factoring in the energy necessary for producing corn.

Naturally, some permanent politicians in Washington are responding to the government-caused gas hikes by calling for even more government power. Republican Sen. John Warner, who lives in the Watergate (a few miles from Capitol Hill), wants the federal government to again set a national speed limit. Our greatest nonrenewable resource is time, which is why Americans routinely broke the Washington-imposed 55 mph speed limit between 1974 and 1995. Sen. Warner may believe that citizens' time is worth nothing, but the Constitution does not empower him and his colleagues to decide how fast people can drive on every road in America. This is something for which federal officials have no competence, and no right to interfere.

69 Congressional Budget Office, "Reducing the Deficit: Spending and Revenue Options," March 3, 1995.

70 Jonathan Adler, "Alternative Fuel Follies with Ethanol Vapors," *The Washington Times*, May 3, 1995.

72 David Biello, "Biofuels Are Bad for Feeding People and Combating Climate Change," Scientific American, February 7, 2008

Conclusion

Increased energy prices and supply uncertainties put America's economic future at risk. We need a president determined to make America's own energy resources available for development. Americans must look outside of the two major parties for the tough, realistic leadership our country needs.

Government intervention, whether through more regulations or more subsidies (or both), hurts consumers in the end. Whatever Washington politicians do to subvert or thwart market practices will undermine the nation's ability to find the energy necessary to fuel American prosperity. The free market, driven by consumer choice and reflecting the real cost of resources, should be the foundation of America's energy policy. Free markets are the best hope for plentiful energy at reasonable prices (as we are already seeing in the ways the marketplace and American consumers are responding to the high price of gasoline, by buying more fuel-efficient vehicles and driving less).

PRESIDENTIAL POWER GRABS

No man in this country is so high that he is above the law. No officer of the law may set that law at defiance with impunity. All the officers of the government, from the highest to the lowest, are creatures of the law, and are bound to obey it. It is the only supreme power in our system of government.

—*United States v. Lee* (US Supreme Court, 1882)

Americans have long understood that their freedom depends on the law. Thomas Paine, in his magnificent 1776 *Common Sense* pamphlet, declared, "Let a crown be placed, by which the world may know, that so far as we approve as monarchy, that in America the law is King. For as in absolute governments the King is law, so in free countries the law ought to be King; and there ought to be no other."

George Washington was perhaps our greatest president in part because he exhibited virtually no appetite for personal power. He set the precedents that helped constrain many of his successors. But George Washington's personal restraint has long since been eclipsed by the pervasive hunger for power that grips most of the modern politicians who come to Washington.

Former president Richard Nixon shocked the nation when he declared in 1977, "When the president does it, that means that it is not illegal." Unfortunately, in the subsequent decades, Nixon's view that the president is above the law seems to have become conventional wisdom inside the Beltway.

Presidents and members of Congress take an oath to uphold the Constitution. And a key principle of this nation's founding document is that government is and must always be *under* the law.

But with each new administration, it seems as if the chief elected official in this land finds more pretexts to slip the leash of the law. We will discuss executive orders and signing statements in this chapter, and then consider in depth some of the worst abuses of the law and Constitution in the following chapters.

Executive Order Edicts

The Los Angeles Times noted on July 4, 1998: "Fresh from what aides view as a triumphant trip to China, Clinton is reportedly eager to exercise his executive powers to the hilt." Senior White House counselor Paul Begala declared: "He always comes back from these trips with a big head of steam . . . This president has a very strong sense of the powers of the presidency, and is willing to use all of them." Begala then offered up a thumbnail summary of the Bill Clinton philosophy of government: "Stroke of the pen. Law of the land. Kind of cool."[72]

Clinton issued more than three hundred executive orders during his eight years in the Oval Office. Clinton signed his most controversial executive order during a May 1998 visit to England. That order established expansive principles to justify federal intrusion in state and local affairs, asserting, "Preserving supremacy of federal law provides an essential balance to the power of the states."[73] This was absurd, since the states have been supplicants to Washington for most of the half century. Clinton's executive order essentially sought to nullify the Tenth Amendment of the Constitution, which states, "The powers not delegated to the United States by the Constitution, nor prohibited by it to the states, are reserved to the states respectively, or to the people." Clinton's 1998 Executive Order would have provided justification for any federal agency to supercede federal or state responsibilities with virtually no limitations. Congress would have none of it: in a rare show of courage and constitutional understanding, the House of

---

72 Elizabeth Shogren, "Clinton to Bypass Congress in Blitz of Executive Orders," *The Los Angeles Times*, July 4, 1998.

73 "Executive Order 13083," White House Office of the Press Secretary, May 14, 1998.

Representatives voted 417 to 2 to block any funds for the order's enforcement. Clinton acted like he recognized the hard political facts and suspended the order.

But he was only playing possum. A year later, in August 1999, Clinton reissued the Federalism Executive Order, now numbered EO 13132. I responded to this executive order by proposing the "Federalism Preservation Act of 1999" to "restore the division of governmental responsibilities between the Federal Government and the States that was intended by the framers of the Constitution by requiring all Federal departments and agencies to comply with former Executive Order 12612."[74] (EO 12612 was the executive order that Ronald Reagan issued on federalism, and it was as different from Clinton's order as high noon from the darkest midnight.)

Reagan issued this executive order while I was serving as US Attorney in Atlanta, and I recall the pride I felt at that time at his concise, eloquent statement of what I believed was a core Republican political value: "The people of the States created the national government when they delegated to it those enumerated governmental powers relating to matters beyond the competence of the individual States. All other sovereign powers, save those expressly prohibited the States by the Constitution, are reserved to the States or to the people . . . The people of the States are free, subject only to restrictions in the Constitution itself or in constitutionally authorized Acts of Congress, to define the moral, political, and legal character of their lives."[75]

Late in Clinton's second term, White House Chief of Staff John Podesta launched "Project Podesta" to maximize the president's opportunity to dictate a legacy via executive orders. Podesta commented, "There's a pretty wide sweep of things we're looking to do, and we're going to be aggressive in pursuing it."[76]

---

74 H.R. 4196, 105th Congress, 2d Session introduced by Barr, July 14, 1998. Accessed at http://bulk.resource.org/gpo.gov/bills/105/h4196ih.txt.pdf.

75 Executive Order 13132 – Federalism, Volume 64, Number 153, August 10, 1999. Accessed at http://www.epa.gov/fedrgstr/eo/eo13132.htm.

76 Catherine Edwards, "Clinton's Abuse of Executive Power," Insight on the News, December 13, 1999.

I counterpunched by proposing the Executive Order Limitation Act of 1999, to require the president to provide Congress with copies of every executive order for review. Legitimate emergencies aside, Congress would then have a thirty-day window within which to modify or reject the proposal. I testified before the House Judiciary Committee that "if the president vetoes [the bill] then we know he has an ulterior motive; one that clearly envisages a continued power grab at the expense of Congress."[77]

My friend, Rep. Ron Paul, was also in the forefront of this fight. Ron warned: "We in Congress have created a monster by allowing the president authority to legislate through executive order."[78]

I continued my efforts to rein in presidents' executive decrees even after George W. Bush—who I supported the first time he ran—was elected in 2000. At a March 2001 House Judiciary subcommittee hearing that I chaired, I declared, "Fidelity to constitutional self-government requires adherence to the formal legislative process the framers skillfully drafted into our founding document. When Congress yields its delegated powers to the president, or fails to check executive overreach, it not only undermines its own power, but mars the constitutional fabric carefully tailored by the Founders to preserve and protect our individual liberties."[79]

Unfortunately, Bush soon picked up one of Clinton's worst habits and raised the ante.

Bush used an executive order to drop an iron curtain around the presidency. His November 1, 2001, executive order, entitled "Further Implementation of the Presidential Records Act," effectively overturned an act of Congress and a Supreme Court

---

77 "Prepared Testimony of Representative Bob Barr Before the House Committee on the Judiciary Subcommittee on Commercial and Administrative Law Subject Executive Orders," Federal News Service, October 28, 1999.

78 Catherine Edwards, "Clinton's Abuse of Executive Power," Insight on the News, December 13, 1999.

80 Hearing on Executive Orders and Presidential Directives, Available at http:// commdocs.house.gov/committees/judiciary/hju72142.000/hju72142_0.htm

decision. In 1978, Congress passed the Presidential Records Act, declaring, "The United States shall reserve and retain complete ownership, possession, and control of Presidential records." The act requires that the unclassified papers of a president be routinely released twelve years after the president's term ends. There are provisions in the act to justify nondisclosure for information that could threaten national security.

But Bush's executive order basically surrounded presidential papers with a series of snares that could thwart all but the most determined—and well-financed—effort to learn how a president used and abused his power. As *White House Weekly* summarized, Bush's order "prohibits the release of records unless and until both the former and incumbent president affirmatively consent to their release."[80] It allows the former or the incumbent president to extend the time to review a document request indefinitely; requires the withholding of records if a former president makes any claim of privilege (regardless of how absurd the claim), allows a former vice president to veto access to presidential papers; and "suggests that a requester under the Presidential Records Act must establish *'a demonstrated, specific need'* for records in order to overcome an executive privilege claim."[81]

Bush's order effectively replaced citizens' right to know with former presidents' right to censor. A federal judge overturned part of the order in 2007, and the House of Representatives voted by a large margin in favor of legislation to nullify much of Bush's order. Bush's friends in the Senate have placed holds on the bill and prevented it coming to a vote. As Vanderbilt University history professor Hugh Graham observed, "Unless this executive order of his is overturned, it will be a victory for secrecy in government so total that it would make Nixon jealous in his grave."[82]

On May 22, 2003, Bush issued Executive Order 13303, with the blasé title, "Protecting the Development Fund for Iraq and

---

80 Linda Gasparello, "House Moves to Rescind Bush Order on Papers," April 30, 2002.

81 Ibid.

82 Carl M. Cannon, "For the Record," *National Journal,* January 12, 2002.

Certain Other Property in Which Iraq Has an Interest." This executive order grants to every company or other entity with any interest—direct or indirect—in Iraqi oil or any proceeds thereof, blanket immunity from any judicial process whatsoever. In layman's terms, according to this presidential edict, companies or individuals with any interest in Iraqi oil cannot be sued for anything, anytime, anywhere.

It is bizarre that a president can, literally with the stroke of a pen, exempt from the reach of judicial process an entire class of persons and businesses. The only authority that Bush cited was that he decided the matter of what to do with Iraqi oil—who profits from it, who can use it, and who finances it—constitutes "an unusual and extraordinary threat to the national security and foreign policy of the United States." The president goes on to simply declare this to be a national emergency and issues the blanket immunity.

On May 5, 2006, ironically less than three weeks before former Enron executives Kenneth Lay and Jeffrey Skilling were convicted in federal court of hiding information from investors and auditors, President Bush signed a directive authorizing the director of national intelligence to exempt any publicly traded corporation from maintaining accurate books and following proper auditing procedures. Bush gave the intelligence director John Negroponte absolute power to decide which large corporations do not have to abide by accounting and auditing principles to which the rest of corporate America is subject. This could help telecommunications companies like Verizon and BellSouth cover up their actions in permitting the NSA to illegally wiretap their customers.

On July 17, 2007, Bush issued his executive order on "Blocking Property of Certain Persons Who Threaten Stabilization Efforts in Iraq." While this sounds like an innocuous title, the order entitles the feds to freeze the property of any American who directly or indirectly aids someone who has committed or "poses a significant risk of committing" violent acts "threatening the peace or stability of Iraq" or who undermines "efforts to promote economic reconstruction and political reform" in Iraq. This could potentially be used against peace activists in this country who criticize the Iraqi regime propped up by the US military. University of Wisconsin political scientist Ken Mayer observed, "Threatening the peace or stability of Iraq or the Government of Iraq,' that could be anything."[83]   Thus, people who unknowingly encourage someone who might do something on the other side of the world could lose their bank accounts. The arbitrariness of the order is compounded because the Treasury Department refuses to disclose whom it will target until after it has frozen their bank accounts.

The continuing trend of using executive orders to legislate without having to bother with the messiness of the legislative process seriously subverts the checks and balances necessary for our magnificent system of government to work properly.

Since FDR, one administration after another, Republican and Democrat alike, has been able to accomplish this perversion of our representative democracy, based in large measure on three disturbing characteristics of modern American government.

First, we have become a nation largely ignorant of constitutional history, with little if any emphasis on civics in our schools and universities. Second, we are in modern decades governed by a Congress with little if any interest in conducting consistent or meaningful oversight of the Executive Branch to ensure it stays within lawful and constitutional bounds. Finally, all this is overseen by a federal judiciary far too deferential to Executive Branch power.

Signing Statement Shenanigans

Presidential signing statements might seem an obscure issue, one of little importance in Americans' daily lives. However, presidential signing statements go to the very heart of our country's system of checks and balances.

---

83 Spencer Ackerman, "Broad New Exec. Order Targets Iraq-Related Finances," *TPM Muckraker*, July 19, 2007. Accessed at http://tpmmuckraker.talkingpointsmemo.com/archives/ 003726.php.

Throughout history, signing statements have been used to thank supporters, provide reasons for signing a bill or express satisfaction or displeasure with legislation passed by Congress. More recently, Presidents Ronald Reagan, George H. W. Bush, and Bill Clinton have used signing statements to express constitutional and other objections to legislation, influence judicial interpretation, and otherwise advance policy goals.

But President George W. Bush has radically transformed the use of signing statements. He has often used this mechanism to challenge or deny effect to legislation that he considers unconstitutional, but nonetheless signs.

He frequently announces that he will not be bound by limits on his power and that he will scorn obligations to disclose how federal power is being used.

While Bush supporters speak glowingly of originalist interpretations of the Constitution, Bush's signing statements have far more in common with George III than with George Washington. The Constitution specifies that Congress shall "make all laws" and that presidents must "take care that the laws be faithfully executed."

Since 2001, Bush has objected on constitutional grounds to more than 1,100 provisions in more than 100 pieces of legislation. This is more than twice as many as the 575 constitutional statements issued by the first 42 presidents of this nation combined.

Getting the Patriot Act renewed in 2006 was one of the Bush administration's highest priorities. After months of negotiations and compromises, and despite concerted opposition by civil liberties groups as diverse as the American Civil Liberties Union and the American Conservative Union, a bipartisan agreement was finally reached, giving the White House almost everything it wanted. As part of the deal, Bush administration officials agreed to disclose to Congress how many Americans' privacy was being violated by various provisions of the law. However, Bush reneged in a "signing statement" quietly released after a heavily hyped White House bill-signing ceremony. Bush announced that he would interpret the law "in a manner consistent with the president's constitutional authority to supervise the unitary executive branch and to withhold information."[84] In Bush's view, any provision in the law that requires disclosure is presumptively null and void. Bush's signing statement decree prevented Congress from learning of hundreds of criminal violations by the FBI before they renewed the Patriot Act's most controversial provisions.

After Congress mandated the appointment of an inspector general in late 2003 to look into the Coalition Provisional Authority then governing Iraq, Bush decreed, "The CPA IG shall refrain from initiating, carrying out, or completing an audit or investigation, or from issuing a subpoena, which requires access to sensitive operation plans, intelligence matters, counterintelligence matters, ongoing criminal investigations by other administrative units of the Department of Defense related to national security, or other matters the disclosure of which would constitute a serious threat to national security."[85] Bush effectively neutered the new IG before he even started work. Unfortunately, this same "expose no waste/fraud/abuse" attitude has permeated Bush's policy on Iraq.

On January 28, 2008, Bush released a signing statement on the National Defense Authorization Act that rejected any restrictions on his ability to establish permanent US military bases in Iraq. Bush announced, "Provisions of the act . . . purport to impose requirements that could inhibit the president's ability to carry out his constitutional obligations to take care that the laws be faithfully executed, to protect national security, to supervise the executive branch, and to execute his authority as commander in chief."[86] The phrase "to take care that the laws be faithfully executed" signaled Bush's right to disregard any law that he believed violated his prerogative. Apparently, being president means being entitled to proclaim perpetual occupations of foreign lands, regardless of what action in opposition a Congress might take.

---

85 Charlie Savage, "Bush challenges hundreds of laws - President cites powers of his office," *The Boston Globe*, April 30, 2006.

85 "Statement on H.R. 3289," White House Office of the Press Secretary, November 6, 2003.

86 "President Bush Signs H.R. 4986, the National Defense Authorization Act for Fiscal Year 2008 into Law," White House Office of the Press Secretary, January 28, 2008.

Bush also rejected any law limiting the president's prerogative "to exercise United States control of the oil resources of Iraq." It was as if the President had made a fair-and-square conquest of Iraqi oil during the 2003 invasion and subsequent occupation, and Congress had no right to try to take it away from him. (Bush and others had previously been adamant that the US had not gone to war to seize control of the oil.) Bush also announced that his administration would not cooperate with a "Commission on Wartime Contracting in Iraq and Afghanistan" that Congress had created "to investigate allegations of waste, mismanagement, and excessive force by contractors." After Blackwater ignited major controversy by killing innocent Iraqis, the Bush White House announced that neither Congress nor anyone else was entitled to the details on how the US government gave contractors a license to kill.

Some people consider Bush's I-am-the-Decider view of his own powers as necessary for the war on terror. But the power Bush claims is actually far broader. As *The Boston Globe's* Charlie Savage (who won a Pulitzer Prize for his coverage of signing statements) noted, "On at least four occasions while Bush has been president, Congress has passed laws forbidding US troops from engaging in combat in Colombia, where the US military is advising the government in its struggle against narcotics-funded Marxist rebels. After signing each bill, Bush declared in his signing statement that he did not have to obey any of the Colombia restrictions because he is commander in chief."[87] Bush seems to believe that his oath of office entitles him to intervene in any nation for any reason, regardless of specific acts to the contrary by the people's representatives.

The right to privacy was also skewered by at least one signing statement. On December 20, 2006, in a statement on the Postal Accountability and Enhancement Act, Bush effectively announced that he had the right to open Americans' mail without a warrant. Such warrantless mail opening has long been

---

87 Charlie Savage, "Bush challenges hundreds of laws *The President* cites powers of his office," *The Boston Globe*, April 30, 2006.

unconstitutional and has been a federal crime since the 1970s. Bush's signing statement effectively gutted provisions in the new act designed to reinforce the privacy of first-class mail. White House spokeswoman Emily Lawrimore declared that Bush's newly announced prerogative would not infringe on Americans' privacy because it "would only be used in extraordinary circumstances."[88] But this is a meaningless assertion in view of the manner in which the Bush administration finds extraordinary circumstances whenever and wherever it wants.

What is probably President Bush's most famous signing statement involved the Detainee Treatment Act of 2005. The White House engaged in long and arduous negotiations with Congress over the legislation that Congress enacted to make it crystal clear that torture was illegal. After Bush signed this law, he announced that he would construe it "in a manner consistent with the constitutional authority of the President to supervise the unitary executive branch and as Commander in Chief and consistent with the constitutional limitations on the judicial power."[89] This was widely interpreted to mean that the law is binding only when Bush pleases, if he pleases. He was reiterating a confidential 2002 Justice Department memo that declared the federal Anti-Torture Act "would be unconstitutional if it impermissibly encroached on the President's constitutional power to conduct a military campaign."[90]

Last year, the Government Accountability Office (GAO) revealed that the president has already violated almost a third of the laws he nullified in his signing statements. For instance, when Congress provided Bush with $500 billion to spend for military operations, the law required "that the Defense Department break down its 2007 budget request to show the detailed costs of global military operations, such as the wars in Iraq and Afghanistan. The

---

88 "Bush: Government Can Open Your Mail: White House Says It Has Always Had Such Power, to Be Used in 'Extraordinary,'" ABC News, January 4, 2007.

89 President's Statement on Signing of H.R. 2863, the "Department of Defense, Emergency Supplemental Appropriations to Address Hurricanes in the Gulf of Mexico, and Pandemic Influenza Act, 2006," White House Office of the Press Secretary, December 30, 2005.

90 "Standards of Conduct for Interrogation under 18 U.S.C. §§ 23402340A," Department of Justice Office of Legal Counsel, August 1, 2002.

department ignored the order."[91] GAO did not examine the most controversial signing statement vetoes.

The crux of Bush's unitary executive doctrine is that all power described in Article II of the Constitution that relates to the president is absolute and cannot be limited within the bounds of the government set forth in the Constitution. According to this unitary executive view of the presidency, checks and balances are an archaic relic. This is something that people might have laughed at if prior presidents had sought to use the same claim. Unfortunately, in today's post-9/11, fear-driven atmosphere, many pundits and intellectuals have been eager to accept whatever the Bush team declared, so long as it was described as necessary to fight terrorism.

In a democracy, presidential assertions of power do not happen in a vacuum. They affect the careful balance of power in our system of government. The executive branch is not free to unilaterally change that balance; our Constitution requires legislative and judicial involvement to ensure public debate and oversight and to guard against centralization of power.

Article I of the Constitution gives Congress the power to make the laws. Under Article II, the president has the duty to take care that the laws are properly ("faithfully") executed. The Constitution also says that if the president objects to a law, he should veto it. This gives Congress the chance to override his veto, enacting the law despite the president's opposition or to sustain the veto and work to address the president's objections. This system drives an ongoing negotiation between the two political branches.

In his first six years in office, Bush did not veto a single bill. Instead, he signed bills into law and then issued signing statements that declare he will not give them, or provisions in them, effect. In doing this, the President is cutting off the negotiation and usurping the power of Congress. He effectively is vetoing the law without giving Congress the opportunity to override his veto or address his concerns, as required by the Constitution.

---

91 Jonathan Weisman, "'Signing Statements' Study Finds Administration Has Ignored Laws," *The Washington Post*, June 19, 2007."

Congress has been unfortunately complicit in this power grab. Congress repeatedly has acquiesced to Bush's unilateral actions. It has failed in its constitutional obligation to make the laws and to oversee the White House's actions to make sure it is implementing those laws and doing so lawfully and constitutionally.

No president has the right to veto provisions of laws via signing statements. The president should immediately abandon these inappropriate uses of presidential signing statements, and be made to publicly announce and explain his intention not to comply with any statute or treaty. Congress should make unmistakably clear the link between a president's inappropriate use of signing statements and the costs of doing so—and then to follow through with specific actions to restore our checks and balances.

Conclusion

Unfortunately, there have been few fundamental objections or challenges to the new concept of boundless presidential power. This in itself is a sign of how few Americans comprehend the invaluable constitutional inheritance our forefathers left us. The Constitution—not the whisperings of anonymous presidential aides —must again be made to set the standard for a president's exercise of power.

★

OVER CRIMINALIZATION: PUTTING CITIZENS IN THE WRONG

Each year, it becomes more difficult for the average American to be a law-abiding citizen. Every year, more and more actions are being criminalized. And the more laws are on the books, the more arbitrary is the power law enforcement agents have over private citizens, since the agents will be able to almost always find some reason to ticket, investigate, or arrest citizens.

Our criminal laws have regressed to the point that they now are something genuinely sinister. This has largely occurred over the last century, with the growth of the regulatory state and federalization of what once was almost exclusively a state and local matter.

For our first century as a nation, federal crimes were limited to treason, perjury in federal courts, bribery of public officials, theft of government property, and revenue fraud. Everything else was a state or local matter. For the next 130-odd years, the picture would change, as the government began to assert itself, primarily using the Commerce Clause.

The number of federal criminal statutes and criminal administrative regulations is so large it is literally uncountable, according to the Congressional Research Service. In 1998—before the onslaught of antiterrorism laws—the American Bar Association estimated that the federal criminal law encompassed perhaps 3,300 separate statutes, and an additional 10,000 scattered administrative regulations, the violation of which carried either criminal or civil sanction.

The results of this obese code include vague and hard to comply with environmental, securities, and other anticorporate and anti-entrepreneurial regime, as well as truly wacky and absurd statutes. For instance, it is a federal crime to use the American flag for advertising purposes in the District of Columbia, a federal crime for a peanut dealer to fail to produce a report on his stock at the request of the government, a federal crime to alter pennies or other coins or banknotes, and a federal misdemeanor to lie about your financial condition in order to bathe in the public bathhouse at the Hot Springs National Park, Arkansas.

On top of the bales of new laws that Congress enacts, there are the truckloads of new regulations that federal agencies issue. Federal agencies issued almost 3,600 new final rules last year. In 2007, the Federal Register contained more than 72,000 pages. On top of the Federal Register, there are tens of thousands of other pages of agency guidance and memos and notices that often end up carrying the force of law—at least when federal agents are going after some hapless citizen or small company that cannot afford a lawyer to fight back.

Laws That Allow the Government to Steal

More than a hundred different federal statutes empower government agents to confiscate private property even if a citizen is not convicted of wrongdoing. The government can seize bank accounts, cars, or other property based solely on an allegation of violating laws on gambling, wildlife controls, immigration, banking offenses, or controlled substances (the most frequently invoked type of law for forfeitures). The federal Bureau of Alcohol, Tobacco, Firearms and Explosives (ATF) gave its agents Leatherman tool kits engraved with the motto *Always Think Forfeiture*. And once the ATF grabs a citizen's guns, it can easily cost thousands of dollars in lawyers' fees to try to get them back.

The feds have also used forfeiture power to seize unapproved medical devices. The Food and Drug Administration claims that any device it has not formally approved is "adulterated" and thus can be seized.

The fixation on grabbing property can actually undermine public safety. The White House drug czar's office recently encouraged local and state police to put more emphasis on collecting intelligence instead of merely grabbing currency. Jack Killorin, chairman of that office's highway enforcement project, recently told National Public Radio: "What we're trying to do is get people to move beyond the stop 'n' grab into the investigation of criminal organizations."[92] But since local and state police agencies are often allowed to keep a large share of what they confiscate for their own use, the incentives will lead lawmen astray.

I fought against forfeiture abuses when I was a member of Congress. At one point, I was the only member of the House Judiciary Committee who objected to a reform bill that would have continued to let law enforcement commandeer private property almost to its heart's content. The final bill that made it through in 2000 made some fixes, but the forfeiture laws continue to be a peril to freedom because of their pro-government slant. Federal agencies and their local law enforcement agencies confiscated more than $1.6 billion in property in 2007, almost three times the amount that was seized in 2002.

Martha Stewart, Poster Girl

Thanks in part to the ever-increasing number of federal criminal laws, law enforcement personnel, prosecutions, and convictions, federal officials can be selective in what cases they choose to bring. Prosecutors often look for the limelight; the result frequently is the quest for indictments based not necessarily on fault, but on flashbulbs and publicity.

Nowhere is this clearer than in the Martha Stewart case. Stewart was not actually convicted for any sort of securities offense. She wasn't busted for insider trading, or fraud, or any

---

92 "Dirty Money: Asset Seizures and Forfeitures," National Public Radio, June 18, 2008.

similar substantive offenses. She was convicted of making false statements and conspiracy and obstruction of an agency proceeding. In other words, the very few months she served in jail —the product of a lengthy and expensive public trial—were the result of her not being forthcoming with investigators. She was convicted of something that is legal for the government agents she spoke to. (FBI agents are taught in an ethics class that subjects of investigations have "forfeited their right to the truth."[93])

Stewart was nailed largely because of the vast sweep of federal laws. As Harvard law professor William Stuntz observes, "The federal criminal code has a generic false statements statute that bans lies told in the course of any matter that falls, directly or indirectly, within the jurisdiction of a federal agency . . . The federal criminal code includes 100 separate misrepresentation offenses, some of which criminalize not only lying but concealing or misleading as well, and many of which do not require that the dishonesty be about a matter of any importance . . . a good deal of ordinary lying fits within the definition of one or another federal felony."[94] Yet the odds that a politician will be held criminally liable for a lie he tells on the campaign trail or on the floor of Congress are slim to none, and "Slim just left town," as Dan Rather used to say.

Though real corporate crime—activity that brings American capitalism into disrepute—should, of course, be prosecuted, the Stewart case made her a poster child for the dangers of overcriminalization.

Criminalizing Home Run Records

In 1990, Congress made possession of anabolic steroids without a doctor's prescription a felony punishable by up to one year in prison. Unfortunately, the federal ban on steroids may be generating more harm than steroids themselves.

---

93 Roberto Suro, "Law Enforcement Ethics: A New Code for Agents," *The Washington Post*, August 21, 1997.

94 "The Pathological Politics of Criminal Law," *Michigan Law Review*, December 2001.

The criminalization of steroid possession converted a health issue into a moral crusade, turning behavior that was often merely foolish into something that is now officially labeled as evil. The criminalization of steroid possession epitomizes the vast extension of criminal law to cover more and more types of nonviolent, voluntary activity. Anabolic steroids pose no real danger to anyone other than the users.

Steroids are often prescribed by physicians to help individuals rebuild damaged muscle tissue, treat reproductive problems, and other illnesses. Steroids have also become increasingly popular with athletes as strength-enhancers. Massive doses of steroids, like heavy doses of many pharmaceuticals, can result in death or severe bodily harm. They can cause liver problems, elevated blood pressure, shrunken testicles, and other problems. But although steroid use is risky, steroids result in a lower rate of permanent injury than do sports such as professional football, according to University of Wisconsin professor of medical ethics, Norm Fost.[95]

In the same way that Prohibition resulted in more people drinking poisonous wood alcohol (instead of alcoholic beverages based on grain alcohol), the steroid ban is resulting in people using far more dangerous substances to enhance athletic performance. Many individuals have responded to the federal restrictions on steroid distribution by seeking out steroid substitutes often made in unsanitary conditions in basement laboratories. The FDA warns that GHB (gamma-hydroxy-butyrate), one such substitute drug, is a "dangerous and powerful hypnotic" that could cause coma, seizures, and cessation of breathing.

The steroid ban is operating as a drug dealers relief act. The federal crackdown is spurring the same hardcore criminal elements who distribute heroin and cocaine to enter steroid distribution. The ban transferred control over the production and marketing of steroids from pharmacists and physicians to the riff-raff of society.

---

95 David Wharton, "Steroid Use Has Proponents," *Spokesman Review*, May 10, 2004. Accessed at: http://www.spokesmanreview.com/allstories-news-story.asp?date=051004& ID=s1518611

The steroids law epitomizes Congress's tendency to try to use blunt force to solve social problems that stem largely from an individual's uninformed or foolish personal choices. Imprisoning steroid users makes as little sense as jailing cigarette smokers for refusing to obey the Surgeon General's latest hectoring.

The ban hit the front pages of the newspapers—especially the sports sections—beginning in 2005. Barry Bonds and Roger Clemens supposedly used steroids or human growth hormones to temporarily improve their on-field performances. If an athlete is willing to mortgage his long-term health in return for a few more home runs or strikeouts, and if the team employing him is willing to pay a ridiculous sum of money to have him do so, more power to him.

Yet we now have a former US senator (Maine's George Mitchell), at least two federal law enforcement agencies (the FBI and the IRS), at least one US Attorney's office, and members of Congress from both major political parties all tripping over themselves to prove they are tougher than the next person at scouring steroids out of American sports.

Politicians' huffing and strutting on steroids is in sharp contrast to an organization in much less repute at Georgetown dinner parties. In June 2007, the WWE (World Wrestling Entertainment) was rocked by the Chris Benoit tragedy, near Atlanta, Georgia. It was speculated that Chris had murdered his family and committed suicide in a steroid or "'roid" rage. It was unclear how much of a role drugs played in Benoit's actions, and whether a mild brain injury may also have been a contributing factor.

In the wake of the tragedy, the head of the WWE, Vince McMahon looked internally to recognize these problems and address them. Although in the two years before Benoit's death, dozens of wrestlers had been suspended, gone to rehab, or been dismissed under the WWE's Wellness Program. The WWE strengthened its drug policy further, reemphasizing that its own internal laws would be enforced.

McMahon didn't wait for Congress to pass a law or parade his wrestlers in front of congressional committee hearings. He took the lead and assumed responsibility over the health and welfare of the individuals who work for the WWE, through rehabilitation, testing, and even anonymous help lines, to deal with any possible problems. While there may be some employees of the organization who may not like random drug tests or being thrown on a treadmill for an EKG, they have the choice of finding a new employer.

That's the beauty of the libertarian solution. It does not take government intervention or our tax dollars. It also does not force anyone to do anything. It only requires voluntary action and decisions.

Sports organizations and leagues can rightfully fine and ban competitors who test positive for steroid use. The private policing of steroid use to prevent unfair athletic competition is far preferable to government's heavy-handed attempts to enforce a steroid ban based on dubious federal interests.

The Failure of the New Prohibition

Perhaps the area in which overcriminalization does the greatest harm is federal narcotics policy. Drug prohibition, like Prohibition and alcohol, has failed. Indeed, the problem is worse today than in 1972, when Richard Nixon first coined the phrase "war on drugs." Whether we like it or not, tens of millions of Americans have used and will continue to use mind-altering drugs. Yet in 2005 we spent more than $12 billion on federal drug enforcement efforts. Another $30 billion went to incarcerate nonviolent drug offenders.

The drug war continually drags more innocent people into its "solutions." Methamphetamine, which is highly abusive and addictive, has become the drug of choice in much of rural America, as well as in a growing number of cities. A key ingredient in its manufacture is pseudoephedrine—a chemical found in many completely legal, over-the-counter cold and allergy medications.

In a typical knee-jerk reaction, state and federal governments are now using antidrug statutes to crack down on such nefarious criminals as convenience store clerks and pharmacists who sell cold medicine to customers who then use it for the illicit manufacture of its illegal derivative.

Even worse, the government is making life difficult for the law-abiding cold or allergy sufferer who simply wishes to purchase a medication containing pseudoephedrine. The heavy hand of government is throwing the baby out with the bathwater. Consumers are now being forced to *prove* their innocence before obtaining a packet of Sudafed or Claritin capsules. In some states, cold and allergy drugs that used to be readily available over the counter are now being treated as prescriptions. In other states, customers are being forced to sign a registry and put their names into a database in order to buy over-the-counter cold medications.

Imagine how long it would take you to clear your name to satisfy some government investigator reviewing the new drug registry, if you bought too much Sudafed and found yourself listed on a national registry of suspected drug dealers.

New drugs have been created that would allow effective cold or allergy relief without pseudoephedrine. But the Food and Drug Administration (FDA)—renowned for its laggardly ways—will likely delay approval of the breakthroughs for at least half a decade. It is easier for the government to treat millions of people as drug abuse suspects than to expedite a real solution.

A Mindless War on Painkillers

The unrecognized casualties of federal drug crackdowns include millions of Americans undergoing surgery who are denied adequate pain relief. *Scientific American* stated in 1990: "Society's failure to distinguish between the emotionally impaired addict and the psychologically healthy pain sufferer has affected every segment of the population. Perhaps the most distressing example is unnecessary pain in children."[96] The American Medical Association concluded in

96 Ronald Melzack, "The Tragedy of Needless Pain; Morphine for Pain Relief is Not Addictive and Should be Prescribed More Often," *Scientific American,* February, 1990.

a report that "inadequate pain relief is only rarely due to the unavailability of effective pain control medications."[97]

Federal agencies have essentially made it a crime to effectively treat chronic or severe pain. Heavily armed DEA teams have raided many doctors' offices. Dr. Ronald Myers, president of the American Pain Institute, observes: "The war on drugs has turned into a war on doctors and pain patients. Such is the climate of fear across the medical community that for every doctor who has his license yanked by the DEA, there are a hundred doctors scared to prescribe proper pain medication for fear of going to prison."[98]

One of the most shocking federal crackdowns involves OxyContin, a revolutionary painkiller that improves the quality of life for legions of people. The feds went all the way up the supply chain with this drug. Shortly after OxyContin gained FDA approval in 1995, it began to be vilified by the DEA and its parent agency, the Justice Department. Federal agents publicly denigrated the pain medication as "hillbilly heroin" because it had achieved a level of abuse in the Appalachian region, and issued incorrect but easily quotable statistics purporting to establish that OxyContin abuse rapidly had become an epidemic.

The feds launched more than four hundred investigations into doctors who prescribed OxyContin. Assistant US Attorney Gene Rossi boasted: "Our office will try our best to root out [certain doctors] like the Taliban."[99]

The news media leaped to follow the script the DEA provided. The US Attorney for the Western District of Virginia launched a relentless investigation of Purdue Pharma. Several years and hundreds of subpoenas and search warrants later, the government got its scalp—or rather, three small strands of corporate hair.

---

97 American Medical Association, "Report on the Council on Ethical and Judicial Affairs of the American Medical Association," Summer, 1994.

98 Frank Owen, "The DEA's War on Pain Doctors," *Village Voice,* November 5, 2003.

99 Melinda Ammann, "The Agony and the Ecstasy: How the OxyContin Crackdown Hurts Patients in Pain," *Reason,* April, 2003.

In July 2007, a Purdue Pharma associated company, Purdue Frederick Co., its former president and CEO, its chief legal officer, and its former chief medical officer, pleaded guilty to the misdemeanor offense of misbranding a drug in violation of FDA regulations. Their actual offensive conduct? Allowing a small percent of the company's large sales force to mischaracterize to some doctors the drug's potential for abuse, even though the company's rules prohibited any deviation from the information FDA requires for approved medicines. The government then publicly and falsely labeled these misstatements as the cause of the drug's abuse epidemic, a charge never made in court.

Government lawyers never even showed that any of the officials charged even knew about the misstatements. However, the risk of catastrophic losses to the company and the threat of jail time if a jury were to convict swayed the company to plead rather than fight.

Four months after the company's officials pled guilty, a research study announced that OxyContin's role in drug abuse is actually quite low, and that the medicine is not any more widely abused than other pain-killing drugs.[100] The media almost completely ignored the study that debunked its own earlier, wrong-way stampede. The 2007 study echoed earlier research debunking federal OxyContin fearmongering. The DEA sanctified its crackdown by claiming that almost five hundred people died from OxyContin overdoses in 2002. However, the *Journal of Analytical Toxicology* reported only a dozen cases in which OxyContin was the sole cause of death for 2002.[101] In all other cases, the fatality resulted from combining OxyContin with cocaine, alcohol, or other substances.

Among the most divisive issues of drug enforcement involves the medical use of marijuana. People suffering from

---

[100] Trevor Butterworth, "New Study on Drug Addiction Exposes Media's Misrepresentation of OxyContin Plague" STATS (Statistical Assessment Service), January 25, 2008

[101] Sally Satel, "Limbaugh's Addiction Blurs Benefits of Drug," *York Daily Record,* (PA), November 16, 2003.

multiple sclerosis, epilepsy, glaucoma, and the nauseating effects of chemotherapy have found relief with marijuana. Harvard Professor of Psychiatry Lester Grinspoon noted, "Between 1839 and 1900, more than a hundred articles on the therapeutic uses of marijuana appeared in scientific journals. As late as 1937 extract of cannabis was still a legitimate medicine marketed by drug companies."[102]

It was politics, rather than true science, that led to the government's classification of marijuana as a Schedule 1 controlled substance, preventing its medical use. The DEA has scorned the scientific evidence of marijuana's benefits time and again. A DEA administrative judge spent two years holding hearings on the medical aspects of marijuana and ruled in 1988, commenting: "The evidence in this record clearly shows that marijuana has been accepted as capable of relieving the distress of great numbers of very ill people and doing so with safety under medical supervision. It would be unreasonable, arbitrary and capricious for a DEA to continue to stand between those sufferers and the benefits of this substance in the light of the evidence of this record."[103] Then-DEA chief John Lawn denounced the judge's rulings as a "cruel and dangerous hoax"[104] and refused to accept his findings. Yet public opinion polls have found that over 70 percent of Americans favor permitting the medical use of marijuana.

Regardless of federal policy, the federal government should accept the decisions of the citizens of the states if they choose to allow the medical use of marijuana. No executive branch official should be permitted to interfere in a state initiative or referendum campaign in order to defeat or undo the will of the people.

None of these criticisms of existing policies mean that I believe drug use to be harmless or appropriate for minors. For that

---

102 Arnold Trebach and Kevin Zeese, editors, *New Frontiers in Drug Policy* (Washington: Drug Policy Foundation, 1991), p. 246.

103 Michael Isikoff, "Appellate Court Panel Orders DEA to Reevaluate Medical Value of Marijuna," *The Washington Post*, April 27, 1991

104 Ibid.

reason I would encourage people and institutions throughout America, from churches to social agencies to sports leagues, to work together to address drug abuse. One of our nation's greatest strengths is the willingness of people to organize outside of government to solve human problems. But treating what is, at base, a moral, spiritual, and health problem as a matter of federal criminal law has solved nothing. We must reestablish the primacy of individual choice and state's rights in deciding these issues.

The so-called federal war on drugs has become a war against the American people as well as the Constitution and the Bill of Rights. It is another manifestation of the concentration of power in Washington and the tendency of government to criminalize conduct that should never end up in court. As such, the war on drugs threatens individual liberty, domestic order, and peace here and abroad.

The federal government should get out of the drug war and allow the people of the states to determine their own drug policies. Rather than continuing to arrest and imprison people for offenses that do not directly harm other people, we should focus federal law on crimes involving serious fraud and violence with identifiable victims. Even then, only where there is a clear and specific federal interest, should the federal government be involved.

It is also time to consider use of the presidential pardon and commutation powers as another way to reduce the number of people in federal prison for nonviolent drug offenses. We can no longer afford the human and economic costs of imprisoning so many thousands of people for drug possession. This is the most destructive impact of drug prohibition. These people must live forever with the stigma of prison. Only luck saved even presidents and candidates for president from bearing the same mark, which would have disqualified them from not only high political office, but also many more commonplace jobs.

Conclusion

For many years now, there simply has been no constituency lobbying against the ever-fattening tomes of federal and state criminal law. The public will never, ever be for fewer laws. People react emotionally to crime—as a concept—and are almost always unimpressed with abstract or academic arguments against overcriminalization.

The countervailing forces against irrational lawmaking—that is, the Congress and the courts—have long since thrown in the towel. Congress, perhaps more than any other body, is responsible for the predicament in which we find ourselves. In its failure to push back against the public and the shrill voices of the mass media, Congress has created and encouraged a regime of criminal law that punishes thousands of acts that carry with them no ill intent.

The costs of overcriminalization are subtle, and the arguments against it sometimes tend to be dry and academic. But the core principle at stake here—a limited government whose sole purpose is to protect our ability to remain self-reliant and free to determine our own path under the dictates of our own conscience —cannot long survive under laws that are increasingly illegitimate.

The problem is not new. Nearly half a century ago, law professor Herbert Packer, in his 1968 classic *The Limits of the Criminal Sanction,* lucidly summarized a wise standard:

> The criminal sanction is the best available device we have for dealing with gross and immediate threats of harm. It becomes less useful as the harms become less gross and immediate. The less threatening the conduct with which it is called upon to deal, the greater the social costs that enforcement incurs. We alienate people from the society in which they live. We drive enforcement authorities to more extreme measures of intrusion and coercion. We taint the quality of life for free men.[105]

---

106 Herbert Packer, *The Limits of the Criminal Sanction* (Stanford: Stanford University Press, 1968), p. 365.

In a free society, citizens have a right to choose their risks and suffer accordingly. It is time for politicians to finally recognize the differences between vices and crimes. As Lysander Spooner, a prominent abolitionist and legendary opponent of political hypocrisy, wrote in 1875, "Vices are those acts by which a man harms himself or his property. Crimes are those acts by which one man harms the person or property of another. Vices are simply the errors which a man makes in his search after his own happiness."[106]

Over the last hundred years, federal government power has mushroomed, and politicians have continually pretended that the ever-growing number of punishments would eventually make people happy. This was simply another in a long series of fraudulent political promises. It is time to repeal the laws that pointlessly subvert both freedom and domestic tranquility.

---

106 Lysander Spooner, *The Lysander Spooner Reader* (San Francisco: Fox & Wilkes, 1992), p. 23.

★

TREATING ALL AMERICANS LIKE TERRORISTS

As an American, I resent an administration taking the position that the burden is on the citizen to show the government has abused power and violated the law, and to otherwise shut up and comply. As a former CIA official and federal prosecutor, I witnessed firsthand how much of our national security apparatus—even our counterterrorism and international intelligence work—is built on very basic policing methods. From your local grafters to the bin Ladens of the world, bad guys are generally found and punished using a system that includes sound intelligence, solid investigation, and responsible prosecution, but all with the framework of basic checks and balances on government power that forces sound police work and that militates against dragnet investigative fishing expeditions. Now, however, throughout the federal war on terror on the home front, there is almost no effort being made to avoid dragging innocent people into the investigations.

With the Patriot Act, we gave a single branch of the government nearly unlimited and certainly unchecked authority to delve into the private lives of ordinary people in the name of the holy grail of national security. History predicted exactly what would happen: that power would be abused to drag in ever-growing numbers of innocent people. That is the natural consequence of a statute that is fundamentally based on the theory of "trust us." As a result, the names of hundreds of thousands, if not millions, of innocent Americans have been added to various government terrorist databases, and untold millions have had—and are having—their private communications monitored and retained in databases.

Americans have fought to keep limits on government power ever since 1775. Throughout this long battle, the federal courts have served as official referees. It has not always been a pretty sight, but our courts have generally stepped in when necessary and done the right thing—correctly interpreting the Fourth Amendment as it applies to executive branch action or legislative branch lawmaking in order to ensure the essential privacy principle embodied therein retains its meaning. But since 9/11, the referees have been largely kicked off the field by the executive branch and their congressional enablers.

The FBI's Magic Muzzling Letters

The Patriot Act made it far easier for the Federal Bureau of Investigation to use National Security Letters (NSLs) to compel private citizens, businesses, nonprofit organizations, and other entities to surrender information upon demand. Every National Security Letter is backed up by an FBI badge, and every badge is backed by the World's Largest Law Firm.

The FBI is issuing fifty thousand NSLs a year. This is more than a hundredfold increase in the rate of such secret searches over the pre-9/11 era. NSLs empower the FBI to seize records that reveal "where a person makes and spends money, with whom he lives and lived before, how much he gambles, what he buys online, what he pawns and borrows, where he travels, how he invests, what he searches for and reads on the Web, and who telephones or e-mails him at home and at work," *The Washington Post* noted.[107]

Each NSL can lasso the records of thousands of people. The FBI used nine NSLs to get eleven *thousand* phone account records. In late 2003 and early 2004, the FBI used NSLs to snare personal data on almost a million people who visited Las Vegas around New Year's Eve. FBI agents also threatened to use NSLs to snare the gambling profiles of casino guests in order to make casinos surrender other information. In 2005, the FBI used one NSL to snare the records for all e-mail and Internet users at three dozen Connecticut libraries.

107 Barton Gellman, "The FBI's Secret Scrutiny," *The Washington Post*, November 6, 2005.

Prior to the Patriot Act, NSLs could only be used to seek information that pertains to a foreign power, or an agent of a foreign power. But there are no such restrictions in the post-9/11 era.

Each FBI field office issues its own letters. Unlike search warrants approved by judges, there is no requirement that probable cause of a crime exist before the FBI forcibly intrudes. Instead, FBI agents need only certify (to themselves) that the records they demand are sought for or relevant to an investigation "to protect against international terrorism or clandestine intelligence activities."[108]

But the relevant standard has no relevance to a standard; it is a standard without a standard. Simply saying that the FBI can use a National Security Letter to obtain information on any person or persons they want, so long as it is relevant to an investigation they have determined is an appropriate one, without any review, without any accountability, without any objective standard, has rendered it meaningless.

FBI agents are issuing NSLs for people two or three times removed from a suspected terrorist without any indication those people have done anything wrong. For example, the FBI could issue an NSL for the terrorist's pizza delivery boy, the delivery boy's coworkers, or every person who has ordered pizza from that same establishment. Under the current standard, these far-reaching contacts are considered relevant.

NSLs are accompanied by a gag order; anyone who discloses that they have received such a letter can be sent to prison for three years. In 2007, federal judge Victor Marrero denounced the NSL gag orders as "the legislative equivalent of breaking and entering, with an ominous free pass to the hijacking of constitutional values."[109] The gag orders effectively keep the targets prostrate before federal investigators, making it far more difficult for them to speak out or challenge a government abuse.

---

109 John Solomon and Barton Gellman, "Frequent Errors In FBI's Secret Records Requests," *The Washington Post*, March 9, 2007.

109 Dan Eggen, "Judge Invalidates Patriot Act Provisions," *The Washington Post*, September 7, 2007.

NSLs also prohibit recipients from disclosing the fact that they have surrendered customers' and other data to the feds. Libraries in Santa Cruz, California, posted warnings to their patrons informing them that the Patriot Act "prohibits library workers from informing you if federal agents have obtained records about you. Questions about this policy should be directed to Attorney General John Ashcroft, Department of Justice, Washington, D.C. 20530."[110]

The NSLs can deep-freeze the First Amendment. The FBI could easily issue an NSL to demand personal information on anyone who maintains or visits an online blog criticizing Bush. I worked with Jameel Jaffer of the ACLU in fighting Patriot Act excesses. He warned: "If the government monitors the Web sites that people visit and the books that they read, people will stop visiting disfavored Web sites and stop reading disfavored books. The FBI should not have unchecked authority to keep track of who visits al-Jazeera's Web site or who visits the Web site of the Federalist Society."[111]

Even though the Patriot Act gave the FBI sweeping power, many FBI agents chose to ignore the remaining legal limits to their intrusions. A 2007 Inspector General report revealed that thousands of NSLs were issued in violation of federal law. The IG also found over seven hundred instances of FBI agents issuing so-called exigent letters, claiming emergency circumstances and the immediate need for records. FBI agents often lied about the existence of an emergency, and never followed up with an actual legal request as promised. None of the FBI agents who lied or violated the law were prosecuted. The IG revealed that the FBI had deceived Congress as to the program's operation and greatly understated the number of NSLs.

In 2004, the FBI hit the Internet Archive, a digital library that maintains records of the previous versions and Web sites on the World Wide Web, with a National Security Letter. The Internet

---

110 Bob Egelko and Maria Alicia Gaura, "Libraries Post Patriot Act Warnings," *San Francisco Chronicle,* March 10, 2003.

111 Barton Gellman, "The FBI's Secret Scrutiny," *The Washington Post,* November 6, 2005.

Archive fought the request, and two years later, the FBI backed down. FBI Assistant Director John Miller justified issuing the information demand to the Internet Archive because the NSLs "permit the FBI to gather the basic building blocks for our counterterrorism and counterintelligence investigations."[112] But the basic building blocks probably include the personal data of hundreds of thousands, if not millions, of Americans. And in the vast majority of cases, this is information a federal judge would not permit the government to seize, since there would be no individual grounds for suspicion.

The FBI is warehousing the information they uproot, even when the data is found to be unrelated to terrorism, and shoveling it out to other federal agencies. Few, if any, Americans know which federal agencies may be pawing through their travel, phone, Internet, financial, or other data. The stockpiled information from NSLs is accessed by tens of thousands of law enforcement and intelligence personnel without restriction.

Your Home as Government's Play Box

In the old days, a man's home was his castle. This helped inspire comments such as Supreme Court Justice Lewis Powell's 1972 observation that breaking and entering by government agents had long been recognized as "the chief evil against which the wording of the Fourth Amendment is directed."

Now, thanks to the Patriot Act, a man's home is the government's play box.

There was a time only a few years ago, when the government, in executing a search warrant, would have to give the home or business owner contemporaneous notice that the search was going to be conducted. The government would also have to hand the person an inventory of what the government agents had seized. Supreme Court Justice Clarence Thomas recognized this procedure as one of fundamental fairness, even if not expressly

---

112 Ellen Nakashima, FBI Backs Off From Secret Order for Data After Lawsuit," *The Washington Post*, May 8, 2008.

required by the Fourth Amendment.

These two requirements, which the government had to follow absent exigent circumstances (emergency, destruction of evidence likely, and so forth), simply gave citizens the knowledge necessary to contest the facts of the search or seizure. The citizen could thus assert any constitutional infirmities in the government's behavior.

But Section 213 of the Patriot Act vastly expanded the ability of federal law enforcement to obtain secret sneak-and-peek search warrants, which allow the authorities to surreptitiously enter our homes or offices, search our belongings, download the contents of our computer, take pictures, seize property, and not tell the target for an indefinite period of time afterward.

Obviously, in the absence of notice and inventory, the constitutional guarantee in the Fourth Amendment that the citizen (or noncitizen alike) be free from unreasonable searches and seizures would be meaningless. If you don't know your home or office has been searched, if you don't know what the government has taken, then you have no way to know if your constitutional rights have been violated.

Section 213 states that searches can now be done in secret if federal agents assert that there is "reasonable cause to believe that providing immediate notification of the execution of the warrant may have an adverse result." All it could take is a simple redundancy: lawmen could claim that a search must be kept secret because otherwise the person will know that they have been searched (the adverse result).

We have no idea how many people's personal belongings have been secretly rummaged through by federal agents thanks to the Patriot Act. But we also have no reason to assume that this power, like many other recent federal conquests, has been abused far more often than the government would like to admit.

In fact, the number of secret sneak-and-peek searches by federal agents doubled after the Patriot Act became law. More telling, however, is the fact that the vast majority of sneak-and-peak search warrants are unrelated to terrorism investigations. Instead, drug cases have been the most frequent use for the new intrusive power. Prosecutors have also managed to persuade judges to let them use sneak-and-peak powers in cases involving cockfighting, judicial corruption, bounced checks, and even health care fraud.

Some defenders of the Patriot Act insist that there have not been ample documented cases of abuses. But this is largely because of the pervasive secrecy of how Patriot Act powers are being used.

In reality, the abuse is in the power itself. For the government to lay claim to such intrusive powers is a violation of this nation's founding compact.

Watch Lists, Blacklists

Federal agencies have a long history of punishing Americans for the agencies' own follies. Nothing illustrates this better than the ballooning of terrorist watch lists in recent years.

Prior to 9/11, the Federal Aviation Administration had not even bothered compiling and forwarding to airlines a list of individuals who had been identified as flight risks by the FBI, CIA, and its own experts. This was simply one more bureaucratic task to which no one got around. The FAA did send out a fax with three hundred names to airlines on the morning of September 12, 2001. "Two of the [9/11] hijackers were on those September 10 lists," *Newsweek* contributing editor Steven Brill noted in his 2003 book, *After: How America Confronted the September 12 Era*. But the FAA "crossed those names off on September 12 to avoid embarrassment," Brill reported. An FAA official explained the agency's disastrous failure: "We just never got around to setting up a protocol for who would control the list and how we would get the airlines to implement it." [113]

---

113 Steven Brill, *After: How America Confronted the September 12 Era* (New York: Simon and Schuster, 2003), p. 46.

The feds compensated for their pre-9/11 shortfall by creating a catchall that, by the summer of 2008, included a million names of terrorist suspects. At a time when the Justice Department is catching and prosecuting few if any bona fide terrorists, the feds are adding twenty thousand names a month to the watch list. The feds determined it is easier, or perhaps simply preferable, to develop a database of law-abiding citizens, rather than a database of known or actually suspected terrorists.

After 9/11, the new Transportation Security Administration took over administration of the "No Fly List." Unfortunately, but typically, TSA is relying on a close-enough-for-government-work standard that bars many innocent Americans from air travel. *The Wall Street Journal* noted: "Many entries on the list lack details that could make it easy to know if a traveler is really the person named. TSA gives airlines little guidance on just when a passenger's name is close enough to one on the list to warrant flagging the person for a law enforcement check."[114] Many travelers are wrongly stopped time and again, and taken aside for intensive questioning, regardless of how many times they have previously proved they are not a member of Al Qaeda or an Aryan Nation kingpin.

The TSA got a black eye when Sen. Ted Kennedy (D-MA) revealed that he had been blocked from flying many times because his name triggered an alarm on the No Fly List. Kennedy's staff had to yank strings with top federal officials before the TSA would lift its attempted travel ban on one of the best-known senators in the nation. According to one Bush administration officials, Kennedy was put on the list because some terrorist suspect had once used "T. Kennedy" as an alias. Rep. John Lewis (D-GA), a long-term congressman and well-known civil rights activist, was also routinely stopped because his name was on the watch list.

John Anderson of Minneapolis has routinely been flagged as a suspected terrorist. His first siderailing at an airport occurred in 2004 when he was four years old and on the way to Disney World

---

114 Ann Davis, "Why a 'No Fly List' Aimed at Terrorists Delays Others," *The Wall Street Journal,* April 22, 2003.

with his family. Since then, ticket agents routinely require his family to undergo special scrutiny before the boy can be trusted to leave the ground. The same happens to many other John Andersons, though perhaps the TSA feels like they have been prudent by not detaining every passenger named John.

Many innocent Americans have been placed on the terror list because of Department of Homeland Security quotas for federal air marshals to add new names to the list. A July 2004 memo from the Las Vegas office of the federal air marshals declared, "Each federal air marshal is now expected to generate at least one SDR [Suspicious Detection Report] per month."[115] The SDRs identify suspected terrorist behavior, which effectively assures that a person will be added to a watch list. One federal air marshal complained to a Denver television station in 2006: "Innocent passengers are being entered into an international intelligence database as suspicious persons, acting in a suspicious manner on an aircraft . . . and they did nothing wrong."[116] A passenger was cited on a SDR because he was "taking a photo of the Las Vegas skyline as his plane rolled down the runway," one marshal said.[117] Marshals' jobs, evaluations, and pay depend in part on how many people they label as terrorist suspects.

The feds pressure private companies to use the watch lists on their customers. A report by the San Francisco Lawyers' Committee for Civil Rights shows that the list connects consumers with suspected terrorists on such tenuous bases as a shared middle name. Tom and Nancy Kubbany were denied a mortgage because Tom's middle name matched an alias of one of Saddam Hussein's sons—despite the fact that Tom was born in Michigan, had never been to Iraq, and is thirty years older than Saddam's son.

When Sandra Cortez, a Colorado grandmother, went to buy a new car, she was barred from the purchase because her name

115 "Marshals: Innocent People Placed On 'Watch List' To Meet Quota," The Denver Channel, July 21, 2006. Accessed www.thedenverchannel.com/news/9559707/detail.html.

116 Ibid..

117 Ibid.

showed up on the terrorist watch list. As National Public Radio recently reported, "she came up as a possible match for Sandra Cortes Quintero, an accused drug trafficker from Colombia. But besides their first names, no other information matched."[118] Even though the Colorado grandmother was obviously born long before 1971—the data of the Colombian alleged trafficker's birth—she was still tainted.

In 2007, the Chicago Police Department fired janitor Arif Sulejmanovski after his name was discovered on a terrorist watch list. Police soon learned that he was placed on the list during a criminal investigation, and that his entry remains despite a federal investigation finding no ties to terrorist activities.

The federal governments' watch list system is so haphazard that it even snares many government employees who should not be suspects. The Electronic Privacy Information Center (EPIC) filed a Freedom of Information Act request and received the logs from TSA's call center. The results, as summarized by Wired.com's Ryan Singel,[119] showed that among the suspects nabbed by the watch list were a person with an Energy Department security clearance, and an active-duty Army officer who had served four combat tours (including one in Afghanistan) and who holds a top-secret clearance.

The Justice Department Inspector General reported in 2008 that many FBI offices continue adding faulty data to the lists. Nor does the government consistently remove regularly outdated names from the watch list. The watch list also has holes because at least two federal investigative agencies—the FBI and the Bureau of Alcohol, Tobacco, Firearms, and Explosives—employed different definitions of terrorism. The ACLU's Tim Sparapani has noted that the IG report is "more confirmation that the watch lists are growing out of control and without controls," and that the watch

---

118 "Terror list prevents many innocent people from buying homes, cars, etc.," CBS Early Show transcript, May 19, 2008.

119 Ryan Singel, "Feds' Watch List Eats Its Own," Wired.com, May 4, 2006. Accessed at http://www.wired.com/science/discoveries/news/2006/05/70783

list "is getting worse over time, not better."[120] The Government Accountability Office reported in 2007 that the Department of Homeland Security may be violating federal laws by failing to inform the public of the methods used to compile watch lists.

In response to tidal waves of complaints, TSA created a Traveler Redress Inquiry Program for people to try to get their names cleared. But the program appears to be a typical triple snafu that is of little—if any—real value to people whose names appear on the lists. At one point, TSA claimed that only fifteen thousand Americans were on the terror watch list. But in the first year of the redress program, almost thirty thousand Americans requested that their names be taken off the list. The TSA refuses to remove many people from the list regardless of how much evidence of their good citizenship they provide.

Terrorism watch lists have been a key vulnerability for the United States for more than a decade. And yet the lists today still cannot pass the laugh test.

Breast Bombs, Facecrime, and Other TSA Boondoggles

In the post-9/11 era, the government needs only the skimpiest of pretexts to intrude deeper into people's lives, or their apparel. After a Russian airliner was apparently blown up by Chechen terrorists in 2004, the TSA decided that the culprits were female and had bombs hidden in their bras. TSA announced that its screeners therefore would conduct far more intrusive searches regardless of whether female travelers set off the metal detector when passing through. The agency decreed: "TSA policy is that screeners are to use the back of the hand when screening sensitive body areas, which include the breasts (females only), genitals and buttocks."[121]

Flying quickly became far more demeaning for millions of

---

120 "Terror Watch Lists are Unworkable," American Civil Liberties Union, March 17, 2008.

121 Joe Sharkey, "When a Pat Down Seems Like Groping," *The New York Times*, November 2, 2004.

women. *The New York Times* columnist Maureen Dowd, in an article entitled "Hiding Breast Bombs," described her airport experience: "A beefy female [TSA] agent runs her hands all the way around your breasts, in between, underneath—with guys standing around staring."[122] Some of the breast pat-downs were done by male screeners. After hundreds of complaints and a tidal wave of bad public relations, TSA relented, instructing screeners "not to touch women between their breasts unless they set off a hand-held metal detector in the chest area," as the *The Washington Post* reported.[123] The Great Chechen Grope found no bombs, but may have alleviated on-the-job boredom for many TSA screeners and nearby passengers.

Unfortunately, the TSA's bosom boondoggle was only the tip of the iceberg of the agency's pointless intrusions.

Approach any major airport in the United States in this brave new post-9/11 world, and there is one message transmitted loud and clear to you—be afraid. Armed police are everywhere. You can't stop your car for more than a few seconds without being warned by an armed police officer that you'd better move on, under threat of arrest or worse. (An Atlanta police officer was videotaped throwing a female driver to the ground after she failed to move on quickly enough when ordered.)

Detached voices over the public address system remind you constantly of the applicable Homeland Security threat level (perpetually stuck at orange), and recount what you can and cannot carry on the plane. Your "government-issued identification card" must always be at the ready to show on demand. You have to partially disrobe and traverse a security gauntlet before even getting to the gate area. The oppressive sense of fear fostered by the airlines and the TSA continues from curbside drop off to exiting the airport in your destination city. Fear has become the currency of modern air travel.

---

[122] Maureen Dowd, Maureen Dowd, "Hiding Breast Bombs," *The New York Times,* November 25, 2004.

[123] Sara Kehaulani Goo, "Airport Pat Down Protocol Changed," *The Washington Post,* December 23, 2004.

Perhaps the government is inducing fear to distract attention from it own incompetence. TSA screeners perennially dismally fail the governments' own security tests. At Newark Liberty International Airport, for example, TSA screeners failed to detect the concealed bombs and guns smuggled through by undercover agents in 90 percent of the tests in 2006. This was consistent with other undercover government tests since 9/11.

TSA responded to the failure of its agents to find planted test bombs by proclaiming a whole new Yukon territory. TSA chief Kip Hawley declared: "There are infinite ways to find things to use as a weapon and infinite ways to hide them. But if you can identify the individual, it is by far the better way to find the threat."[124] Thus, TSA embarked on the Great Search for Dangerous People.

Hundreds of undercover TSA Behavior Detection Officers, or BDOs, are now roaming America's air terminals, peering into the faces of people to discern slight facial movements or other behavior characteristics indicating a possible lawbreaker or terrorist. Government agents who don't notice the bomb or the gun in the backpack are redeemed when they notice a one-twentieth of a second rise of an eyebrow. This sounds suspiciously like what Orwell described in 1984 as a NewSpeak offense: *Facecrime.*

The TSA is keeping the details of its Rosetta Stone to airline passengers secret. But some details of the new surveillance program have leaked out. *The Washington Post* reported that "screeners, former screeners and consultants say the officers are looking for people traveling without bags, sweating and constantly checking out every person passing by, especially those with badges and guns. People who avoid eye contact or veer away when police approach also draw their attention."[125] Avoiding TSA intrusions is now evidence of hostile intent! The number of people who fear flying outnumber Al Qaeda associates by at least a few thousandfold, yet visible anxiety could be enough for the TSA to

124 Eric Lipton, "Faces, Too, Are Searched at U.S. Airports," *The New York Times*, August 17, 2006.

125 Del Quentin Wilber and Ellen Nakashima, "Searching Passengers' Faces for Subtle Cues to Terror," *The Washington Post*, September 19, 2007.

justify taking people aside for a far more intensive examination.

TSA personnel now believe it their duty to watch for anybody at an airport who might be committing any crime whatsoever. A BDO operative at the Orlando airport who detected four illegal immigrants traveling with fake driver's licenses told *The Washington Post:* "It wasn't that unusual . . . Every day, that is what I'm looking for."[126]

TSA is using its BDOs to legitimize its pervasive surveillance of everyone. They seek to make Americans view other passengers as grave perils, as if flying with a bad driver's license was the equivalent of setting off a shoe bomb.

The TSA is adapting the method used by floundering police forces around the nation— vindication-via-endless-tickets for petty offenses. The more people they hassle, the more obvious their public service. They create pointless measures of their success, and the media and the public swallow the new bogus yardstick almost every time. It is only a matter of time until the TSA begins bragging about apprehending scofflaws in possession of overdue library books.

People who refuse to play twenty questions with the TSA after being selected by BDOs have been threatened with detention or arrest.

But even the TSA lacks faith in the omniscience of its BDO squad.

Jay Cohen, undersecretary of Homeland Security for Science and Technology, indicated in 2007 that he "wants to automate passenger screening by using videocams and computers to measure and analyze heart rate, respiration, body temperature and verbal responses as well as facial micro-expressions," according to a McClatchy news report.[127] Homeland Security is now soliciting proposals from companies to develop just such technology.

---

126 Del Quentin Wilber and Ellen Nakashima, "Searching Passengers' Faces For Subtle Cues to Terror," *The Washington Post*, September 19, 2007.

127 Kaitlin Dirrig, "New airport agents check for danger in fliers' facial expressions," McClatchy News Service, August 14, 2007.

On top of the BDOs and other hoops travelers must jump through, the TSA also claims the right to slap fines on anyone who shows a bad attitude when submitting to its inquisitions.

A fine of up to $1,500 can be levied (after the fact, of course) against an air traveler for something called "non-physical interference with screening." What is that? Looking at the screener the wrong way? Failing to jump high enough when told to jump? Or maybe, just maybe, non-physical interference with screening consists of a bad attitude, perhaps failing to greet a screener with appropriate deference or subservience as he or she arbitrarily forces you to disrobe publicly or submit to an additional, random inspection?

One of eight aggravating factors listed in TSA's guidelines is the "attitude of violator." Of course, you may not know until long after you've departed the airport, landed, and gone home that your attitude sufficiently rankled some TSA employee after he or she found an item of contraband mistakenly left in your carry-on, to warrant a hefty fine.

Remember, we're not talking of deliberately bringing weapons through a security checkpoint. That would be a criminal offense, not a civil infraction, and should be prosecuted. What we're talking about here are mistakes committed by law-abiding but harried men and women trying their best to comply with vague, even unknown, security guidelines in the crowded and pressure-filled atmosphere that permeates all airports in the post-9/11 world. But TSA rules are sufficient to give the bureaucrats what they want: more arbitrary power over other American citizens.

These fines have little, if anything, to do with preventing terrorist attacks. The terrorists studied airport security before 9/11 and easily evaded the official snares.

TSA's Latest, Greatest Intrusion: Full-Body X-Rays

And, for those who thought it could not get any worse, the TSA is becoming far more intrusive in selected airports across the land. In Phoenix, Boston, Chicago, and other high-traffic locales, the TSA is installing millimeter wave scanners that provide the equivalent of full-body X-rays. The Electronic Privacy Information Center complained: "These machines, which show detailed images of a person's naked body, are equivalent to a 'virtual strip search'," with photos "detailed enough to show genitalia."[128] While this is the type of technology that might be a juvenile boy's dream, it poses more than superficial risks to Americans' privacy, and possibly to their health. If some smarmy guy in a trench coat was caught using the same technology to photograph children at an elementary school playground, he would probably be sent to prison for many years. The American Civil Liberties Union rightly declared: "Passengers . . . should not be required to display highly personal details of their bodies such as evidence of mastectomies, colostomy appliances, penile implants, catheter tubes and the size of their breasts or genitals as a prerequisite to boarding a plane."[129]

The TSA says that Americans should not be concerned about its photographing their bodies because the agency will assure that the personal pictures are not abused. But this is the same agency that has created one scandal after another because of its violations of federal law with confidential personal data. There is no reason to expect that the TSA will do a better job of safeguarding pictures of movie stars' backsides than it does safeguarding the average citizen's confidential data.

Moreover, the potential health risks to passengers passing through a device taking a full-body x-ray is not at all clear. Of course, the government assures us there is no risk whatsoever. Will everyone who feels assured by that declaration please raise his hand?

There is no evidence that TSA needs to make records of every traveler's body in order to keep hijackers off of planes. Unfortunately, both Republicans and Democrats have slumbered while TSA sticks its nose ever further into Americans' privacy.

---

128 Kaitlin Dirrig, "New Airport Agents Check for Danger in Fliers Facial Expressions," McClatchy News Service, August 14, 2007.

129 Rapiscan Systems, Rapiscan Secure 1000. Accessed at http://epic.org/privacy/surveillance/spotlight/0605/rapiscan.pdf.

Conclusion

It has become far too easy to simply raise the specter of national security to kill any discussion about what methods of delving into private lives are appropriate. The power to take away one's privacy necessarily carries with it the power to demean, control, and even jail a person. The largely government-induced fear now pervading our society has created the perfect storm in which government agents stop anybody, anytime, anyplace for suspect activity based on a behavior pattern, all in the name of fighting terrorism. And that ought truly to make a person nervous and stressful (even without BDOs watching you).

Even as our leaders in Washington claim we cannot allow terrorists to change our way of life, they are planning and implementing policies that do precisely that. We have rendered virtually meaningless the Fourth Amendment's prohibition against government collecting evidence on law-abiding citizens unless there is reason to suspect the citizen engaged in criminal behavior. To pass constitutional muster and sound public policy based on respect for our Constitution, there must be some link between an individual and a reason to invade his or her privacy; that connection has been all but severed since 9/11.

Americans need to wake up to how their rulers are shredding their rights year by year, day by day. A recent survey by Privacy International, a well-respected watchdog organization based in London, listed the United States as among the worst performers in terms of protecting citizens' privacy. The US—along with China, Russia, Thailand, and a few other nations—was labeled as an "endemic surveillance society." Who would have thought a decade ago that the United States would have stooped to Red China's level?

Can government agents be trusted to know everything about everyone? The Founding Fathers certainly didn't think so. I hope my fellow citizens will not be naive enough to trust government agencies to cease and desist out of their sheer good-heartedness. There have been far too many criminal violations by the FBI and other federal agencies, and there have been no real penalties for any of the agents or agencies that scorned the law. To trust self-policing is to surrender to a government far more powerful than it should be, than it needs to be, and than our Founding Fathers contemplated.

★

THE WAR ON
FINANCIAL PRIVACY

It was not so many years ago that Americans could open a bank account and rest assured its contents would be free from prying government eyes unless federal agents could convince a federal judge that the bank customer had violated the law. Even the Internal Revenue Service was severely limited in how it could use the tax-related data and with whom it could share the information. In other words, as a man's home was his castle, so too his finances were his secret. No more.

Financial privacy is perhaps the most important privacy to the average citizen. Most Americans do not engage in political activism or make speeches that the government would want to suppress. But the privacy of one's finances is something that is valuable to every citizen.

This is an issue of principle. Liberty is far more than just a bank account, e-mail, or Social Security number. It is our birthright to keep personal affairs private from others, and especially from the government. It is our constitutional right not to have our privacy invaded and evidence gathered against us without the government having a good reason for doing so. Unfortunately, these core principles of good Americanism are increasingly confined to history books.

Stopping a Federal Roundup Before 9/11

My first experience battling excessive federal financial intrusions occurred in the final years of the Clinton presidency. In late 1998, four federal agencies issued proposed regulations that would have treated ordinary citizens like drug kingpins. The regulations—

known as "Know Your Customer" (KYC)—would have forced banks to report far more personal data on their customers to the federal government. Working together with my friend, Texas congressman Ron Paul, we helped stir up a political firestorm and gave federal bureaucrats one of their worst whippings of the 1990s.

Though the KYC regulations were supposedly needed to combat illicit activities, they would in reality have compelled banks to become snitches against their customers, even when there was no evidence of wrongdoing. The proposed regulations specified that a bank had to "determine its customers' sources of funds, determine, understand and monitor the normal and expected transactions of its customers, and report appropriately any transactions of its customers that are determined to be unusual or inconsistent."[130] Banks would have been obliged to create profiles of each customer and undertake "a risk assessment of the customer and the intended transactions of the customer." Even someone who merely deposited a bonus check from his regular job could be reported to the government.

Had these regulations been finalized, banks would have been obliged to disclose any data on their customers within forty-eight hours after receiving a request from law enforcement—no search warrant required. In other words, the Fourth Amendment would have been abolished for Americans' bank accounts.

The proposed regulations were based on the Bank Secrecy Act of 1970, which made it a federal crime for banks to keep secrets from the government. That law required banks and other financial institutions to submit a Currency Transaction Report (CTR) to the government for every transaction involving more than $10,000. This provision results in many home buyers being reported to the government as potential money launderers after they use a cashier's check at a closing to buy a new home. Banks and other institutions delivered more than 100,000 pounds of Currency Transaction Reports (77 million reports) to the government between 1987 and 1995, but only 580 people were

---

130 American Civil Liberties Union, "See-Through" Body Scanners. Accessed at http://www.aclu.org/privacy/35506res20080603.html.

convicted of money laundering in those years.[131]

The paperwork that subsequently flooded the government actually subverted law enforcement. The notorious CIA-turncoat Aldrich Ames, for example, was receiving wire transmissions of more than $50,000 from Switzerland in the early 1990s, prior to his arrest. His local bank notified the government of suspicious transactions, but the bureaucrats were so swamped by other reports they ignored alarm notices about a tidal wave of KGB money flowing to a key CIA official.

On March 4, 1999, the House Banking Committee passed an amendment I proposed to eliminate the Know Your Customer regulations. I commented that day: "It is ludicrous to assume that profiling the salary deposits, ATM fees, and mortgage payments of millions of Americans will have a significant impact on the activities of criminals. These regulations assume that millions of law-abiding Americans are potential criminals, simply because they have a checking account. Existing law already provides more than adequate authority to fight money-laundering." I hailed the amendment's passage as "a resounding defeat for those who want a Big Brother government to snoop in every aspect of our lives."[132]

Unfortunately, there are no permanent victories for freedom in Washington. Though federal bureaucrats were routed in 1999, they did not abandon their scheme. Instead, they bided their time, waiting for a more favorable season for legalizing their intrusions.

9/11 Snuffs the Right to Privacy

In Washington, nothing succeeds like failure. The 9/11 hijackings were preceded by the biggest failure ever by US financial watchdogs.

A United Nations 2002 report on terrorist financing noted

---

131 "Bob Barr Kills 'Know Your Customer' Regulation," Congressional Press Releases, March 4, 1999.

132 "Bob Barr Kills 'Know Your Customer' Regulation," Congressional Press Releases, March 4, 1999.

that a suspicious activity report had been filed with the US government over a $69,985 wire transfer that Mohamed Atta, leader of the 9/11 hijackers, received from the United Arab Emirates. Unfortunately, "this particular transaction was not noticed quickly enough because the report was just one of a very large number and was not distinguishable from those related to other financial crimes,"[133] according to the report. *The Wall Street Journal* reported that Mohamed Atta was on a Customs Service watch list, and that he "had been implicated in a 1986 bus bombing in Israel and had traveled in and out of the US on an expired visa,"[134] according to an FBI investigator. Any large wire transfer to Atta from an Arab nation should have set off a whole series of alarms, but as *Insight* magazine reported in March 2002, "Treasury sources say there is a two-year backlog of Suspicious Activity Reports still waiting to be entered into the agency's computers."[135]

It is beyond dispute that government investigators and analysts failed to properly sift and analyze the data they possessed on the 9/11 hijackers before their fatal attack. But the failure of bureaucrats to do their job would not be held against them when they then sought even more power over average Americans. The failure to stop the hijackers on 9/11 provided a blank check for politicians and regulators to revive their attempts to impose the Know Your Customer dragnet.

The Patriot Act greatly expanded the federal government's pretexts and prerogatives to intrude into Americans' financial lives. While administration officials and members of Congress invoked the terrorist threat, the actual provisos of the new legislation allowed bureaucrats to target individuals and businesses who posed no threat to national security. *Money Laundering Alert* newsletter described one financial provision of the Patriot Act as a "dream-come-true information gathering tool for US agencies," extending

133 Edith M. Lederer, "U.N. Experts Investigating Allegations That al-Qaida Has Moved Assets into Gold, Diamonds and Other Precious Stones," Associated Press, May 22, 2002.

134 David Armstrong and Joseph Pereira, "FBI Gives Carriers Access to Watchlists," *The Wall Street Journal,* October 23, 2001.

135 Quoted in John Berlau, "Show Us Your Money," *Reason,* November 2003.

a "welcome mat to the Central Intelligence Agency, National Security Agency and other US counterparts"[136] to look at the new financial information on American citizens and others.

The Patriot Act also created a new crime—bulk cash smuggling. Anyone who transports more than $10,000 into or out of the United States must fill out FinCEN (the Treasury Department's Financial Crimes Enforcement Network) Form #105 to notify the US government. Failure to fill out the form subjects a person to up to $500,000 in fines and up to ten years in prison, and, of course, seizure of any money he is transporting. Many foreigners and US travelers are unaware of this regulation and end up being stripped of their property at the US border.

The Patriot Act empowered the feds to commandeer all available financial data on Americans merely on a bureaucratic whim. The Electronic Frontier Foundation's Kevin Bankston observes: "There is no probable cause here. There is no judicial oversight. Yet the government can immediately query financial institutions across the nation to find out where you have an account or who you've done business with. It's not just if you have an account there, but any record of a financial transaction."[137]

Here again, most warrantless financial searches the feds have ordered under the Patriot Act have no connection to terrorism. In 2003, two-thirds of the thousands of Patriot Act financial searches "were in money-laundering cases with no apparent terror connection," including searches by the IRS for tax fraud, the Postal Service for postal fraud, the Secret Service for counterfeiting, and the Agriculture Department for food stamp fraud, according to *Newsweek*.[138]

Government investigators used Patriot Act financial dragnet powers in Operation G-String, an investigation of bribes involving

---

136 "BSA Gets Great Expansion in Coverage, Reach and Strength," *Money Laundering Alert*, November 2001.

137 Sam Stanton and Emily Bazar, "Patriot Act's Broad Brush," *The Sacramento Bee*, December, 21, 2003.

138 Michael Isikoff, "Show Me The Money," *Newsweek*, December 1, 2003.

Las Vegas strip clubs. One businessman bribed local politicians to deter them from enacting regulations that limited intimate contact during lap dances. The FBI used the Patriot Act to compel banks around the nation to report any information on financial transactions by Las Vegas politicians and other targets in the probe. Rep. Shelley Berkley (D-NV) complained: "It was never my intent to have the Patriot Act used as a kitchen sink for all of the law enforcement tool goodies that the FBI has been trying to get for the last decades."[139] Berkley observed that, back when the Patriot Act was considered, "Never . . . did the FBI say we needed additional tools to keep this nation safe from strip-club operators." [140]

The Patriot Act gives federal agencies new pretexts by which to confiscate private property without a criminal conviction. The Justice Department is exploiting the Patriot Act's powers for confiscations for alleged crimes with no relation to terrorism (such as seizing the bank accounts of Canadian telemarketers accused of fraud.)

Congress crafted a law that empowers the government to punish thousands of people for breaking the regulations for every terrorist who might get caught laundering money. Under the Patriot Act, a vast array of businesses, from travel agencies to pawn shops, must designate a compliance officer, develop internal anti–money-laundering policies, and arrange for independent audits of their efforts. Company officials who fail to hop through the right hoops can be hit with long prison sentences.

In today's climate of fear and arbitrary power, whether wielded directly or indirectly by the government, institutions that used to operate on the maxim that the customer is always right, now start from the premise, "every customer is a lawbreaker, and we will treat them as such." Welcome to post-9/11 America, friends.

---

139 Sam Stanton and Emily Bazar, "Patriot Act's Broad Brush," *The Sacramento Bee,* December, 21, 2003.

140 Michael Isikoff, "Show Me The Money," *Newsweek,* December 1, 2003.

Banks are mandated under the Patriot Act to require every customer, even those who have been customers in good standing for twenty years, to produce government-issued identification to open an account (even if they already have several). Some banks reportedly are requiring customers to produce their original Social Security card. Others are taking the opportunity to ask for other, even more irrelevant and intrusive forms of identification, as some sort of fishing expedition.

Banks are under increasing pressure to file more and more Suspicious Activity Reports, or SARs, with the federal government. The Patriot Act greatly expanded the category of suspicious activities that would trigger such filings. In 2007, banks and other firms covered by the Bank Secrecy Act submitted more than 1.2 million Suspicious Activity Reports to Uncle Sam, a 16 percent jump from the prior year. Yet at the same time SARs are cascading into the government, the reported allegations of terrorist financing are down sharply. The new reporting requirements are putting average citizens, not Al Qaeda, in the bureaucratic crosshairs.

Now, these and other federal reporting forms by law must be filed whenever any person—terrorist, criminal or simply law-abiding student, housewife or lawyer—engages in a broadly defined financial transaction at an equally broadly defined financial institution. The SAR, for example, is triggered whenever someone in the employ of, or connected with, that institution concludes there is something suspicious about a transaction (either alone or in conjunction with other, perhaps nonsuspicious, activities). If the suspicions of the employee are aroused while the customer is actually engaged in the questionable transaction, then the law requires that the act be reported immediately.

Any suspicion by a bank employee, for example, that a transaction is intended to violate or evade any federal law or any federal regulation (of which there are tens of thousands on the books) could prompt a report. Reportable suspicions clearly need have nothing to do with suspected terrorist activities or even suspected violations of federal felonies. Transactions as small as $2,000 must be reported.

Of course, the law prohibits financial institutions from notifying anyone that a suspicious activity has been reported to Uncle Sam. The official SAR report does its best to make mountains out of molehills. Among the whistle-blowing obligations are:

a). Describe supporting documentation and retain for five years.

b). Explain who benefited, financially or otherwise, from the transaction, how much, and how.

c). Retain any confession, admission, or explanation of the transaction provided by the suspect and indicate to whom and when it was given.

d). Retain any confession, admission, or explanation of the transaction provided by any other person and indicate to whom and when it was given.

e). Retain any evidence of cover-up or evidence of an attempt to deceive federal or state examiners or others.

. . . i) Recommend any further investigation that might assist law enforcement authorities.

. . . l) Indicate whether any information has been excluded from this report; if so, why?

The last proviso effectively creates a burden on banks and other institutions to overreport reams of information in order to cover themselves against subsequent federal crackdowns, with all that largely (if not totally) irrelevant data, going into a public database.

Also, as a result of defensive filings by banks, the types of transactions that are coming under scrutiny are often routine and not indicative of any unlawful activity. This reporting represents little more than just plain snooping by bank officials eager to curry favor with federal regulators, and reflects the federal government's increasing desire to gather data on all of us for no reason or any reason.

It has gotten so bad that one banker recently told me his bank has set quotas for increased numbers of SARs to be filed each reporting period. Banks file suspicious reports on customers who merely heavily use ATM machines. The federal government is now prosecuting banks for not filing enough SARs.[141] The same bureaucrats who failed to notice the Suspicious Activity Report on Mohamed Atta are now empowered to slap million-dollar penalties on bankers who fail to satisfy the government's latest definition of due diligence against money laundering.

Federal investigators are increasingly ruling financial institutions by fear. In a 2008 settlement with Sigue Corp., a California money transmitter, the Justice Department imposed a $15 million fine in part because the company failed to do the government's job. Sigue, in fact, reported many suspicious transactions, but, with a newly announced standard, that did not satisfy the feds. Sigue's general counsel, Robert Pargac, complained that the Justice Department "is saying you just don't have to have your AML [anti–money-laundering] compliance program, detect suspect activity, and report it to law enforcement, but it goes a step further, and they are requiring institutions to *prevent* money laundering"[142] (emphasis added). Ralph Sharpe, an former federal money laundering investigator, told *American Banker* magazine that the settlement's implications for anyone filing a SAR is "that is it is not enough to file a SAR or a good SAR, but you've got to take the next step to see if there is something there—some pattern, some abuse—and you have to act on it."[143]

The web of snooping in which federal investigators and regulators are now able to ensnare any person who engages in any form of financial transaction has become so complex and pervasive that almost no person anywhere in the world can escape its clutches. This explains how the FBI got wind of former New York

---

141 Asset Protection Corporation, "Banking, Privacy, and the USA PATRIOT Act." Accessed at http://www.assetprotectioncorp.com/bankingandprivacy.html.

142 Cheyenne Hopkins, "BSA Decree Sets New Compliance Bar," *American Banker*, January 28, 2008.

143 Ibid.

Governor Eliot Spitzer's withdrawals of a few thousand dollars to pay for a prostitute. The ability of the government to manipulate this vast power is magnified manyfold by virtue of the manner in which our laws and regulations require the active complicity of the entire cadre of persons working in or connected with banks and other entities that provide financial transactions.

It only takes a vague suspicion of money laundering for the feds to confiscate your bank accounts. In April 2008, *Forbes* reported two cases of hapless business owners torpedoed by such action:

> The feds seized $400,000 in late 2006 from bank accounts of Jennifer and Jeremy Marshall, the owners of Aquagrill, a SoHo seafood restaurant . . . The government said the funds traced to deposits of $9,950 or less and began a criminal structuring investigation. The Marshalls' lawyer argues they weren't trying to hide money and shouldn't be charged. She adds that an independent expert has confirmed "every penny" was earned legitimately and taxes were properly paid.
>
> In Texas the feds seized $330,000 from the owners of Executive Taxi, Dallas Taxi and Golden Taxi on suspicion of structuring. Allen Mansourian, Barry Sangani and Ahmad Sangani insist that the cash was deposited as it came in from the cab business. In court papers they say they could lose their liability insurance and be forced to shut down if they don't get their money back.[144]

Bureaucratic Greed at Its Worst?

In 2006, *The New York Times* revealed that the Bush administration was secretly vacuuming up Americans' personal records passing through a Belgian hub for international banking, begun in 2001 by the US Treasury and the Central Intelligence Agency. After *The*

---

144 Janet Novack, "My Big Fat IRS case," *Forbes*, April 7, 2008.

Times exposed the secret program, the administration quickly redubbed the intrusion the Terrorist Finance Tracking Program.

But there is no requirement that people be suspected of links to terrorism before the government impounds their personal data. The program was a typical, post-9/11 grab-everyone's-data roundup. Treasury Undersecretary Stuart Levey said, "We've done a large number of searches . . . I don't know the exact number but it's . . . at least tens of thousands, maybe hundreds of thousands of searches."[145] If the government official in charge of the intrusion has no idea whether the number of searches is tens or hundreds of thousands, this is strong circumstantial evidence the government is grabbing too much information.

The feds did not have a warrant for any of the tens or hundreds of thousands of searches it conducted, only a secret presidential authorization. The Terrorist Finance Tracking Program violates both a 1978 federal law, the Right to Financial Privacy Act, and the Fourth Amendment. The Bush administration is almost certainly carrying out other financial surveillance efforts that far surpasses what has so far leaked out.

Like other post-9/11 information info grabs, this roundup was largely a failure—at least against the purported targets. *The Los Angeles Times* reported that even government officials admitted "the effort has been only marginally successful against al-Qaida, which long ago began transferring money through other means, including the highly informal banking system common in Islamic countries."[146]

Conclusion

At the same time the government is tightening the thumbscrews on the penny ante spending of average Americans, the government itself could not be acting more irresponsibly. In 2004, the US

145 Karen DeYoung, "Officials Defend Financial Searches," *The Washington Post*, June 24, 2006.

146 Greg Miller and Josh Meyer, "U.S. Secretly Tracks Global Bank Data," *The Los Angeles Times*, June 23, 2006.

government flew almost $12 billion in crisp hundred-dollar bills into Baghdad in C-130 planeloads. It made little or no effort to track how the pallets of shrink-wrapped cash were spent. The dollars were passed out willy-nilly to buy support for the US occupation, or for the new interim Iraqi government. A report by the House Committee on Oversight and Government Reform noted, "Some of the funds could have enriched both criminals and insurgents fighting the United States."[147] It was far more likely that some of the US-dumped cash ended up in the coffers of groups such as Al Qaeda in Iraq than that typical Americans would provide even a nickel in aid to Osama bin Laden. Yet the government entitles itself to treat almost every bank account owner as a potential terrorist financier, at the same time it makes scant effort to prevent US tax dollars dumped into Iraq from falling into the hands of terrorist groups.

The issue is not whether the federal government should detect and block terrorist financing; everyone favors such efforts. Instead, the issue is whether the government can invoke the terrorist threat to exempt itself from all statutory and constitutional restraints, and thereby destroy all privacy of American citizens.

Federal financial investigators have long been overwhelmed by too many reports from all manner of financial institutions. Unfortunately, the Bush administration, the bureaucrats, and Congress responded to the failure to find needles in the haystack prior to 9/11 by mandating vastly larger haystacks. But seizing more personal data is no substitute for competent, focused analysis of real threats.

Groveling to bureaucrats will not make Americans safe. The penalties the Treasury Department and banking regulators inflict do little or nothing to deter aspiring foreign enemies. The Bush administration has been far more effective at destroying financial privacy than at protecting Americans.

---

147 David Pallister, "How the US sent $12bn in cash to Iraq. And watched it vanish," *The Guardian* (United Kingdom), February 8, 2007.

Suspicious Activity Report

July 2003

Previous editions will not be accepted after December 31, 2003

FRB: FR 2230 OMB No. 7100-0212

FDIC: 6710/06 OMB No. 3064-0077

OCC: 8010-9,8010-1 OMB No. 1557-0180

OTS: 1601 OMB No. 1550-0003

NCUA: 2362 OMB No. 3133-0094

TREASURY: TD F 90-22.47 OMB No. 1506-0001

ALWAYS COMPLETE ENTIRE REPORT

(see instructions)

Part I Reporting Financial Institution Information

1. Check box below only if correcting a prior report.

Corrects Prior Report (see instruction #3 under "How to Make a Report")

2. Name of Financial Institution

3. EIN

4. Address of Financial Institution

5. Primary Federal Regulator

    a. Federal Reserve

    b. FDIC

    c. NCUA

    d. OCC

    e. OTS

6. City 7. State 8. Zip Code

9. Address of Branch Office(s) where activity occurred Multiple Branches (include information in narrative, Part V)

10. City 11 State 12 Zip Code

13. If institution closed, date closed_____ / _____ / _____

14. Account number(s) affected, if any

Part II. Suspect Information

15. Last Name or Name of Entity 16 First Name 17 Middle

18. Address

19. SSN, EIN or TIN

20. City 21. State 22. Zip Code 23. Country

24. Phone Number—Residence (include area code)

25. Phone Number—Work (include area code)

26. Occupation/Type of Business

27. Date of Birth_____ / _____ / _____

28. Admission/Confession? a Yes b No

29. Forms of Identification for Suspect:

    a. Driver's License/State ID Number _____ Issuing Authority _____

    b. Passport

    c. Alien Registration

    d. Other _____

30. Relationship to Financial Institution:

    a. Accountant

    b. Agent

    c. Appraiser

    d. Attorney

    e. Borrower

f. Broker

g. Customer

h. Director

i. Employee

j. Officer

k. Shareholder

l. Other _____

31. Is the relationship an insider relationship? a Yes b No

c. Still employed at financial institution

d. Suspended

e. Terminated

f. Resigned

32. Date of Suspension, Termination, Resignation_____ /
_____ / _____

Part III. Suspicious Activity Information

33. Date or date range of suspicious activity

From ____ / _____ / _____ To ____ / _____ / _____

34. Total dollar amount involved in known or suspicious activity
$____.00

35. Summary characterization of suspicious activity:

a. Bank Secrecy Act/Structuring/Money Laundering

b. Bribery/Gratuity

c. Check Fraud

d. Check Kiting

e. Commercial Loan Fraud

f. Computer Intrusion

g. Consumer Loan Fraud

h. Counterfeit Check

i. Counterfeit Credit/Debit Card

j. Counterfeit Instrument (other)

k. Credit Card Fraud

l. Debit Card Fraud

m. Defalcation/Embezzlement

n. False Statement

o. Misuse of Position or Self Dealing

p. Mortgage Loan Fraud

q. Mysterious Disappearance

r. Wire Transfer Fraud

s. Other

t. Terrorist Financing

u. Identity Theft

36. Amount of loss prior to recovery _____.00

37. Dollar amount of recovery (if applicable)_____ .00

38. Has the suspicious activity had a material impact on, or otherwise affected, the financial soundness of the institution? a Yes b. No

39. Has the institution's bonding company been notified? a Yes b No

40. Has any law enforcement agency already been advised by telephone, written communication, or otherwise?

a. DEA

b. FBI

c. IRS

d. Postal Inspection

e. Secret Service

f. US Customs

g. Other Federal

h. State

i. Local

j. Agency Name (for g, h or i)

41. Name of person(s) contacted at Law Enforcement Agency

42. Phone Number (include area code)

43. Name of person(s) contacted at Law Enforcement Agency

44. Phone Number (include area code)

Part IV. Contact for Assistance

45. Last Name

46. First Name

47. Middle

48. Title/Occupation

49. Phone Number (include area code)

50. Date Prepared_____ / _____ / _____

51. Agency (if not filed by financial institution)

Part V. Suspicious Activity Information Explanation/Description

Explanation/description of known or suspected violation of law or suspicious activity.

This section of the report is **critical**. The care with which it is written may make the difference in whether or not the described conduct and its possible criminal nature are clearly understood. Provide below a chronological and **complete** account of the possible violation of law, including what is unusual, irregular or suspicious about the transaction, using the following checklist as you prepare your account. **If necessary, continue the narrative on a duplicate of this page.**

a. **Describe** supporting documentation and retain for 5 years.

b. **Explain** who benefited, financially or otherwise, from the transaction, how much, and how.

c. **Retain** any confession, admission, or explanation of the transaction provided by the suspect and indicate to whom and when it was given.

d. **Retain** any confession, admission, or explanation of the transaction provided by any other person and indicate to whom and when it was given.

e. **Retain** any evidence of cover-up or evidence of an attempt to deceive federal or state examiners or others.

f. **Indicate** where the possible violation took place (e.g., main office, branch, other).

g. **Indicate** whether the possible violation is an isolated incident or relates to other transactions.

h. **Indicate** whether there is any related litigation; if so, specify.

i. **Recommend** any further investigation that might assist law enforcement authorities.

j. **Indicate** whether any information has been excluded from this report; if so, why?

k. If you are correcting a previously filed report, describe the changes that are being made.

For Bank Secrecy Act/Structuring/Money Laundering reports, include the following additional information:

l. **Indicate** whether currency and/or monetary instruments were involved. If so, provide the amount and/or description of the instrument (for example, bank draft, letter of credit, domestic or international money order, stocks, bonds, traveler's checks, wire transfers sent or received, cash, etc.).

m. **Indicate** any account number that may be involved or affected.

Paperwork Reduction Act Notice: The purpose of this form is to provide an effective and consistent means for financial institutions to notify appropriate law enforcement agencies of known or suspected criminal conduct or suspicious activities that take place at or were perpetrated against financial institutions. This report is required by law, pursuant to authority contained in the following statutes. Board of Governors of the Federal Reserve System: 12 USC. 324, 334, 611a, 1844(b) and (c), 3105(c) (2) and 3106(a). Federal Deposit Insurance Corporation: 12 USC. 93a, 1818, 1881-84, 3401-22. Office of the Comptroller of the Currency: 12 USC. 93a, 1818, 1881-84, 3401-22. Office of Thrift Supervision: 12 USC. 1463 and 1464. National Credit Union Administration: 12 USC. 1766(a), 1786(q). Financial Crimes Enforcement Network: 31 USC. 5318(g). Information collected on this report is confidential (5 USC. 552(b)(7) and 552a(k)(2), and 31 USC. 5318(g)). The Federal financial institutions' regulatory agencies and the US Departments of Justice and Treasury may use and share the information.

Public reporting and recordkeeping burden for this information collection is estimated to average 30 minutes per response, and includes time to gather and maintain data in the required report, review the instructions, and complete the information collection. Send comments regarding this burden estimate, including suggestions for reducing the burden, to the Office of Management and Budget, Paperwork Reduction Project, Washington, DC 20503 and, depending on your primary Federal regulatory agency, to Secretary, Board of Governors of the Federal Reserve System, Washington, DC 20551; or Assistant Executive Secretary, Federal Deposit Insurance Corporation, Washington, DC 20429; or Legislative and Regulatory Analysis Division, Office of the Comptroller of the Currency, Washington, DC 20219; or Office of Thrift Supervision, Enforcement Office, Washington, DC 20552; or National Credit Union Administration, 1775 Duke Street, Alexandria, VA 22314; or Office of the Director, Financial Crimes Enforcement Network, Department of the Treasury, P.O. Box 39, Vienna, VA 22183. The agencies may not conduct or sponsor, and an organization (or a person) is not required to respond to, a collection of information unless it displays a currently valid OMB control number.

Tips on SAR Form preparation and filing are available in the SAR Activity Review at www.fincen.gov/pub_reports.html

Suspicious Activity Report Instructions

Safe Harbor Federal law (31 USC. 5318(g)(3)) provides complete protection from civil liability for all reports of suspicious transactions made to appropriate authorities, including supporting documentation, regardless of whether such reports are filed pursuant to this report's instructions or are filed on a voluntary basis. Specifically, the law provides that a financial institution, and its directors, officers, employees and agents, that make a disclosure of any possible violation of law or regulation, including in connection with the preparation of suspicious activity reports, "shall not be liable to any person under any law or regulation of the United States, any constitution, law, or regulation of any State or political subdivision of any State, or under any contract or other legally enforceable agreement (including any arbitration agreement), for such disclosure or for any failure to provide notice of such disclosure to the person who is the subject of such disclosure or any other person identified in the disclosure".

Notification Prohibited Federal law (31 USC. 5318(g)(2)) requires that a financial institution, and its directors, officers, employees and agents who, voluntarily or by means of a suspicious activity report, report suspected or known criminal violations or suspicious activities may not notify any person involved in the transaction that the transaction has been reported.

In situations involving violations requiring immediate attention, such as when a reportable violation is ongoing, the financial institution shall immediately notify, by telephone, appropriate law enforcement and financial institution supervisory authorities in addition to filing a timely suspicious activity report.

WHEN TO MAKE A REPORT:

1. All financial institutions operating in the United States, including insured banks, savings associations, savings association service corporations, credit unions, bank holding companies, nonbank subsidiaries of bank holding companies, Edge and Agreement corporations, and US branches and agencies of foreign banks, are required to make this report following the discovery of:

   a. **Insider abuse involving any amount.** Whenever the financial institution detects any known or suspected Federal criminal violation, or pattern of criminal violations, committed or attempted against the financial institution or involving a transaction or transactions conducted through the financial institution, where the financial institution believes that it was either an actual or potential victim of a criminal violation, or series of criminal violations, or that the financial institution was used to facilitate a criminal transaction, and the financial institution has a substantial basis for identifying one of its directors, officers, employees, agents or other institution-affiliated parties as having committed or aided in the commission of a criminal act regardless of the amount involved in the violation.

   b. **Violations aggregating $5,000 or more where a suspect can be identified.** Whenever the financial institution detects any known or suspected Federal criminal violation, or pattern of criminal violations, committed or attempted against the financial institution or involving a transaction or transactions conducted through the financial institution and involving or aggregating $5,000 or more in funds or other assets, where the financial institution believes that it was either an actual or potential victim of a criminal violation, or series of criminal violations, or that the financial institution was used to facilitate a criminal transaction, and the financial institution has a substantial basis for identifying a possible suspect or group of suspects. If it is determined prior to filing this report that the identified suspect or group of suspects has used an "alias," then information regarding the true identity of the suspect or group of suspects, as well as alias identifiers, such as drivers' licenses or social security numbers, addresses and telephone numbers, must be reported.

c. **Violations aggregating $25,000 or more regardless of a potential suspect.** Whenever the financial institution detects any known or suspected Federal criminal violation, or pattern of criminal violations, committed or attempted against the financial institution or involving a transaction or transactions conducted through the financial institution and involving or aggregating $25,000 or more in funds or other assets, where the financial institution believes that it was either an actual or potential victim of a criminal violation, or series of criminal violations, or that the financial institution was used to facilitate a criminal transaction, even though there is no substantial basis for identifying a possible suspect or group of suspects.

d. **Transactions aggregating $5,000 or more that involve potential money laundering or violations of the Bank Secrecy Act.** Any transaction (which for purposes of this subsection means a deposit, withdrawal, transfer between accounts, exchange of currency, loan, extension of credit, purchase or sale of any stock, bond, certificate of deposit, or other monetary instrument or investment security, or any other payment, transfer, or delivery by, through, or to a financial institution, by whatever means effected) conducted or attempted by, at or through the financial institution and involving or aggregating $5,000 or more in funds or other assets, if the financial institution knows, suspects, or has reason to suspect that:

i. The transaction involves funds derived from illegal activities or is intended or conducted in order to hide or disguise funds or assets derived from illegal activities (including, without limitation, the ownership, nature, source, location, or control of such funds or assets) as part of a plan to violate or evade any law or regulation or to avoid any transaction reporting requirement under Federal law;

ii. The transaction is designed to evade any regulations promulgated under the Bank Secrecy Act; or

iii. The transaction has no business or apparent lawful purpose or is not the sort in which the particular customer would normally be expected to engage, and the financial institution knows of no reasonable explanation for the transaction after examining the available facts, including the background and possible purpose of the transaction.

The Bank Secrecy Act requires all financial institutions to file currency transaction reports (CTRs) in accordance with the Department of the Treasury's implementing regulations (31 CFR Part 103). These regulations require a financial institution to file a CTR whenever a currency transaction exceeds $10,000. If a currency transaction exceeds $10,000 and is suspicious, the institution must file both a CTR (reporting the currency transaction) and a suspicious activity report (reporting the suspicious or criminal aspects of the transaction). If a currency transaction equals or is below $10,000 and is suspicious, the institution should only file a suspicious activity report.

2. **Computer Intrusion.** For purposes of this report, "computer intrusion" is defined as gaining access to a computer system of a financial institution to:

a. Remove, steal, procure, or otherwise affect funds of the institution or the institution's customers;

b. Remove, steal, procure or otherwise affect critical information of the institution including customer account information; or

c. Damage, disable or otherwise affect critical systems of the institution. For purposes of this reporting requirement, computer intrusion does not mean attempted intrusions of websites or other non-critical information systems of the institution that provide no access to institution or customer financial or other critical information.

3. A financial institution is required to file a suspicious activity report no later than 30 calendar days after the date of initial detection of facts that may constitute a basis for filing a suspicious activity report. If no suspect was identified on the date of detection of the incident requiring the filing, a financial institution may delay filing a suspicious activity report for an additional 30 calendar days to identify a suspect. In no case shall reporting be delayed more than 60 calendar days after the date of initial detection of a reportable transaction.

4. This suspicious activity report does not need to be filed for those robberies and burglaries that are reported to local authorities, or (except for savings associations and service corporations) for lost, missing, counterfeit, or stolen securities that are reported pursuant to the requirements of 17 CFR 240.17f-1.

HOW TO MAKE A REPORT:

1. Send each completed suspicious activity report to:
   Detroit Computing Center, P.O. Box 33980, Detroit, MI 48232-0980

2. For items that do not apply or for which information is not available, leave blank.

3. If you are correcting a previously filed report, check the box at the top of the report (line 1). Complete the report in its entirety and include the corrected information in the applicable boxes. Then describe the changes that are being made in Part V (Description of Suspicious Activity), line k.

4. **Do not include any supporting documentation with the suspicious activity report.** Identify and retain a copy of the suspicious activity report and all original supporting documentation or business record equivalent for five (5) years from the date of the suspicious activity report. All supporting documentation must be made available to appropriate authorities upon request.

5. If more space is needed to report additional suspects, attach copies of page 1 to provide the additional information. If more space is needed to report additional branch addresses, include this information in the narrative, Part V.

6. Financial institutions are encouraged to provide copies of suspicious activity reports to state and local authorities, where appropriate.

ILLEGAL WIRETAPS
VS. FREEDOM

The right of the people to be secure in their persons, houses, papers, and effects, against unreasonable searches and seizures, shall not be violated, and no Warrants shall issue, but upon probable cause, supported by Oath or Affirmation, particularly describing the place to be searched, and the person or things to be seized.

—Amendment IV, US Constitution

For more than two centuries, Americans have considered privacy a cause worth fighting for. Federal judge Gerhard Gesell, in a ruling in the case of a burglary authorized by the Nixon White House, declared: "The American Revolution was sparked in part by the complaints of the colonists against the issuance of writs of assistance, pursuant to which the King's revenue officers conducted unrestricted, indiscriminate searches of persons and homes to uncover contraband."[148]

At the time the Bill of Rights became the law of the land, the fledgling country was at risk at every turn. But in the exercise of the kind of vision and courage that has been our trademark throughout our history, our Founding Fathers did not flinch from their belief in a freedom such as the world had never seen, and has yet to be duplicated. They fashioned a fair but strict set of prohibitions that focused its force on the power of the government to intrude upon the rights and privacy of its citizens.

Unfortunately the words of the Fourth Amendment now appear to be in disrepute, their meaning denigrated, their import in

---

148. *United States v. Ehrlichman*, 376 F. Supp. 29, 32 (D.D.C. 1974).

disrepair. America, in the twenty-first century, appears to have become afraid of—or disinterested in—the grand experiment in freedom begun almost 250 years ago by a group of patriots determined to govern themselves free from the control of an overweening and powerful government. Virtually the entire range of policy decisions within the purview of our federal government at this time in our history appears to be governed by fear, deception, or mistake—not by the courage exemplified by our forefathers.

One of the first principles of our republic is that a United States citizen in this country is clothed with a sphere—an aura—of privacy that the federal government cannot invade absent a good and sufficient reason. This was the rule that the US government lived by for more than two hundred years. After 9/11, however, Uncle Sam secretly placed all Americans in a brave new world of electronic surveillance.

The Bush administration failed to allow something as mundane as the Bill of Rights to restrain its intrusions. And a law passed by Congress in 2007 to ratify and legalize a Bush surveillance program shatters the foundation of the Fourth Amendment as surely as if a keg of dynamite were lit beneath it. In the name of fighting terrorism the Bush administration appears to have succeeded in convincing Congress that to succeed in the global war on terror, the Fourth Amendment must not only yield, but be disassembled.

Echelon and Onwards

I have been gravely concerned about warrantless wiretaps of Americans since my time in Congress. In 2000, for example, I testified before the House Intelligence Committee about the dangers of Echelon—a spy satellite system run by the National Security Agency along with the United Kingdom, Australia, New Zealand, and Canada. Echelon scans millions of phone calls, e-mails, and faxes each hour, searching for keywords. I warned, "By all appearances, what we have is a massive government program that scoops up unbelievably huge numbers of private communications, indiscriminately, without any oversight or court involvement. There's a very fine, but extremely important, line between legitimate foreign intelligence gathering and unconstitutional eavesdropping on American citizens, and it appears that line has been crossed." I persuaded my colleagues to support my amendment to an appropriations bill that required NSA and the CIA to report to Congress on the standards Echelon used to tap Americans' communications. NSA responded by sending a letter to all members of Congress containing this boilerplate language: "We want to assure you that the NSA's activities are conducted in accordance with the highest constitutional, legal and ethical standards, and in compliance with statutes and regulations designed to protect the privacy rights of US persons."[149]

At the same hearing at which I testified, Air Force General Michael Hayden, the NSA chief, also testified. Hayden was asked whether the government could intercept communications of an American citizen in this country. Hayden replied: "If that American person is in the United States of America, I must have a court order before I initiate any collection against him or her."[150]

Six years later, General Hayden had an extra star on his shoulder and he was working for a new president. And he had turned inside-outside his interpretation of federal law.

9/11 and the Right to Listen In

In the months and years after the Patriot Act was passed, many critics accused the federal government of trampling civil liberties. Attorney General John Ashcroft mocked any concerns about the feds going too far. In stump speeches in his 2003 Patriot Act salvation tour, he would sneer, "I heard a fellow said his car wouldn't start the other day, and he blamed the Patriot Act."

---

149 Alice Ann Love, "NSA Defends Eavesdropping Policy," Associated Press, February 27, 2000.

150 Quoted in "Testimony by Former Rep. Bob Barr concerning Opposition to S. 1927, 'The Protect America Act,'" Senate Judiciary Committee, September 5, 2007.

During his 2004 reelection campaign, Bush declared, "Any time you hear the United States government talking about wiretap, it requires—a wiretap requires a court order. Nothing has changed, by the way. When we're talking about chasing down terrorists, we're talking about getting a court order before we do so."[151] Such assurances were potentially disingenuous, but they helped keep civil liberties off the front burner in the 2004 election campaign.

But a year after Bush secured a second term, *The New York Times* revealed that since 2002 the National Security Agency had carried out a massive warrantless wiretapping scheme, listening in to as many as five hundred Americans' phone calls at the same time without a warrant. The Bush administration secretly decided it need not be bothered with providing any justification to spy on American citizens.

Some of my former Republican colleagues in Congress reacted to the revelation by forming a legal lynch mob—urging that the reporters and publisher who revealed this massive, illegal program be arrested for treason. I appreciated that the paper had the gumption to expose federal crimes, but it seemed such perspective was a distinctly minority view. When Bush bragged of his Terrorist Surveillance Program a few weeks later during the State of the Union, Republican members of Congress leaped to their feet and gave him a thundering ovation.

President Bush responded to the exposé by portraying himself as heroically rising above the statute book to protect the American people. Bush declared: "This is a limited program designed to prevent attacks on the United States of America and, I repeat, limited. I think most Americans understand the need to find out what the enemy's thinking."[152] But Bush's program automatically treated vast numbers of Americans like the enemy. The president originally claimed only people connected to Al Qaeda were tapped, but that has subsequently been shown to be false.

---

151 "Remarks by the President in a Conversation on the USA Patriot Act, Kleinshans Music Hall, Buffalo, New York," White House Office of the Press Secretary, April 20, 2004.

152 "Bush defends NSA spying program," CNN.com, January 1, 2006.

After 9/11, the Bush administration decided that the president could surveil whomever he pleased in the name of national security and his role of choice—Commander in Chief. Bush declared, "We believe there's a constitutional power granted to presidents as well as, this case, a statutory power. And I'm intending to use that power."[153] It was as if Article II of the Constitution was rewritten: *The President shall be commander in chief of the Army and Navy of the United States and when carrying out duties in such capacity shall not be subject to the laws of these United States or of this Constitution.*

Bush and Attorney General Alberto Gonzales claimed that the warrantless wiretaps were based on Congress's authorization to use military force against the people who attacked the United States. But if that measure actually nullified all domestic limits on the president's power, Americans have been living under martial law since September 18, 2001, when Congress passed the resolution (and for which I voted). Moreover, if the authorization to use military force actually authorized the administration to surveil anyone it chose, there would have been no reason to propose the Patriot Act, since presumably all of those powers also were included. The Bush administration, and President Bush in particular, believes a president truly does inherently possess such expansive and unreviewable power. But they also recognize it strengthens (even if legally contradicting) their case if they propose statutory measures explicitly providing for some of these powers. In this manner also, the case is made easier for successor presidents to claim and use such broad powers.

Bush's program blatantly violated existing federal law. In 1978, responding to scandals involving political spying on Americans in the name of counterespionage (especially during the Nixon administration), Congress passed the Foreign Intelligence Surveillance Act (FISA). This act prohibited wiretapping of domestic phone calls without a warrant. The law created a special, secret FISA court that set a much lower standard for securing

---

153 Dan Eggen and Walter Pincus, "Varied Rationales Muddle Issue of NSA Eavesdropping," *The Washington Post*, January 27, 2006.

search warrants than is required by other federal courts.

The FISA court has approved almost every one of the more than twenty-two thousand search warrant requests the feds have submitted since 1978. In emergencies, time-sensitive situations, federal agencies can even submit retroactive requests up to seventy-two hours after they begin surveilling someone. The number of FISA-approved wiretaps almost doubled after 2001. Yet the Bush administration whined that FISA made the US government a helpless giant against terrorists. One government official told *The Washington Post* that the administration complained bitterly that the FISA process "demanded too much: to name a target and give a reason to spy on it." The official explained: "For FISA, they had to put down a written justification for the wiretap. They couldn't dream one up."[154] Heaven forbid that the federal government has to have an articulable reason before it could spy on its own citizens!

FISA was enacted in part because of the NSA's long history of abuses. The NSA had created files in the late 1960s, for example, on such threats as Dr. Benjamin Spock, Joan Baez, and Martin Luther King, Jr. The NSA attempted to surveil all Quakers in the United States (because of their antiwar philosophy), except, of course, the Quaker president, Richard Nixon. Had it included Nixon in its effort, the NSA might have prevented Watergate.

The Supreme Court rebuked Nixon in 1972, unanimously rejecting the assertion that a president may conduct electronic surveillance of American citizens without judicial approval for national security, declaring that our "Fourth Amendment freedoms cannot properly be guaranteed if domestic security surveillances may be conducted solely within the discretion of the Executive Branch."[155] Former White House Counsel John Dean noted: "Nixon was charged in Article II of his bill of impeachment with illegal wiretapping for

154 Carol D. Leonnig and Dafna Linzer, "Judges on Surveillance Court To Be Briefed on Spy Program," *The Washington Post*, December 22, 2005.

155 David G. Savage and Bob Drogin, "Legality of Wiretaps Remains in Question," *The Los Angeles Times*, December 18, 2005.

what he, too, claimed were national security reasons."[156]

Bush reincarnated the same policy that Richard Nixon used —having the NSA snoop on American citizens and others the president considered a threat; but he's put the program on steroids.

"Judges need not apply" might as well be the motto of the Bush wiretapping program. The question of who gets wiretapped is now determined by shift supervisors at the National Security Agency.

The Terrorist Surveillance Program apparently was largely the brain child of Vice President Dick Cheney's office. Cheney has made clear that he believes the president is not bound by the law. Cheney's chief counsel, David Addington, repeatedly told Jack Goldsmith, a top appointee at the Justice Department: "We're one bomb away from getting rid of that obnoxious [FISA] court."[157] Goldsmith noted that Addington and Cheney "abhorred FISA's intrusion on presidential power ever since its enactment in 1978. After 9/11 they and other top officials in the administration dealt with FISA the way they dealt with other laws they didn't like: They blew through them in secret based on flimsy legal opinions that they guarded closely so no one could question the legal basis for the operations."[158] Those secret and flimsy legal opinions the Bush administration has relied on to conduct a broad range of questionable (if not blatantly illegal) activities since the 9/11 attacks were drafted largely by or under the direction of loyal political appointees at the Department of Justice (this certainly is one factor accounting for the low esteem in which the DOJ is held by a large majority of Americans).

Yet the White House insisted that its terrorist-surveillance program has been thoroughly reviewed by the Justice Department to determine its legality. (Prior to the Bush administration, the

---

156 John Dean, "George W. Bush as the New Richard M. Nixon," Findlaw.com, December 30, 2005.

157 Glenn Greenwald, "Dick Cheney's top aide: 'We're one bomb away' from our goal," Salon.com, September 4, 2007.

158 Michiko Kakutani, "Former Law Adviser Speaks Out on Bush," *The New York Times*, September 11, 2007.

courts, not federal agencies, were the final arbiters of the lawfulness of agencies' actions.)

But in May 2006, Congress was notified that the White House throttled an investigation by the Justice Department's Office of Professional Responsibility (OPR), the agency's pseudo-watchdog, into "whether DOJ lawyers had behaved unethically by interpreting the law too aggressively—by giving a legal green light to coercive interrogations and warrantless eavesdropping," as *Newsweek* reported.[159] Attorney General Gonzales said the investigation was unnecessary because the Justice Department had decided the wiretaps were legal.

In the summer of 2007, the Bush administration decided to railroad through Congress legislation effectively rubberstamping its perverse reading of the law and the Constitution. The result was the Protect America Act—a label almost as bogus as the original Patriot Act. This act gave the Bush team a legal license to do almost anything it pleased, surveillance-wise, for six months. To spur Congress to enact the law, Bush administration officials helped spread false rumors of a possible terrorist attack on Capitol Hill itself. On August 2, 2007, the Capitol Police announced they were boosting security "in response to intelligence indicating the increased possibility of an Al Qaida terrorist attack on Congress sometime between now and Sept. 11," *Roll Call* (a Capitol Hill newspaper) reported.[160]

Rep. Jane Harman (D-CA), a former ranking member of the House Intelligence Committee, declared the following month that the National Counterterrorism Center knew the terror alert was bogus but said nothing to undercut the administration's fearmongering.

After Congress—predictably—caved and passed the Protect America Act, Director of National Intelligence Mike McConnell told the *El Paso Times* that "some Americans are going to die

---

159 Mark Hosenball and Evan Thomas, "Hold the Phone," *Newsweek*, May 22, 2006.

160 http://thinkprogress.org/2007/09/20/harmanterrorattack

because of the public debate over FISA."[161] Inquiring what the government is doing and asking questions about the constitutionality of the government's actions became the equivalent of a WMD attack on the American people.

The Protect America Act expanded the federal government's power to listen in to any of your calls or e-mails, so long as a government official "reasonably believed" one party was outside the United States. Any call you made with or e-mail you sent to someone in another country—a friend, a relative, a business associate or anyone else—could be monitored by the government without any suspicion you were doing something wrong or that you were conspiring with a member of Al Qaeda.

If an American soldier stationed in Iraq e-mails his wife back in Omaha, the government can intercept and keep copies of his correspondence. If an American college student is spending a semester studying in London, the government can automatically listen to her phone calls home to her parents. If a doctor is traveling on vacation to Mexico and e-mails one of his patients, that can go into the massive federal database as part of both his and his patient's permanent record.

The Bush administration decided—and Congress agreed in 2007—that "there's no reasonable expectation of privacy in any communication with a foreign person or somebody outside the country."

The Protect America Act was also perilous because it authorized the attorney general (without court approval) to order Internet service providers and other types of companies to give the NSA access to communications and equipment regarding information on its customers, without any proof that American customers whose communications are acquired are conspiring with terrorists.

These measures destroy the fundamental notion that American citizens enjoy a right to privacy in their homes, persons,

---

161 "Harman: Conservatives Falsely Hyped Terror Threat Against U.S. Capitol to Pass FISA Expansion," ThinkProgress.com, September 20, 2007. Accessed at http://thinkprogress.org/2007/09/20/harman-terror-attack/.

and businesses to be free from arbitrary government surveillance and searches. That may sound apocalyptic, but believe me, it is not. It is a fact.

Sadly, in July 2008, a bipartisan Congress passed a somewhat modified version of the Protect America Act. This new law provides retroactive immunity to telephone companies for breaking federal law and betraying their customers via the Terrorist Surveillance Program since 2001. The new law, which amends FISA, contains the essence of the Protect America Act, making it far easier for the government to wiretap Americans without any evidence of their wrongdoing or connection to terrorism. The new law requires only reasonable belief, rather than evidence, that a wiretapped phone call might involve only Americans calling each other within this country. And we have seen too many examples of what the Bush administration considers a reasonable belief (such as Dick Cheney's assertion that Saddam possessed a "reconstituted nuclear weapon"). Congress's failure to uphold a proper constitutional standard in passing this law creates a golden invitation for future administrations to similarly take the law into their own hands.

Rounding Up Everyone Else's Records

The NSA wiretaps are occurring in cahoots with a program that tracks the calls of millions of Americans and has created the biggest database in history. Most of America's largest phone companies illegally delivered to Uncle Sam the records of phone numbers of incoming and outgoing calls that tens of millions of Americans had made.

Two days after *USA Today* revealed the existence of this surveillance program, Bush declared, "We are not trolling through the personal lives of millions of innocent Americans."[162] But the only way that this could be true is if almost all Americans are guilty—or at least guilty enough to spy on—because we subsequently discovered they *were* trolling through massive

---

162 Andrea Stone, "Lawsuit over phone records may grow," *USA Today*, May 14, 2006

quantities of phone calls, e-mails, and records of both.

Former AT&T employee Mark Klein revealed in 2006 that equipment was attached to AT&T core operations that empowered the NSA to conduct "vacuum-cleaner surveillance of all the data crossing the Internet." Klein explained,

> In 2003 AT&T built "secret rooms" hidden deep in the bowels of its central offices in various cities, housing computer gear for a government spy operation which taps into the company's popular World-Net service and the entire internet. These installations enable the government to look at every individual message on the internet and analyze exactly what people are doing. Documents showing the hardwire installation in San Francisco suggest that there are similar locations being installed in numerous other cities. [163]

It is a federal crime for providers of electronics communications to "knowingly divulge a record or other information pertaining to a subscriber or customer . . . to any government entity" without a valid warrant or subpoena, thanks to the Electronic Communications Privacy Act of 1986, without a valid warrant or subpoena. The 1986 act mandates that companies who betray privacy can be fined up to $1,000 for each customer they wrong.

Qwest was the only major phone company that spurned the government's demand for it to betray its customers. Perhaps because of Qwest's refusal to kowtow, the Justice Department prosecuted Qwest CEO Joe Nacchio for insider trading—one of the vaguest crimes on the books. Nacchio's conviction was overturned by a federal appeals court in March 2008.

The Electronic Freedom Foundation sued the feds over the illegal call tracing. The Justice Department asked a federal judge to

163 Chris Roberts, "Debate on the Foreign Intelligence Surveillance Act," *El Paso Times*, August 22, 2007. Accessed at http://www.elpasotimes.com/news/ci_6685679.

throw the lawsuit out of court, claiming "the lawfulness of the alleged activities cannot be determined without a full factual record, and that record cannot be made without seriously compromising US national security interests."[164] In other words, national security entitles government officials to cover up how they are intruding into Americans' lives.

Both the terrorist surveillance program and the call-tracking program are the result of secret orders from the Oval Office. We have no way of knowing what other surveillance edicts may have come out of the White House since 9/11.

Surveillance vs. Democracy and Freedom

People will usually never know how much information the government has gathered on them unless and until the government openly takes some punitive action against them. There is power in information. The more information the government gathers, the greater the temptation to exploit it.

We must not forget the dark history of illegal surveillance in this country. During J. Edgar Hoover's later years, the FBI's COINTELPRO program carried out thousands of surveillance and subversion operations against Americans, and used the information to undermine groups and individuals with viewpoints out of favor in Washington. A 1976 Senate report noted that, "many of the techniques used [by the FBI] would be intolerable in a democratic society even if all of the targets had been involved in violent activity, but COINTELPRO went far beyond that . . . the Bureau conducted a sophisticated vigilante operation aimed squarely at preventing the exercise of First Amendment rights of speech and association, on the theory that preventing the growth of dangerous groups and the propagation of dangerous ideas would protect the national security and deter violence."[165]

---

164 Bob Egelko, "U.S. opens assault on wiretap suit," *San Francisco Chronicle*, May 16, 2006.

165 *Intelligence Activities and the Rights of Americans,* Senate Select Committee to Study Governmental Operations with Respect to Intelligence Activities, April 14, 1976.

Unrestricted government surveillance undermines democracy itself. Congressional oversight of the FBI was stillborn for many years in part because congressmen feared retaliation with derogatory information the FBI stockpiled on them. The 1976 Senate report on Intelligent Activities and the Rights of Americans noted: "The FBI's ability to gather information without effective restraints gave it enormous power. That power was inevitably attractive to politicians, who could use information on opponents and critics for their own advantage, and was also an asset to the Bureau, which depended on politicians for support."[166]   Hale Boggs, the Majority Leader of the House of Representatives, described in 1971 the effect of congressional fear of the FBI: "Freedom of speech, freedom of thought, freedom of action for men in public life can be compromised quite as effectively by the fear of surveillance as by the fact of surveillance."[167] This reflects the important principle enunciated earlier by famed philosopher and author Ayn Rand, who recognized that "if you take away a man's privacy, you gain the ability to control him."

Any information the feds stockpile can be used against people the government does not like—or people the government seeks to silence or suppress. If Americans acquiesce to the feds warehousing their phone-call data, this will simply encourage the seizure of far more personal information.

Conclusion

The president's warrantless wiretapping brought out the worst in our political system. When the administration's abuses and falsehoods were exposed, there was scant interest on Capitol Hill in seeking to hold anyone accountable. When push came to shove, most members of Congress were happy to rubber-stamp and retroactively legalize the president's abuses. Both political parties were more interested in exploiting the warrantless wiretapping for partisan advantage, rather than stopping it.

---

166 Ibid.

167 Ibid.

The response of the American people and the American legal and political system to Bush's warrantless wiretaps is a bellwether for the future of American liberty. Unfortunately, many people are inclined to trust the government even after evidence surfaces of official misconduct.

Too many Americans have forgotten why the Founding Fathers opposed government intrusions *on principle*. The Supreme Court nailed the issue in 1886: "It is not the breaking of his doors, and the rummaging of his drawers that constitutes the essence of the offense; but it is the invasion of his indefeasible right of personal security, personal liberty, and private property."[168] A principled opposition to warrantless searches is the only way to respect what Supreme Court Justice Louis Brandeis rightfully labeled as the "right to be alone—the most comprehensive of rights, and the right most valued by civilized man."[169]

We should not forget that it was not privacy that failed in the months and years before the Al Qaeda hijackings of US airliners. Prior to 9/11, the government had ample information to detect a conspiracy to hijack four airplanes, and it had more than significant lawful tools to do so. The congressional Joint Intelligence Committee concluded in 2002: "To much of the Intelligence Community, everything was a priority—the US wanted to know everything about everything all the time."[170] The CIA, NSA, and FBI failed to focus on the gravest terrorist threats. Because the government failed to analyze and exploit the information in its possession, it entitled itself to seize vastly more information and to snuff Americans' privacy. As Thomas Powers, a historian of the CIA, observes: "The request for broader powers is the excuse of first resort of anyone who's failed at national security or law-enforcement tasks."[171]

---

168 Otto Friedrich, "The Individual Is Sovereign," *Time*, July 21, 1986.

169 Ibid.

170 Eleanor Hill, Joint Inquiry Staff Statement," Hearing on the Intelligence Community's Response to Past Terrorist Attacks Against the United States from February 1993 to September 2001, October 8, 2002.

171 Tim Weiner, "The C.I.A.'s Domestic Reach," *The New York Times*, January 20, 2002.

What lawyers in the Bush administration apparently fail to grasp—in the government's zeal to intrude into the private lives of Americans by (among other things) the NSA electronic spying program in the so-called war on terrorism,—is that the law, and its attendant lawful behavior, provides all the weapons needed to fight terrorism; no sacrifices are necessary. This principle has been embraced by people who know far more about history than the political appointees in the Justice Department. The former chief judge of the Foreign Intelligence Surveillance Court, Royce Lamberth, a Ronald Reagan appointee, for example, warned of the danger of unfettered electronic surveillance in the name of fighting the war on terrorism: "We have to understand you can fight the war [on terrorism] and lose everything if you have no civil liberties left when you get through fighting the war . . .[b]ut what we have found in the history of our country is that you can't trust the executive . . . Judges are the kinds of people you want to entrust that kind of judgment to more than the executive."[172]

Alleged associates of Al Qaeda are the purported targets of recent breathtaking assertions of presidential power. Tomorrow, it may be your phone calls or e-mails that will be swept up into our electronic infrastructure and secretly kept in a growing file attached to your name. Then everyone you contact could become a suspect, a link in an ever lengthening chain that would ensnare us all in the files of the largest database ever created.

---

172 Department of Justice Report Regarding Internal Investigation of Shootings at Ruby Ridge, Idaho during Arrest of Randy Weaver," Released through Lexis Counsel Connect/ American Lawyer Media, June 1995.

THE MILITARIZATION OF LAW ENFORCEMENT

After President Reagan appointed me as US Attorney for the Northern District of Georgia in 1986, I worked closely with the FBI and other federal agencies as they conducted investigations and as they planned and carried out searches of homes, businesses, and other targets. I recognized that the fact a federal judge had granted a search warrant did not nullify the rights of the people living in the homes to be searched. The fact the raid was being conducted in the United States meant the government was obliged to respect Americans' rights. Law enforcement agents could not punish people as guilty simply because they resided where there was probable cause to believe evidence of a crime existed.

Unfortunately, such basic notions of fair play now seem like ancient relics. And the federal government itself has paved the way; both by example and by flooding local and state law enforcement agencies with military equipment that should never be routinely used against American citizens. We have the militarization of Mayberry.

The Ruby Ridge Robot: The New Symbol
of Federal Law Enforcement

The federal targeting of and attack on the Randy Weaver family at Ruby Ridge, Idaho, in 1992 was a bellwether of the radical change in law enforcement procedures. An undercover informant working for the federal Bureau of Alcohol, Tobacco and Firearms entrapped Weaver into selling him a sawed-off shotgun. The government then sent Weaver the wrong court date. After he did not show up, they launched a massive campaign that seemingly came out of some Bizarro comic book.

Weaver and his family holed up on their mountaintop home. Federal marshals never attempted to serve a warrant and arrest him. Instead, they called in the Pentagon, which conducted aerial reconnaissance and provided photos that were scrutinized by the Defense Mapping Agency. Surveillance cameras were erected surrounding Weaver's property, creating reams of photographs proving beyond a shadow of the doubt that the Weavers used the outhouse behind their cabin.

In August 1992, a team of six heavily armed marshals trespassed onto Weaver's land. They provoked a firefight by killing the Weavers' dog; the clash ended with one US marshal dead and fourteen-year-old Sammy Weaver shot in the back and killed as he was leaving the scene.

The marshals panicked and called in the FBI's Hostage Rescue Team (HRT), the most militarized branch of the Bureau. The FBI's elite snipers were told that "any armed male adult observed in the vicinity of the Weaver cabin could and should be killed."[173] This was death by law enforcement; jury and judge need not apply. FBI sniper Lon Horiuchi then killed forty-two-year-old Vicki Weaver with a head shot as she stood in the door of her cabin holding her ten-month-old baby. Moments earlier, Horiuchi had shot her husband, Randy Weaver, in the back without warning or provocation.

The FBI laid siege to the survivors. FBI spokesmen continually told the media that Randy Weaver refused to negotiate with the feds. But the authorities never told them about the FBI robot outside the cabin holding a 12-gauge shotgun in one arm and a phone in the other. FBI siege negotiators continually summoned Weaver to exit the cabin and pick up the robot's phone and talk to FBI agents. However, the shotgun in the robot's other hand was

173 Wikisource.com, "Activities of Federal Law Enforcement Agencies Toward the Branch Davidians/Submission by Hon. Steven Schiff. Accessed at http://en.wikisource.org/wiki/ Activities_of_Federal_Law_Enforcement_Agencies_Toward_the_Branch_Davidians/ Submission_by_Hon._Steven_Schiff.

pointing directly at the cabin door. It is difficult to imagine a more intimidating collect call.

This robot with the shotgun epitomized the overreach of federal officials at Ruby Ridge. But the feds suppressed the evidence of the robot until long after Weaver had surrendered.

An Idaho jury later rejected almost all charges against Weaver, in part because of the perception that the federal government's use of force was clearly excessive.

Waco: The FBI Revs Up

The following year, the law enforcement-on-steroids mentality pervaded federal action at Waco. The Bureau of Alcohol, Tobacco and Firearms could easily have arrested David Koresh, the leader of the Branch Davidians, on gun charges and, after he was in custody, carried out a search of the Davidians' residence. Koresh had cooperated with authorities on numerous occasions; he was seen frequently in Waco, and he had even gone target shooting with undercover ATF agents (who he knew were G-men) just days before the fatal raid.

Instead, on February 28, 1993, seventy-six ATF agents arrived unannounced in front of the Branch Davidians' residence in two large cattle trailers. Federal law normally requires that agents knock and announce their purpose before entering a residence. But the ATF never gave a whit about serving the residents with the warrant and giving them a chance to peacefully comply with the search. Instead, ATF agents rehearsed at a military base a plan for one group of agents to storm the front door while a second group climbed ladders and smashed in through second-story windows. Media had been alerted as well.

Like the Weaver raid the previous year, the Branch Davidian raid also reportedly began with federal agents shooting dogs, and it quickly deteriorated. Four ATF agents ended up dead, more than twenty were wounded, and six Davidians were killed.

After the ATF botched the initial assault, the FBI's Hostage Rescue Team (HRT) was called in to take charge and begin surrender negotiations; this, even though there were no hostages, insofar as all persons at the compound remained there voluntarily. The FBI preferred to rely on intimidation and force instead of reason. The FBI brought in a dozen tanks and armored personnel carriers that were soon smashing cars and toys and anything else in their path outside the Davidians' front door.

The local sheriff had dealt with Koresh amicably for years and had his trust. But the FBI cut off his contact with the Davidians. The Davidians also respected the Texas Rangers, but the FBI quickly also pushed the Rangers out of the picture. If the local sheriff or the Texas Rangers had negotiated a peaceful settlement, it would have been far more difficult for federal prosecutors to justify the ATF's initial violent raid in court.

The siege ended after the FBI sent in tanks that smashed into the Davidians' residence and pumped it full of a potentially toxic and highly volatile combination of CS gas and methyl chloride. Then-Republican Rep. Steven Schiff (NM) commented in a dissent, based in part on information supplied by me, that "no rational person can conclude that the use of CS gas under any circumstances against children, would do anything other than cause extreme physical problems and possibly death . . . I believe the deaths of dozens of men, women and children can be directly and indirectly attributable to the use of this gas in the way it was injected by the FBI."[174]

FBI tank drivers continually smashed into the building, collapsing at least a quarter of the residence upon the women, children, and men holed up inside. The FBI was also firing pyrotechnic grenades into the building. Eventually, but predictably, a raging fire burst out and ended with more than seventy people dead, including many children.

---

174 Wikisource.com, "Activities of Federal Law Enforcement Agencies Toward the Branch Davidians/Submission by Hon. Steven Schiff. Accessed at http://en.wikisource.org/wiki/ Activities_of_Federal_Law_Enforcement_Agencies_Toward_the_Branch_Davidians/ Submission_by_Hon._Steven_Schiff.

The Clinton administration and the media responded to the fiery debacle by making a hero out of Attorney General Janet Reno, who had approved the final assault. Two years later, during congressional hearings, Reno asserted that the fifty-four-ton tanks that smashed through the Davidians' ramshackle home should not be considered military vehicles; instead, they were "like a good rent-a-car."[175]

I was deeply frustrated during those congressional hearings on Waco because I sensed the government was continuing to withhold key information. The Pentagon refused to cooperate with the congressional investigation, even though it had been far more involved at Waco than the Clinton administration initially disclosed. In 1997, I called on Congress to open a new investigation into what happened at Waco, but received no support from senior House Republicans at that time. After new evidence surfaced in 1999, a new investigation finally commenced. But the Pentagon claimed that six thousand pages of documents regarding its activity at Waco were classified because of national security. (The Pentagon's elite Delta Force was present during the FBI's final assault.) Many questions remain unanswered to this day.

Militarizing Against Drugs

Unfortunately, there has been scant examination of the dangers of the federal law enforcement's militarization after Waco. Two of the groups that did stand up against this new peril were the American Civil Liberties Union and the National Rifle Association—an unlikely alliance that showed how some conservatives and liberals recognized the growing peril to fundamental liberty.

In the mid-to-late 1990s, the Pentagon deluged local and state law enforcement with thousands of machine guns, more than one hundred armored personnel carriers, scores of grenade launchers, and more than a million other pieces of military hardware. Local police departments also received surplus military helicopters. The

---

175 James Bovard, "Hearings Show Waco Defense is Wacky," *The Wall Street Journal*, August 2, 1995.

Justice Department also flooded local police agencies with money that allowed them to ramp up their armaments.

While SWAT teams were not common in local police forces before the 1980s, there were more than thirty thousand such teams by the late 1990s. The SWAT acronym originally stood for Special Weapons Attack Team but was sanitized and relabeled: Special Weapons and Tactics. *The Washington Post* noted in 1997, "The explosive growth and expanding mission of SWAT teams has, in turn, led to complaints that an occupying army is marching through America's streets—that they are too aggressive, too heavily armed, too scary."[176]

The hardware was soon driving the policy: the fact that so many cities have police all dressed up for war makes it easier for departments to rely on massive intimidation rather than old-fashioned police work. The existence of the team spurred calling them out on the flimsiest of pretexts. The Greenwich, Connecticut, SWAT team was routinely deployed any time the state lottery prize exceeded a million dollars—as if local authorities expected the jackpot would induce mass insanity. By far the most common use for SWAT teams was to carry out drug raids.

The Ignored Lesson from Columbine

The follies of relying on a highly militarized law enforcement shined through in the worst high school shooting in US history.

During the April 1999 Columbine High School shooting at Littleton, Colorado, eight local SWAT teams quickly descended on the high school parking lot after the shooting started. But none of the SWAT teams confronted the killers during their forty-five-minute killing spree, which concluded with their own suicides. TV footage showed one heavily armed SWAT team crouching and advancing like molasses behind an armored personnel carrier—as if they expected that the teenage gunman possessed shoulder-fired missiles instead of civilian firearms.

---

176 William Booth, "Exploding Number of SWAT Teams Sets Off Alarms," *The Washington Post*, June 17, 1997."

Jefferson County, Colorado, SWAT team commander Terry Manwaring, whose team eventually entered the school, explained: "I just knew [the killers] were armed and were better equipped than we were."[177] The SWAT team members were decked out in flak jackets and carried submachine guns—as well as many other weapons. The two teen-aged killers had one unreliable handgun, a single semiautomatic rifle, and two shotguns. And their trench coats were not bulletproof. It seemed as if the SWAT teams had gotten bogged down by the sheer weight of their armor and accouterments.

The Columbine debacle should have been a warning on the danger of focusing on new accessories instead of old-time savvy. There were probably numerous cops at the scene who would have willingly risked their lives by charging into the school to stop the crime in process. But the ultracautious and heavily armed SWAT mentality prevailed.

Amazingly, Columbine was invoked in the following years to justify more police departments creating SWAT teams.

The Elián Gonzáles Raid

The feds set another dreadful example for law enforcement when more than 130 federal agents carried out a raid in Miami's Little Havana section on April 22, 2000, to seize six-year-old Elián González.

Heavily armed federal agents of the Immigration and Naturalization Service and the Border Patrol, using a battering ram and outfitted in full military hardware, including submachine guns, broke down the front door of the modest home. The agents burst in yelling obscenities and breaking personal belongings. This major operation was conducted in every respect as a military strike. The agents wore full battle gear and carried enough firepower to stage a military coup in a small country.

---

177. Barbara Vobejda, "Response In Littleton Was Swift, But Unsure," *The Washington Post*, 12 May 1999.

The raid was a tactical success and the agents got their prize, young Elián. But an Associated Press photographer captured a haunting image of a federal agent dressed in paramilitary gear pointing a submachine gun at the boy, cowering in the arms of Donato Dalrymple, the fisherman who plucked him from the sea and brought him ashore to America to be free.

Attorney General Reno called a press conference a few hours after the raid and, when asked about the photo, stressed that the agent's finger was not on the trigger. The submachine gun at issue —a Heckler and Koch MP-5—can fire more than six hundred rounds a minute, and the agent's finger could easily have slipped if he was bumped or otherwise surprised. This submachine gun is known as a "room broom" because of its ability to instantly sweep away any opposition.

This raid never made any sense. In a nation full of illegal aliens, Reno's Department of Justice felt that this single six-year-old child, who barely escaped drowning while trying to flee Cuba, posed the gravest of all threats to American national interests and that no expense should be spared in removing him from American soil and returning him to Fidel Castro's control. The action was lawless as well as absurd. Harvard law school constitutional scholar laurence Tribe concluded that "no judge or neutral magistrate had issued the type of warrant or other authority needed for the executive branch to break into the home to seize the child . . . Ms. Reno's decision to take the law as well as the child into her own hands . . . strikes at the heart of constitutional government and shakes the safeguards of liberty."[178]

The Post-9/11 Era of Militarization

After the 9/11 attacks, federal bankrolling of local and state law enforcement went into overdrive. While the militarization of the 1990s was driven by drug war concerns, the militarization of the new century is justified in the name of fighting terrorism. Since its creation shortly after the 9/11 attacks, the Homeland Security

---

178 Laurence Tribe, "Justice Taken Too Far," *The New York Times,* April 25, 2000.

Department has inundated local and state law enforcement with money to buy practically any "toys" they please.

Some states set up regional SWAT teams to collect the windfalls. Robert Cormier, the commander of the Central New Hampshire Special Operations Unit, says, "We had to explain to Homeland Security that we do have risks here, even though it's New Hampshire." Cormier justified the build-up because "[a]nyone can become a terrorist at a moment's notice."[179]

Thus the government is entitled to always be a hair-trigger away from using overwhelming force against anyone and everyone.

Many local police departments are using federal Homeland Security grants to purchase Ballistic Engineered Armored Response vehicles, nicknamed the BEAR. The BEAR is twenty-four feet wide and seven feet long and weighs almost fifteen tons. In order to assure safe policing in the many small towns and crossroads that are buying BEARs, the vehicle possesses "hardened steel armor plate and ballistic glass, 12 specially designed gunports, a roof hatch with a rotating turret, and gun mount platforms."[180] The rigs cost more than $300,000 apiece.

Pittsburgh is using its BEAR for routine patrols and sweeps in relatively high-crime black neighborhoods. It also leaves it parked outside major events in order to dissuade anyone from causing trouble.

Professor Peter Kraska of Eastern Kentucky University, one of the nation's top SWAT experts, noted that most police departments do not have a "credible, justifiable reason for buying these kinds of vehicles," but purchase them anyhow because they "tap into that subculture within policing that finds the whole military special-operations model culturally intoxicating."[181]

---

179 Peter Jamison, "Regional SWAT Teams in N.H. Under Scrutiny," *Valley News* (White River Junction, VT), 17 August 2008.

180 Carlos Illescas, "Aurora Cops Loaded with 'The BEAR'," *The Denver Post*, December 11, 2007.

181 Ramit Plushnick-Masti, "Too militaristic? Growing police use of armored vehicles raises concerns in US cities," Associated Press, 9 May 2007.

More Militarization Nonsense

Federal law enforcement continues paving the way for using massive force against targets that would not even qualify as paper tigers. In early 2003, federal agents carried out a raid on the home of legendary comedian Tommy Chong (of Cheech and Chong fame) because the feds decided that the glass bongs he sold were illegal drug paraphernalia. Chong had been openly selling the bongs over the Internet and in stores for years. The Drug Enforcement Agency hit Chong's home in Pacific Palisades, California, at 5:30 a.m., while Chong and his wife were asleep. Chong later commented, "It was a full-on raid. Helicopters, them bangin' on the door. They come in with loaded automatic weapons, flak jackets, helmets, visors, about 20 agents. They bust in the house. They took all my cash, took out my computers, and they took all the glass bongs they could find."[182] If the feds had simply sent a couple DEA agents to knock on the door and carry out a peaceful search, the story might have gotten far less splash in the media.

Local law enforcement managed to one-up the feds with the notorious drug raid that occurred in November 2003 at Stratford High School in Goose Creek, South Carolina. Dozens of SWAT-team members barged into the school with guns drawn. The videotape of the raid shows dozens of students lying prone in the school's hallways with armed officers clearly shouting at them to "get down and put your hands up" while searching vainly for the drugs that were the apparent justification for the raid in the first place. "They hit that school like it was a crack house, like they knew that there were crack dealers in there armed with guns," one fourteen-year old student said.[183]

What did it take to unleash the SWAT team on the high school children? Apparently, all it takes is a report of suspicious activity. The school's principal heard reports that some students

---

182 Chris Brunner, "Libertarians Are Terrorists, Says the State of Alabama," ChrisBrunner.com, May 9, 2007. Accessed at http://www.chrisbrunner.com/2007/05/09/libertarians-are-terrorists-says-the-state-of-alabama.

183 American Civil Liberties Union, "Profile of Le'Quan Simpson," December 15, 2003. Accessed at http://www.aclu.org/drugpolicy/gen/10679res20031215.html.

were acting suspiciously, so he called the cops to come search for drugs. The police failed to find any illicit drugs, despite searching in every nook and cranny of the school.

In high schools, there is an awful lot of behavior that goes on in the hallways that would fall into the category of suspicious activity. If such activity now provides the predicate for SWAT-type raids, then be prepared for the Great Stratford High School Raid of 2003 to become commonplace. Is the term *measured response* no longer a part of our vocabulary?

We should also ask what lesson this is teaching our youngsters. That government power can properly be exercised arbitrarily? That you raid first and ask questions later? That preemptive strikes are the best course of action? That overwhelming force is a proper response to any problem?

This incident illustrates the degree to which America is now gripped by a climate of fear and overreaction. It also bears testimony to the unbridled power with which our society has clothed government, both locally and nationally.

On January 24, 2006, Fairfax County, Virginia, police carried out a SWAT raid to nab a thirty-seven-year-old optometrist (who worked at two different Wal-Marts) accused of wagering over sports events. An undercover policeman had met Salvatore Culosi in a bar and had swayed him to continually up the ante on bets on football games. The undercover policeman stopped by in the evening to settle some accounts for the weekend's wagers. When Culosi stepped out of his apartment to talk with the undercover policeman, he was dressed in jeans and a t-shirt. The police knew that Culosi had no firearms. Yet Fairfax County authorized a SWAT raid for the arrest. At least one policeman had his .45-caliber handgun drawn. Even though Culosi made no threatening movements and offered no resistance, he was shot in the chest and died almost instantly. Fairfax County police later said that the policeman who shot Culosi bumped into his vehicle door as he was climbing out and involuntarily fired. The only penalty he received for killing Culosi was a three-week suspension without pay. An editorial from *The Washington Post*, entitled "Killing Without Cause," remarked: "One wonders if the

SWAT team in Fairfax, lacking frequent opportunities to respond to situations involving imminent danger and threats, is deployed simply to give its officers something to do."[184]

Another example of this trend occurred just outside of Washington, DC on July 29, 2008. Prince George's County police launched an attack on the home of the mayor of Berwyn Heights, Maryland. County police targeted the mayor's house after he was apparently victimized by a drug smuggler who shipped marijuana to that address and five others in the county. Rather than carefully checking the facts, including talking to the local police department, the Prince George's County Police effectively and unilaterally declared war on the mayor and his family, even though the mayor was completely ignorant of what the drug smuggler had done.

The police broke down the door rather than knocking, and charged in with guns drawn. They killed the couple's two Labradors, one while it was running away. Mayor Cheye Calvo spent two hours in handcuffs while in his boxer shorts; his mother-in-law was handcuffed in another room, left beside one of the dead dogs. Absent exigent circumstances, so-called no-knock raids are an affront to the Constitution. So is a shoot-first-ask-questions-later philosophy by the police. The police falsely claimed on the day of the raid that they possessed a no-knock warrant. Apparently, the police did not possess any warrant at the time they attacked the mayor's house. Instead, a police detective stopped by the house a few days later to show the mayor the original warrant. This makes a mockery of any notion that citizens can peacefully challenge the power of law enforcement agents before they rampage into their homes.

The Prince George's police have done this before—in late 2007 they invaded a house at the wrong address and shot the family dog. All Americans are at risk when the police behave this way. Just ask yourself what might happen if a suspicious package is delivered to your home and the cops bust in. The Prince George's County police had probably the highest rate of wrongfully shooting innocent people of any major police department in the country during the 1990s.

---

184 Editorial, "A Killing Without Cause," *The Washington Post*, November 30, 2006.

Conclusion

We all want police to do their jobs well, but part of doing their job well is respecting the people's constitutional rights. Joseph McNamara, a former police chief and current Hoover Institution fellow, observes, "Policing is not about victory, it's about enforcing the law and maintaining order. The soldier's duty is to kill the enemy, but a peace officer's duty is to protect human life. You cannot be the public servant when you're strutting around like an occupying army."[185] Michael Mello, a criminal law professor at Vermont Law School, warns, "There's a real danger in shifting the focus from local community policing, which is what really works —cops on the beat, building and developing relationships between law enforcement and the communities in which they operate—to the sort of flashier, sexier approach to law enforcement where you get to play with a lot of really cool toys, and feel like you're in Baghdad."[186]

Federal law enforcement agencies should set a good example for the rest of the country. It is vital that government officials never forget that it is a free people they are protecting. Uncle Sam should stop militarizing local law enforcement and financing local oppression.

---

185 Jim Nesbitt, "Are police too quick to call in the SWAT team?" *Raleigh News and Observer*, January 7, 2007.

186 Peter Jamison, "Regional SWAT Teams in N.H. Under Scrutiny," *Valley News* (White River Junction, VT), August 17, 2008.

GUNS: THE BULWARK OF AMERICAN LIBERTY & SELF-RELIANCE

A well-regulated militia, being necessary to the security of a free state, the right of the people to keep and bear arms, shall not be infringed.

—Amendment II, Constitution of the United States

For the framers of our Constitution, the Second Amendment clearly served as a core foundation of our other freedoms embodied in the Bill of Rights. To Americans in the era of the Revolution, the Second Amendment was no second-class right. On the contrary, St. George Tucker described it as "the true palladium of liberty." Patrick Henry caught the spirit of the era: "The great object is that every man be armed . . . everyone who is able may have a gun." James Madison, writing in the Federalist Papers, derided European kings who were "afraid to trust the people with arms."

The Second Amendment is the bulwark of Americans' self-reliance. Surrendering the responsibility for self-preservation to the government would affect not only all those who choose to own firearms, but every citizen who believes individuals have basic rights and responsibilities that trump government power.

Fighting Clinton's Antigun Machinations

I became a member of Congress during the most antigun administration in American history. The Clinton administration never let the law or the Constitution stand in the way of its antigun agenda. Year after year of his presidency, Clinton pressured Congress to enact broad new prohibitions on guns and sweeping restrictions on gun owners.

The Clinton administration was so antigun it believed that gun owners should be presumed guilty by definition. This came through lucidly in a 1994 Supreme Court case involving Harold Staples, an Oklahoma gun owner prosecuted by the Alcohol, Tobacco and Firearms agency after it seized his AR-15 rifle, rebuilt it, and claimed it fired more than one bullet per trigger squeeze. Staples's lawyer, Stephen Halbrook, noted that the ATF, after it confiscates a person's guns, routinely tampers with them to make them shoot automatically, and then drags the person into court on trumped-up charges of owning a machine gun. [187]

In the Staples case, federal prosecutors argued that "one would hardly be surprised to learn that owning a gun is not an innocent act." Justice Clarence Thomas, who wrote the majority decision for the Supreme Court rebuking the Clintonites, derided their presumption "that a defendant's knowledge that the item he possessed 'was a gun' is sufficient for a conviction."[188] This disdain for gun owners shone through in practically everything the Clinton administration said and did regarding Waco. There was a presumption of guilt that pervaded federal action even before the Bureau of Alcohol, Tobacco and Firearms launched their surprise attack on the Branch Davidians' home in February 2003. And the fact the Davidians owned plenty of guns somehow made irrelevant the actions of the FBI using tanks and flammable, toxic gas on women and children in their final assault on April 19, 2003. Congress finally held hearings on this atrocity more than two years later. But the Democrats swayed the media to focus on red herrings while the Republican leaders on the committees were far more interested in appearing to be nice guys than in finding the truth about federal action.

---

187 James Bovard, "Kafkaesque world of gun control," *The Washington Times,* August 8, 1994.

188 Staples v. United States, 511 U.S. 600 (1994).

Early in his administration, Clinton cheered on efforts to forcibly disarm public housing residents and ban them from owning firearms. After the Chicago Housing Authority began conducting warrantless searches of residents' apartments to seize their guns, Clinton visited Chicago, endorsed the searches and seizures, and declared, "The most important freedom we have in this country is the freedom from fear. And if people aren't free from fear, they are not free."[189] Presumably, public housing residents had no right to have any apprehensions about housing police charging into their homes at any hour, day or night, to give them freedom from fear. The Clinton administration acted as if people were obliged to surrender their Second Amendment rights merely because a government agency was their landlord.

The crackdown was the ultimate hollow gesture, perhaps designed to appeal to bleeding heart liberals living in affluent and safe neighborhoods. The crime rate in some public housing projects is more than twenty times higher than the national average. HUD's ban would have prevented mothers and fathers from defending their own families in a very dangerous crime environment. HUD was stopped from stripping residents' constitutional rights because there was nothing in the Department's enabling legislation that authorized it to operate in that manner.

In my first term in Congress (1995–1996), Speaker Newt Gingrich designated me as chairman of the Speaker's Task Force on Firearms Legislation. The task force spearheaded the legislation to repeal the 1994 Clinton gun ban. I was the primary sponsor on the gun ban repeal, which passed the House but not the Senate because Majority Leader Dole did not bring it to a vote, despite his promise to do so if it passed the House. I was also the point person in the House working to remove antigun and other noxious provisions from the Antiterrorism and Effective Death Penalty Act of 1996.

One of Clinton's biggest triumphs was the 1994 Brady Handgun Violence Prevention Act, which instituted a nationwide

---

189 "Remarks by President Clinton to Residents of the Robert Taylor Homes in Chicago," *U.S. Newswire*, June 17, 1994.

waiting period for handgun buyers. At the initiative of pro-Second Amendment members of the House and Senate, and at the urging of the NRA, however, the Brady Act banned law enforcement agencies from using background-check information to compile registration lists of gun owners. But the Federal Bureau of Investigation, which runs the instant-check system, announced in 1998 that it would retain records of approved gun buyers for eighteen months. The FBI's contempt for the clear language of the federal gun law alarmed many gun owners. Foreign dictators have used gun registration lists to disarm their victims. We must prevent our politicians from creating a list of Americans who could be targeted for gun confiscation in the coming years.

The FBI also announced plans to impose a fee of $16 to conduct the mandatory checks. I introduced a bill called the No Gun Tax Act to prohibit the FBI from compiling lists of gun owners and from imposing a fee for background checks. The FBI's policies were part of "a long-standing policy of this administration to discourage firearms ownership," I noted at the time.

One of the problems with contemporary Big Government is that there are so many agencies and so many political appointees with a hunger for abusing power.

In December 1999, the White House announced that HUD would be bankrolling lawsuits against gun manufacturers. The Clinton team acted as if companies like Smith & Wesson, Colt, and Glock were the true sources of public housing's high crime rates. The Justice Department reportedly advised HUD that there was no legal basis for HUD's involvement in the lawsuits. But that didn't matter: there were headlines to grab and photo-ops to be scheduled.

I responded to the announcement by sending a letter warning HUD Secretary Andrew Cuomo: "As you are surely aware, the notion that the federal government can sue companies for negligence for simply manufacturing a legal, extensively regulated product is the worst kind of legal quackery. There is no basis in precedent or law for the suit you are planning, and one is left to conclude your only goal is to bully gun manufacturers into making changes . . ."[190]

On March 17, 2000, Clinton announced that Smith & Wesson, the nation's largest gun manufacturer, agreed to sweeping new controls over its gun designs, marketing, and new restrictions on gun buyers. HUD Secretary Cuomo, the prime architect of the deal, declared of the new specifications for firearms: "This is a product that did not exist last week . . . This will do to the [gun] industry what FedEx did to the [delivery] industry. This is a better mousetrap."[191]

But the Clinton administration apparently wanted a firearm "mousetrap" that was simply more difficult to fire, as if that would make people safer. The agreement required that, "within 12 months, handguns will be designed so they cannot be readily operated by a child under 6."[192] The feds seemed to think that it would be a big improvement to redesign a firearm so that it resembled a bottle of aspirin with a childproof cap. But people struggling to get the trigger lock off a revolver cannot request a time-out from some assailant.

As a result of the settlement, Smith & Wesson imposed draconian new restrictions on retailers selling its guns. The settlement also created an Oversight Commission stocked with government officials to perpetually keep their thumb on the company.

When the agreement was revealed, I counterpunched: "Once again we see that the Clinton administration will go to any length to chip away at the Second Amendment rights of law abiding citizens . . . They are trying to cajole, threaten, and use every trick

---

190 "Barr Calls for Investigation of HUD Gun Lawsuit," Congressional Press Release, December 8, 1999.

191 "Press Conference with Secretary Andrew Cuomo; Subject: Gun Agreement with Smith and Wesson," Federal News Service, March 22, 2000.

192 "Agreement Between Smith & Wesson and the Departments of the Treasury and Housing and Urban Development, Local Governments, and States; Summary of Terms," HUD press release, March 17, 2000.

in the book to try to get gun control enacted before Bill Clinton leaves office."[193]

After the Bush administration took office, HUD allowed the Memorandum of Understanding with Smith & Wesson to lapse.

Clinton succeeded in making guns a moral issue, at least for most of the media. Once guns became a simple question of good and evil, specific details of federal policy or of individual shootings became completely irrelevant. The morality-play narrative buries all the facts that do not sanctify the gun grabbers.

A Worldwide Threat to Gun Owners

In 1775, the Sons of Liberty set bonfires throughout the American colonies to signal that they would not kowtow to the British king.

On July 9, 2001, in capitals around the world, governments and antigun groups celebrated Small Arms Destruction Day by making bonfires of handguns and rifles to celebrate the start of a United Nations conference on the evil of guns. But the UN bonfires, in contrast to those of 1775, signaled the resolve of politicians around the globe to destroy citizens' ability to resist government tyranny.

Since its efforts to achieve nuclear disarmament had been a dismal failure, UN officials decided to chase after small arms instead. On July 9, 2001, the United Nations Conference on the Illicit Trade in Small Arms and Light Weapons in All Its Aspects convened in New York. They were assisted by non-governmental organizations (NGOs) such as the Coalition to Stop Gun Violence, Gun-Free South Africa (which favors banning all private gun ownership), and the International Action Network on Small Arms (INANSA), an entity financed by European governments that is campaigning to severely restrict civilian gun ownership around the world.

The UN conference was another steppingstone on the UN's long-term effort to turn private gun ownership into the moral

---

193 "Barr Claims Extortion by Clinton," *Congressional Press Releases*, March 17, 2000.

equivalent of child porn. In 1995, the UN's Commission on Global Governance recommended that countries "encourage the disarmament of civilians." In 1999, the UN Report of the Group of Governmental Experts on Small Arms called for the "prohibition of . . . private ownership of small arms and light weapons" around the globe.

I had the opportunity to observe the festivities firsthand in 2001 as an official member of the US delegation. Many attendees were openly disdainful of the American constitutional right to keep and bear arms. They vehemently object to the reality this right represents—that a free citizenry must have the power to defend itself against threats, whether from inside or outside the country's borders. Instead, many UN member nations want to enact a legally binding protocol to eventually outlaw legally owned firearms in *all* member nations.

The 2001 conference got off to a bumptious start when US Undersecretary of State John Bolton declared that the United States government would not acquiesce to any UN agreement that threatened Americans' constitutional rights. *The New York Times* damned Bolton's statement as a "shameless subordination of diplomacy to domestic political pandering."[194] *The Washington Post* wailed that Bolton "delivered an opening address that appeared designed to cater to the most extreme domestic opponents of gun control, for whom the UN conference has conjured up the usual paranoid fantasies about international shock troops in black helicopters confiscating handguns and hunting rifles."[195] Obviously, anyone who did not trust the UN as much as *Post* editorial writers must be a rube.

Many American gun owners saw the UN conference as a step towards worldwide gun confiscation. Such fears were not soothed by an op-ed by UN Secretary-General Kofi Annan published in the *International Herald Tribune* on July 10, 2001. Annan wrote, "The world is flooded with small arms and light

---

194 Editorial, "An American Retreat on Small Arms," *The New York Times*, July 11, 2001.

195 Editorial, "Free Fire at the United Nations" *The Washington Post*, July 10, 2001.

weapons numbering at least 500 million . . . Most of these are controlled by legal authorities, but when they fall into the hands of terrorists, criminals and irregular forces, small arms bring devastation."[196] Perhaps Annan was not aware that the militia that fought at Lexington and Concord were "irregular forces." Annan called for a worldwide campaign against small arms—modeled after the UN campaign to ban land mines. Annan specified revolvers as a type of gun that must be restricted.

The multiyear UN series of meetings were based on the notion that there was a huge distinction between licit and illicit weapons. UN officials claimed that law-abiding Americans should not be concerned about the UN convention, because it was only targeting illegal firearms. But it only takes one meeting of the legislature or one edict from a bureaucracy to convert a legal firearm into a prohibited weapon.

When I returned to Washington after the UN summit, I introduced an amendment to an appropriations bill that would have banned using any US taxpayers' money to implement UN gun control proposals. I issued a press release: "The Bush administration's refusal to allow the United Nations to trample on the Constitutional rights of American citizens reflects a new and welcome respect for the Second Amendment after eight years of the Clinton administration. If this conference had been held just one year ago, the US delegation would have caved, and the UN would have gained unprecedented power over the way America would be allowed to conduct its foreign affairs."[197]

The United Nations may be laying the groundwork to eventually strangle international firearms trade. Many governments favor a UN agreement to effectively outlaw all arms shipments to nongovernments. This would make it much more difficult for Americans to aid victims of foreign tyranny. If firearms can be sold internationally only to governments, or to government-approved buyers, then the only thing a government need do to deprive its

---

196 Kofi Annan, "Small arms, big problems," *International Herald Tribune*, July 10, 2001.

197 "Barr Thanks President for Standing Up to U.N. Gun Grab," Congressional Press Release," July 21, 2001.

citizens of the means of defense is to shut down or otherwise suppress domestic arms producers.

Innocent people have already perished because of UN gun grabbing. *The Washington Post* reported of Kosovo in 1999, "Under UN regulations, it is illegal to hold any weapon without written permission from the NATO-led Kosovo Force, KFOR, or UN civilian police."[198] The UN forcibly disarmed many of the Serbs remaining in Kosovo, and then stood by while Serbian women, children, and men were slaughtered by rampaging ethnic Albanians. For the UN, the measure of success was how many weapons it seized, not whether the people who lost the guns were subsequently murdered. The UN refers to such gun roundups from civilians as "micro-disarmament."

The UN's aversion to civilian gun ownership is especially galling considering the growing record of UN peacekeepers raping defenseless women and children in Liberia, the Congo, Haiti, and other nations. UN troops caught committing such atrocities are rarely punished; at worst, they are sent back to their native land.

After the 2001 conference, the UN and its antigun NGO allies are moving forward on other fronts in their relentless drive for limitations on domestic firearms possession under the auspices of the United Nations. Unfortunately, few in our nation's capital have the backbone, interest, or knowledge to challenge the powder-blue bureaucrats. International bureaucrats at the UN have become masters at couching their endeavors to illicitly infringe the sovereignty of individual nations in flowery, high-sounding rhetoric that camouflages their true aims. But the danger continues, and will become especially severe if a majority in the Congress or an individual takes office as president who actually buys into the UN's self-serving dogma.

The worst part of the increasingly bold international antigun movement is how so much of its platform is fueled by irrational antifreedom sentiment. There's an elitist air to the whole process, the sort of rarified certainty you see in career diplomats who have

---

198 Robert Reid, "Although NATO says KLA has surrendered weapons, no shortage of guns in Kosovo," Associated Press, October 3, 1999.

194

spent their entire working life eating cheeses and drinking fine wines at ornate receptions. At the least, the UN should postpone blessing the world with a solution to the gun problem until it discovers a solution for a problem that destroys far more lives: political tyranny.

Bush Era Perils to Gun Owners

When the Clinton administration left town, many gun owners thought that Valhalla had arrived. I commented to *USA Today* in August 2001: "It's been a virtual sea change. In terms of the tone and the general feeling of appreciation and understanding of the Second Amendment, it represents a complete reversal of the last eight years."

But as time went on, the new administration increasingly abandoned gun owners and Second Amendment principles.

After the apocalyptic failure of airport security on 9/11, the Air Line Pilots Association sought federal permission for pilots to carry handguns to defeat hijackers. Capt. Steve Luckey, chairman of the association's flight-security committee, explained, "The only reason we want lethal force in the cockpit is to provide an opportunity to get the aircraft on the ground. We don't have 911. We can't pull over."[199]

The Bush administration rejected the request, preferring instead to rely on jet fighters to shoot down hijacked civilian planes.

Congress eventually trumped the administration, passing a law in September 2002 to create a program to train pilots to use firearms to defend their planes. But the Transportation Security Administration buried the program with red tape. After grumbling about TSA's policies spilled into the media, a TSA official sent an e-mail warning to all pilots authorized to carry guns prohibiting

---

199 Alan Levin, "Lawmakers Add Pressure to Let Pilots Have Guns," *USA Today*, May 3, 2002.

them even from communicating to their congressmen about their concerns about the program.

Those pilots who finally receive official permission to be armed are under so many foolish TSA-mandated restrictions the pilots might not be able to use the weapon even if faced with a deadly peril. In March 2008, a pilot accidentally fired his weapon during a US Airways flight because of the idiotic padlock and holster that TSA requires using on guns. TSA requires far more Rube Goldberg–like restrictions on pilots' firearms than it requires for its own federal air marshals.

The Bush administration has repeatedly placated the antigun crowd by putting gun owners' rights at risk. In 2007, Attorney General Alberto Gonzales endorsed legislation that would ban an American from buying a gun based on any suspicion or groundless accusation that he is somehow connected with acts of international or domestic terrorism. The Senate sponsor of the administration proposal, Frank Lautenberg (D-NJ), promised that the bill would "close the terror gap." Rep. Pete King, a cosponsor and the top Republican on the House Committee on Homeland Security, announced: "The safety of the American people should always come before giving terrorists access to guns, and that is why the terror loophole must be closed."

The title of the bill, Denying Firearms and Explosives to Dangerous Terrorist Act of 2007, implies that but for this legislation becoming law, dangerous terrorists can lawfully obtain firearms and explosives, both of which require government approval to acquire. If someone is a dangerous terrorist, wouldn't the government already be prosecuting him, or shouldn't he already be in jail?

The answer to this puzzle lies in the nature of government power, and in the details of the legislative proposal. The government seeks to gain control over a much larger and more amorphous category—persons who *might* be terrorists or somehow connected with a disfavored organization. The government could henceforth prohibit anyone suspected of being engaged in some sort of activity perhaps related to terrorism, from purchasing a firearm based on nothing more than an unelected federal employee deciding in secret he fits such a description. The attorney general need never reveal to the person denied the ability to purchase a firearm precisely why he or she was so treated.

This law could imperil anyone outside of the political mainstream. For instance, the Web page of the federally funded Alabama Department of Homeland Security in 2007 equated American "anti-government groups" with terrorists. The state Homeland Security agency warned, "In general, these terrorists claim that the US government is infringing on their individual rights, and/or that the government's policies are criminal and immoral. Such groups may hold that the current government is violating the basic principles laid out by the US Constitution."[200] This is the type of definition that could be used to ban all members of the Libertarian Party from buying guns.

With the definition in the proposed legislation, a person could also forfeit his Second Amendment rights merely by raising doubts about the war on terror. In a May 2003 terrorist advisory, the federal Homeland Security Department warned local law enforcement agencies to keep an eye on anyone who "expressed dislike of attitudes and decisions of the US government."[201] If this becomes the litmus test to deny permission to purchase a firearm, then only sheep will be permitted to have guns.

I joined a number of conservative leaders in publicly calling for Attorney General Gonzales's resignation shortly after he endorsed this legislation.

This pseudo-antiterrorist legislation illustrates that when it comes to increasing government power to control individuals and diminish civil liberties, there is hardly a hair's breadth of difference between the two major parties. The Bush administration also abandoned gun owners on the most important Supreme Court Second Amendment case in American history.

---

200 Accessed at www.chrisbrunner.com/2007/05/09/libertariansareterroristssaysthestate ofalabama

201 Jack Douglas, "U.S. Security Memos Warn of Little Things," *Fort Worth Star-Telegram,* May 25, 2003.

The District of Columbia has both one of the highest crime rates and one of the harshest bans on owning firearms. Dick Heller, a security guard, sued, claiming this ban on possessing a gun in his own home violated his constitutional rights. After a federal appeals court struck down the DC law, all eyes turned to the Supreme Court.

The Bush administration stunned gun owners across the land when its Solicitor General filed a brief with the Supreme Court urging that the Court *not* uphold the appeals court decision. Solicitor General Paul Clement feared that clearly recognizing an individual's right to own a gun in his own home might somehow undercut existing federal gun-control laws. The Bush administration brief stressed that the court's review should keep in mind "the strength of the government's interest in enforcement" of antigun laws.

But the Supreme Court made the right decision even though the Bush team fled the scene. Until this decision, the high court had never explicitly held that the Second Amendment directly applied to individuals. The decision marked a new era for gun rights in America. It was also a positive ruling because the right to self-defense is particularly important for women and minorities in a city like Washington. Where crime rates are high, a gun may be the only means for law-abiding citizens to safeguard themselves and their families. The court's decision in the Heller case reinforced the truth that the individual's right to keep and bear arms helps ensure all of our freedoms. The decision had too many caveats and leaves politicians too many remaining pretexts to muddle with this right, but at least it was a major step in the right direction.

Conclusion: Guns and Freedom

I am encouraged that more Americans are understanding that guns are not just about hunting and self-defense. Instead, guns help preserve the republic itself against threats both domestic and foreign.

Robert Cottrol, a George Washington University professor who has conducted groundbreaking work on the true, often-racist origins of various state gun control statutes, observed in 1997, "For most of human history, the individual has all too often been a helpless dependent of the State, dependent on the State's benevolence and indeed competence for his physical survival. The notion of a right to arms . . . takes the individual from servile dependency on the State for survival to the status of participating citizen capable of making intelligent choices in defense of one's life and ultimately one's freedom."[202]

If an explicitly recognized constitutional right—to keep and bear arms—can be taken away from us, where does it end? Is there any right we can count on after that? Many liberals who are incensed by the slightest hint of an attack on the First Amendment, would do well to remember it will be next in line if the Second Amendment is allowed to fall. At a time when other checks and balances are failing, an armed citizenry remains the final surety that the government cannot go too far.

At the same time, one lesson gun owners should take from the post-9/11 world is that the Second Amendment is not an island. Its survival and vitality requires a strong Fourth Amendment. If the government can search and seize wherever and whatever it pleases, then it is only a matter of times until guns are grabbed. Permitting the government to trample one constitutional right puts all other constitutional rights in peril.

---

202 Robert J. Cottrol, "The Gun Control Debate: The Overlooked Civil Rights Dimension," paper presented at American Shooting Sports Council conference, October 18, 1997, Washington.

FOREIGN POLICY, FOREIGN ENTANGLEMENTS

In his farewell address in 1796, President George Washington warned against "the insidious wiles of foreign influence . . . since history and experience prove that foreign influence, is one of the most baneful foes of republican government." Washington warned Americans that "a passionate attachment of one nation for another . . . gives to ambitious, corrupted, or deluded citizens (who devote themselves to the favorite nation), facility to betray or sacrifice the interests of their own country, without odium, sometimes even with popularity." President Thomas Jefferson, in his 1801 inaugural address, put Washington's doctrine into a famous epigram when he called for "peace, commerce, and honest friendship with all nations, and entangling alliances with none."

Unfortunately, George Washington's foreign policy wisdom has long been unpopular in the capital city that bears his name. Both major political parties have dragged the United States into unnecessary foreign conflicts, leaping at almost any opportunity to intervene abroad. This has been a disaster for American taxpayers, American soldiers, American power abroad, and American liberty at home.

The United States vs. the United States

American freedom is at risk from the growing power and intrusions of international organizations. And the United Nations is the granddaddy of all such threats.

The United Nations, and the ideals that underpin its very existence, is intractable. It cannot be fixed, because it is inherently and fundamentally the wrong way to do business in the modern international system. In today's world, it is particularly dangerous and damaging to *American* interests and sovereignty.

Our membership in that body hangs like a millstone around our necks, hampering our ability to act in our national interest, and threatening the domestic institutions that vouchsafe our freedoms. And so it has been for more than half a century.

Yet, after this half century that has witnessed the growth of a massive, expensive and corrupt international bureaucracy on the banks of the East River, the Washington–Jefferson "no entanglements" policy has been vindicated. The United Nations is a hulking mass of nepotism, waste, hypocrisy, corruption and virulent anti-Americanism. It has proved itself not the savior of world peace, but a blockage to that end. Its General Assembly is dominated by small and undemocratic countries that use their one vote—the same vote given to the world's great nations—as an outlet for their loathing envy of the United States, and the Security Council is inherently unworkable with its member state veto.

It is one massive failure. And worse, its failure continues to threaten America's first freedoms. The forces of the international community continue to encroach on American institutions, on our constitutional freedoms, on American law, and on American sovereignty. We are beholden to the failed dream of internationalism. And we pay in both money and, dare I say, national pride.

The United Nations will never be even close to cost effective. It has a ballooning budget, a highly redundant and ineffectual bureaucracy, virtually no outside accountability or transparency and—at the end of the day—a dysfunctional product worth far less than what it costs. If a government agency were as ineffectual as the UN, it would be in the midst of a scandal of epic proportions.

The United States government is currently paying roughly $3 billion a year to underwrite United Nations activities—far more than any other nation. And the UN is up to a great deal more mischief than Americans suspect. It is pushing the Law of the Sea

201

Treaty, which could result in international bureaucrats seizing control over the resources of most of the earth's surface. The UN Committee for Sustainable Development recently kowtowed to Zimbabwean dictator Robert Mugabe—whose idea of sustainability seems to be starving his political opponents. UNESCO (the United Nations Educational, Scientific and Cultural Organization) became such a bastion of left-wing nonsense that President Ronald Reagan formally withdrew US government sponsorship of the organization. Reagan was especially offended by UNESCO's proposal for a "new world information order" involving government licensing of journalists and pervasive new controls over the media. The US rejoined UNESCO in 2002, but has had no effect in deterring the agency from designating World Heritage Sites—which can include mountains, buildings, or other landmarks of bureaucratically certified importance. The United Nations has also sought to get its paws on the Internet, which could undermine one of the greatest information revolutions in modern times. And as noted in chapter 13, the UN has been conspiring for more than a decade to undermine private ownership of firearms around the globe.

Take the UN's historical record. Let's look at the preamble to the United Nations Charter.

First, the United Nations was to prevent the "scourge of war, which twice in our lifetime has brought untold sorrow to mankind." Considering the fact that since its founding, the UN has failed to prevent or end over three hundred wars, or protect the twenty-two million casualties of those wars, one must conclude the institution's success as a peacemaker has been less than stellar.

Second, the United Nations was "to reaffirm faith in fundamental human rights, in the dignity and worth of the human person, in the equal rights of men and women and of nations large and small." On this score, it's done a particularly odious job. In 2003, the United Nations Commission on Human Rights appointed Libya as chair, just one year after it rejected the United States for membership. In 2004, it rejected *Canada* for membership. Yet every year since 1947 it has anointed the Soviet Union or, later,

Russia, a member in good standing of its watchdog human rights body.

Third, the United Nations was to "establish conditions under which justice and respect for the obligations arising from treaties and other sources of international law can be maintained." But the United Nations has done the exact opposite. The double standards at the United Nations have done more to undermine the conditions for an effective and equitable system of international law on this planet than anything else before it.

Clearly, the General Assembly is an untrustworthy body for the resolution of international disputes—and most of us are terrified about what could happen to American troops in an International Criminal Court. Yet, in a bizarre twist that could only happen at an institution divorced from reality, the rest of the world sees the UN as a lapdog of the United States. International law should not rest on such a house of cards: the proper and lawful functioning of international relations should rest on the bilateral or directly multilateral creation of a true meeting of the minds among wholly voluntary partners.

Personally, I favor pulling the United States out of the United Nations. However, I recognize that given the support it enjoys by a large majority of lawmakers on both sides of the political aisle and by every modern president whether Republican or Democrat, that is not currently feasible. However, we must at least scale back its powers and jurisdiction.

The only hope for the United Nations is to cut back its role to the core functions of diplomacy and cooperation on such international problems as health care and refugee relief. That means dramatic and deep cuts in the UN's bureaucracy and budget. We must stop wasting the money of hard-working Americans on the activities of a corrupt elite.

The United States government has given more than one trillion dollars in foreign aid since the end of the Second World War. The US keeps shoveling out the money even though it has long recognized that foreign aid is a dismal failure.

In 1989, the US Agency for International Development (USAID) confessed that "only a handful of countries that started receiving US assistance in the 1950s and 1960s has ever graduated from dependent status."[203]

In 1993, a Clinton administration task force concluded, "Despite decades of foreign assistance, most of Africa and parts of Latin America, Asia, and the Middle East are economically worse off today than they were 20 years ago."[204]

In 2002, President Bush declared, "The old way of pouring vast amounts of money into development aid without any concern for results has failed, often leaving behind misery and poverty and corruption."[205]

These findings merely remind us of the wisdom of the book of Ecclesiastes—that there is nothing new under the sun. More than forty years ago, Ronald Reagan, in his famous speech in favor of Barry Goldwater's presidential candidacy, complained, "We have spent 146 billion dollars [on foreign aid]. Some of that money bought a $2 million yacht for [Ethiopian emperor] Haile Selassie . . . We bought one thousand TV sets with 23-inch screens for a country where there is no electricity, and some of our foreign aid funds provided extra wives for Kenya government officials."[206]

But presidents have continually poured more billions of US tax dollars down this rat hole. Even Reagan, once elected president, did not have the resolution to end foreign aid. The Bush administration has fizzled away more than $100 billion in foreign aid.

Foreign aid not only wastes tax dollars, it destroys the lives of those living in the recipient countries. US food aid routinely

---

203 Doug Bandow, "Foreign aid is broke, so don't fix it," *The Washington Times*, November 13, 1997,

204 Ibid.

205 "Remarks on Compassionate Conservatism in San Jose, California," Public Papers of the Presidents, 34 April 2002.

206 Ronald Reagan, "Rendezvous with Destiny," Address on behalf of Senator Barry Goldwater. Accessed at http://reaganlibrary.com/reagan/speeches/rendezvous.asp

bankrupts foreign farmers. In 2007, CARE, one of the world's largest charities, announced it would cease participating in a US program to dump US food on Third World countries, thereby driving down local crop prices. CARE official George Odo declared, "If someone wants to help you, they shouldn't do it by destroying the very thing that they're trying to promote."[207] The Government Accountability Office condemned US food aid as wasteful and "inherently inefficient"[208] last year. The harmful effect of American food aid has been obvious for decades, but the farm lobby, some aid groups, and politicians profit so much from the scam that the foreign victims count for nothing in Washington.

Foreign aid has long been recognized as a geyser of corruption. A 2007 study by Australia's Centre for Independent Studies in Australia concluded that foreign aid is "a major cause for the rising tide of graft" in Third World nations: "Huge aid flows to Africa have only rewarded incompetent despots and kleptocratic elites . . . In countries which derive over half their national budget from foreign aid transfers—as is now the case in many African and South Pacific countries—genuine democracy has no chance."[209]

Kenyan economist James Shikwati explained the impact of aid: "Huge bureaucracies are financed [with foreign aid], corruption and complacency are promoted, Africans are taught to be beggars and not to be independent. In addition, development aid weakens the local markets everywhere and dampens the spirit of entrepreneurship that we so desperately need." Shikwati noted that "the countries that have collected the most development aid are also the ones that are in the worst shape."[210]

In 2002, President Bush told journalists: "Listen, I can assure you we won't be putting money into a society which is not

207 Celia W. Dugger, "CARE Turns Down Federal Funds for Food Aid," *The New York Times*, August 16, 2007. Accessed at http://www.nytimes.com/2007/08/16/world/africa/16food.html.

208 Ibid.

209 "Make Poverty History: Tackle Corruption," Centre for Independent Studies (Australia), 2007.

210 "Spiegel Interview with African Economics Expert: "For God's Sake, Please Stop the Aid!" *Spiegel* Online, July 4, 2005.

transparent and corrupt, and I suspect other countries won't either."[211] Bush's promise did not stop his administration from bankrolling many of the most corrupt governments in the world, including Nigeria, Bangladesh, Tajikistan, Paraguay, Indonesia, Azerbaijan, and Kyrgyzstan.

Bush responded to the perennial pitfalls of foreign aid in 2002 by launching his Millennium Challenge Account (MCA) to reward foreign governments that "govern justly, invest in their people and encourage economic freedom." The MCA effectively offered foreign rulers a bribe to reward them for not overtly plundering their own countrymen.

But even this program quickly became another in a long history of farcical foreign aid reforms. The latest round of MCA recipients include one-horse island nations like Vanuatu and Cape Verde. The government of Georgia is cashing in under this program—even though that country is widely criticized as one of the most corrupt regimes in the world.

The Bush administration itself may recognize the failure of the Millennium Challenge Account to revolutionize foreign aid. In July 2008 it came up with a new accountability project that generated positive press.[212] The Bush administration called for "developing an international monitoring mechanism for African assistance." President Bush announced, "When people say they're [going to] make a pledge to feed the hungry or provide for the ill, we ought to honor that pledge." Bush's new system simply aimed to track whether western governments fulfill their promises to boost handouts aid to African regimes.

Instead of assuring that African rulers did not loot the aid, the US is now concerned solely with photo op promises about guaranteeing more aid.

It is naive to expect foreign aid to be used only as a reward

---

211 "Remarks Prior to Discussions With Prime Minister Tony Blair of the United Kingdom and an Exchange With Reporters in Kananaskis," Public Papers of the Presidents, 26 June 2002.

212 Michael Abramowitz, "G-8 Plans to Address Aid Accountability," The Washington Post, 7 July 2008.

for good behavior when US government officials and politicians cannot control themselves. Congressmen are perennially voting "earmarks" in legislation that require the US to give certain amounts of money to foreign groups or projects regardless of how badly they perform. The chief of the US Agency for International Development, Randall Tobias, resigned in 2007 after his personal foreign aid program was revealed. Tobias, who was married, was linked to a prostitution ring he repeatedly phoned to send over women to visit him in an apartment for personal services. (Tobias claimed he only paid for massages, not sex, and stressed that he requested Central American women). Ironically, as AID chief, Tobias had required organizations receiving US aid to formally pledge to refuse to fund organizations aiding prostitutes.

The best way to curtail foreign corruption is to end US foreign aid. Our politicians have no right to be generous by giving away our tax dollars to foreign regimes that cannot be trusted with a wooden nickel. And it is especially unjustified to be compelling American citizens to bankroll the governments of middle-income countries with sound market economies (such as Israel) that need no handouts from this nation.

Racketeering with Foreign Elections

In 1996, Chinese government money poured into the Clinton reelection campaign. John Huang raised more than a million dollars for the Clinton campaign, but much of the stash came from illegally laundered foreign contributions. Huang, who had close ties to a corporate giant tied to the Red Chinese military, was rewarded with a high-level job at the Commerce Department, where he had access to top secret intelligence.

Huang's machinations and the role of Chinese cash in the Clinton reelection campaign was a key charge in my initial inquiry on impeaching then-President Clinton, which I filed in November 2007.

Unfortunately, Attorney General Janet Reno refused to seriously investigate these crimes, and they were swept under the rug, in part because Republican congressional leadership did not have the stomach to fight to get the whole truth on this matter. This should have been perhaps the most explosive and appropriate charge in the impeachment of Bill Clinton.

It was self-evident that the Chinese meddling in the 1996 US presidential election was illegal, immoral, and corrupt. Interestingly, there is a US government agency that routinely interferes in foreign elections, bankrolling favorites of US political parties.

Congress created the National Endowment for Democracy (NED) in 1983. Congress and President Reagan pretended NED was a private organization in order to allow US government officials to deny that they were directly involved with NED's efforts to influence politics in foreign countries. But almost all of the agency's money comes directly from the federal Treasury, and its policies are controlled by Congress and the executive branch. Much of the budget of this agency is laundered to two nonprofit entities controlled by the two major American political parties. The National Democratic Institute routinely intervenes in favor of left-wing candidates, and the International Republican Institute (IRI) jumps in foreign elections to provide aid to favored conservative politicians.

Sen. John McCain has long been the chairman of IRI. He bragged in 1997: "When we provide the democratic opposition in Albania with 12 Jeep Cherokees and they win an election, I'm incredibly proud."[213] But even though the total amount of US aid to a small country may not be large, targeted political handouts can tilt the election playing field. How would McCain feel if the Mexican government openly bankrolled candidates in US elections who were in favor of giving more handouts to illegal immigrants?

The National Endowment for Democracy and its grantees have helped spark violent coups in recent years. NED quadrupled its aid to Venezuelan opponents of president Hugo Chavez in 2001 and early 2002. On April 12, 2002, NED grantees were heavily involved in a military coup that left forty people dead, hundreds wounded, and Chavez temporarily deposed. The IRI's Venezuela

213 Andrew Mollison, "Overseas political gifts? It's U.S. policy," *Austin American-Statesman*, February 23, 1997.

subsidiary issued an endorsement, saluting the bravery of the new rulers and "commending the patriotism of the Venezuelan military." On the day after the coup, IRI president George Folsom proclaimed, "Led by every sector of civil society, the Venezuelan people rose up to defend democracy in their country."[214] But such bluster did not prevent the coup from collapsing and Chavez from quickly retaking power. The IRI had received $340,000 in US government grants for political party building in Venezuela, and much of that money had bankrolled one local organization that was heavily involved in the short-lived coup.

In February 2004, an array of NED-aided groups and individuals played key roles in a coup that left one hundred people dead and toppled Haitian president Jean-Bertrand Aristide. Prior to the coup, Brian Dean Curran, the US ambassador to Haiti, warned Washington that the International Republican Institute's actions "risked us being accused of attempting to destabilize the government."[215] But the IRI was rewarded for its meddling in Venezuela and Haiti with even more federal grants.

The US government intervened on a massive scale to assure that a US-favored candidate won in 2004 in the Ukraine. In the two years prior to the election, the US government spent over $65 million "to aid political organizations in Ukraine, paying to bring opposition leader Viktor Yushchenko to meet US leaders and helping to underwrite exit polls indicating he won a disputed runoff election," according to the Associated Press.[216] Rep. Ron Paul (R-TX) complained that "much of that money was targeted to assist one particular candidate, and . . . millions of dollars ended up in support of the presidential candidate, Viktor Yushchenko."[217] Paul was also outraged at the effectively covert nature of much of the US intervention: "There are so many cut-out organizations and sub-

---

214 Christopher Marquis, "U.S. Bankrolling Is Under Scrutiny for Ties to Chavez Ouster," *The New York Times*, April 25, 2002.

215 Walt Bogdanich and Jenny Nordberg, "Mixed U.S. Signals Helped Tilt Haiti Toward Chaos," *The New York Times*, January 29, 2006.

216 Matt Kelley, "U.S. Money Helped Opposition in Ukraine," Associated Press, December 10, 2004.

217 Rep. Ron Paul, "U.S. Hypocrisy on Ukraine," Antiwar.com, December 9, 2004.

grantees that we have no idea how much US government money was really spent on Ukraine, and most importantly how it was spent."[218] At the same time the US was funneling money to Yushchenko's cause, the US government loudly fretted that the Russian government might aid the opposing candidate. Unfortunately, hypocrisy is nothing new for US democracy promotion efforts.

The United States could do far more to aid the worldwide advance of democracy by setting a good example here than by meddling abroad. Instead, recent US government policies are creating a "democracy backlash" around the globe, according to Thomas Carothers, the director of the Carnegie Endowment's Democracy and Rule of Law Project.

The National Endowment for Democracy should be abolished and the US government should stop pretending it has a magic wand that can uplift—or even purify—foreign elections.

The Peril of Creeping Militarization

Defense Secretary Robert Gates recently warned of a "creeping militarization" of American foreign policy. Gates declared that "the US military should never be mistaken for a Peace Corps with guns." Gates sought to enlighten those who believe that greater military force can solve all American problems: "We cannot kill or capture our way to victory."[219]

It is time to reemphasize the word *defense* in national defense. By maintaining a military presence in more than 130 nations around the world in more than 700 installations, with hundreds of thousands of troops deployed overseas, the US spends more to protect the soil of other nations than our own. Bringing these soldiers home would better protect America while saving lives and money. The vast majority of US military bases abroad should be significantly reduced or closed down. The US requires a

---

218 Ibid.

219 Ann Scott Tyson, "Gates Warns of Militarized Policy," *The Washington Post*, July 16, 2008.

military strong enough to defend this nation, not to support and defend much of the rest of the world.

The regular Pentagon budget now exceeds $500 billion a year, not counting the hundreds of billions of dollars of extra "emergency, supplemental" appropriations Congress offers up for the cost of conflicts in Iraq and Afghanistan. The spending has skyrocketed out of control and few people in Congress or elsewhere in Washington are paying close attention to the details. Much, if not most, of this spending is unnecessary for a prudent policy of defending our nation and its vital interests.

The US government needs to honestly admit that the Cold War against the deceased Soviet Union is over. At this point, the North Atlantic Treaty Organization (NATO) is a meaningless jumble of military and civilian bureaucracies from nations with little in common, and possessing goals that shift from crisis to crisis. Both the Clinton administration and the George W. Bush administration sought to make NATO more relevant simply by adding more nations to the membership roll. But it is absurd for the US government to pretend it has any vested interest in risking American lives and treasure to defend the jerry-rigged national borders that popped up throughout Eastern Europe in the past century. We can wish the new nations well without offering perilous guarantees of their domains.

It is time to bring American troops home from foreign lands where they are no longer urgently needed. South Korea is exhibit number one of where the US should immediately withdraw troops. After more than fifty years of American support, South Korea is well able to defend itself. The South has an economy that is estimated to be forty times as large as that of North Korea; South Korea has twice the North's population and a vast technological edge. Maintaining a large and costly American military presence in Korea largely because that's the way it's been done for more than half a century makes little sense, especially if we, as we should, maintain the capability to respond quickly to actual threats against us when necessary and where necessary. South Korean citizens seem far more obsessed with the prospect of beef imports from the

US than with the reality that the US taxpayers have underwritten their defense for more than half a century. Besides, South Korea has been sending money and food to the government in Pyongyang. That is a peculiar way to treat a supposed enemy.

We also must abandon the doctrine of preemptive war. Historically, the United States did not go around the globe attacking nations based on vague—and ultimately false—threats. Americans must recognize that the occupation of Iraq became a bloody debacle not because of some fluke or one-time circumstance in that ancient land, but because of the inherent limits of seeking to forcibly impose our will half way around the world.

American foreign policy should emphasize swift, decisive, and winning action against those who vow to harm us. This means defense, not foreign intervention. America should not be the world's policeman. We should stop attempts at nation building abroad, and we should swear off foreign crusades, no matter how seemingly well intentioned.

We should encourage private involvement around the world, particularly through free trade. The most effective way to preserve peace is through an expanding free market, backed by a full range of cultural and other private relationships, not by maintaining a permanent military presence around the globe.

Focusing on the Real Terror Threat

On September 11, 2001, Al Qaeda hijacked four airplanes and wreaked devastation on our nation. President Bush was correct that the United States must vigorously pursue Osama bin Laden and destroy Al Qaeda's ability to ever attack America again.

Unfortunately, the Bush administration failed to keep Al Qaeda in the crosshairs. The Bush military planners allowed many of Al Qaeda's top leaders and fighters to escape from Afghanistan at Tora Bora, in part because they were busy planning the invasion of Iraq. The Iraq war itself has proven to be a profound distraction to finishing off the organization that killed thousands of Americans.

A few weeks after 9/11, President Bush announced: "So long as anybody's terrorizing established governments, there needs to be a war."[220] Bush told American troops in 2002: "This is about fighting terror wherever it hides. . . . The world must understand that this nation won't rest until we have destroyed terrorism."[221] This is one of the worst follies of the war on terror. Many governments are oppressive and unjust; the fact that people rebel against dictators does not mean the United States should aid regimes in repressing their victims. As former National Security Advisor Zbigniew Brzezinski observed, "Terrorism is a technique, a tactic. You can't wage war on a technique."[222]

In the same way the US must honor George Washington's wisdom in not supporting foreign regimes, the US military must not be sent on wild goose chases against any organization that does not kowtow to US commands in any corner of the world. The recent US bombings and attacks in Somalia exemplify how the notion of attacking any terrorists anywhere can spiral out of control and lead to potentially new quagmires.

President Bush promised to "rid the world of evil," and justified significantly increasing US military intervention abroad to achieve that goal. We must recognize that neither the US government nor anyone else will be able to rid the world of evil as long as human beings act like humans. Making grandiose promises should no longer entitle an American president to throw away the lives of American soldiers.

---

220 "Remarks by the President in Roundtable Interview with Asian Editors," White House Office of the Press Secretary, October 17, 2001.

221 "President Rallies the Troops in Alaska," White House Office of the Press Secretary, February 16, 2002.

222 David Wood, "Analysis: War on Terrorism Lacks an Overarching Strategy," Newhouse News Service, June 18, 2002.

Conclusion

Americans can once again enjoy a sense of safety at home if the US government remembers and respects the wisdom of the era of the founders. Perhaps no clearer statement of the best role for the United States in the world was ever made than John Quincy Adams' Fourth of July 1821 oration: "Wherever the standard of freedom and Independence has been or shall be unfurled, there will her heart, her benedictions and her prayers be. But she goes not abroad, in search of monsters to destroy. She is the well-wisher to the freedom and independence of all. She is the champion and vindicator only of her own." [223]

---

[223] The Future of Freedom Foundation, "John Quincy Adams on U.S. Foreign Policy," *Freedom Daily*, October, 2001. Accessed at http://www.fff.org/freedom/1001e.asp.

IRAQ

The Iraq war is one of the greatest debacles of the US government in the post-World War Two era. We should not have invaded, we should not have occupied, and we should no longer delay exiting.

Though it was the Bush administration that charged into Iraq, this has become a bipartisan boondoggle. Most Democrats have either cheered on the war or exerted little or no effort to curtail US involvement. Politicians of both parties have come up with one excuse after another to perpetuate the American occupation (and to thereby boost the number of Americans and Iraqis killed) and to continue spending some $400 million per day of US taxpayer monies.

Why I Voted for the Iraq War

On October 10, 2002, I voted in favor of the resolution authorizing President Bush to use military force to topple the regime of Saddam Hussein. My support—like that of many members of Congress—was secured via bait-and-switch tactics employed by the Bush administration. If I had known the facts the White House possessed at the time of the vote, I would not have endorsed attacking Iraq.

On the day I voted for the war resolution, I declared, "Saddam Hussein and his regime pose an imminent threat to our national security—a threat which has gone unchecked for too many years now. Iraq has continued developing nuclear, biological, and chemical weapons since throwing out arms inspectors. Without taking action, Iraq's weapons programs will only increase and improve, and the longer we wait to intervene, the more seriously our troops and our security interests will be threatened by Iraq's nuclear, biological, and chemical warfare programs." I warned that if Saddam were left unchecked, "I am certain it will only be a matter of time before he unleashes [WMDs] on the US, either through a direct attack or through funneling weapons of mass destruction to terrorist groups such as Al Qaeda."[224] Neither I nor most of my colleagues knew that the intelligence presented to us in support of—and to secure our votes—was woefully, if not deliberately, mischaracterized by those Bush administration officials briefing us.

One of the most thorough exposés of the charades by which the Bush White House sold the war came out in June 2008 from the Senate Intelligence Committee. The bipartisan committee concluded that, prior to the US attack on Iraq, US intelligence agencies emphatically agreed that Saddam did *not* possess nuclear weapons and was nowhere near being able to acquire or develop them. Yet, in March 2002, President Bush announced that Saddam "possesses the world's most dangerous weapons." On August 26, 2002, Vice President Dick Cheney told the Veterans of Foreign Wars that Saddam could have nuclear weapons "fairly soon." On October 7, 2002, Bush warned, "Facing clear evidence of peril, we cannot wait for the final proof—the smoking gun that could come in the form of a mushroom cloud."[225] Other top administration officials also deceitfully used the mushroom cloud image to frighten people into supporting war.

The nuclear card was one of the two aces that the Bush administration played on Congress—without a trace of scruples. The other key was the notion that Saddam could give nuclear weapons, anthrax, or other WMDs to Al Qaeda or other terrorist groups.

In that October 7, 2002, speech, Bush announced that Saddam Hussein's regime had "trained Al Qaeda members in bombmaking and poisons and deadly gases."[226] However the

---

224 "Barr Statement on Iraq Resolution Joins Colleagues in Supporting Resolution Authorizing Military Force," Congressional Press Release, October 10, 2002.

225 "Remarks on the Iraq Threat to America," *Public Papers of the Presidents,* October 7, 2002.

226 Ibid.

evidence supporting this charge came solely from a tortured confession of an Al Qaeda operative in Egypt. The CIA warned the White House before Bush's speech that the detainee "seems to have fabricated information."[227] Two weeks earlier, on September 25, 2002, Bush declared that "you can't distinguish between Al Qaeda and Saddam when you talk about the war on terror." There was absolutely no support for this conclusion from the confidential information Bush received from the nation's intelligence agencies. The Senate Intelligence Committee concluded that "[s]tatements by the President and Vice President indicating that Saddam Hussein was prepared to give weapons of mass destruction to terrorist groups against the United States were contradicted by available intelligence information." The Committee also bluntly concluded that "[s]tatements and implications by the President and the Secretary of State suggesting that Iraq and Al Qaeda had a partnership, or that Iraq had provided Al Qaeda with weapons training, were not substantiated by the intelligence."[228] The CIA and other intelligence agencies informed the Bush White House before the war started that Saddam would likely use WMDs against the US only if he was "sufficiently desperate" because of an ongoing United States attack. And yet, Bush and team invoked the terrorists with WMDs connection to frighten the Congress and the nation into supporting an attack on a country that posed no imminent threat to the United States.

In hindsight, I and many others on the Hill should have been more skeptical of the Bush administration's claims. I simply did not think that the president's team would be making so many false charges on a subject that would quickly become a life-and-death issue for so many American soldiers and their families. Here again, we were proved sadly wrong.

---

227 Andrew Tilghman, "Senate Report Shows Intel Debunked Al Qaeda-Iraq Link Before Bush's Speech," *TPM Muckraker*, June 16, 2008. Accessed at http:// tpmmuckraker.talkingpointsmemo.com/2008/06/intel.php.

228 U.S. Senate Select Committee on Intelligence, "Senate Intelligence Committee Unveils Final Phase II Reports on Prewar Iraq Intelligence," Press Release of Intelligence Committee, June 5, 2008. Accessed at http://intelligence.senate.gov/press/record.cfm?id=298775.

Spurring Terrorism

Americans should not forget that the Iraq war was not commenced as part of a crusade to spread democracy or to bring liberty to the Arabic world. Instead, President Bush said the war was forced on us to prevent further terrorism attacks.

In 2002 and early 2003, Bush constantly invoked the terrorism threat to justify attacking Iraq. In his May 1, 2003, Mission Accomplished speech on the USS *Abraham Lincoln,* Bush portrayed the defeat of Saddam as a devastating blow against Al Qaeda: "The liberation of Iraq is a crucial advance in the campaign against terror. We have removed an ally of Al Qaeda and cut off a source of terrorist funding. . . . No terrorist network will gain weapons of mass destruction from the Iraqi regime, because the regime is no more." Bush invoked the Al Qaeda threat even though no evidence had surfaced before, during, or after the war to substantiate any link between Saddam and bin Laden.

There were plenty of experts who warned the Bush team that invading Iraq was far more likely to increase rather than to alleviate the terrorist threat. And their forebodings have been fulfilled many times over.

In January 2004, the Army War College published a report that concluded that the war on Iraq undermined the war against Al Qaeda and "created a new front in the Middle East for Islamic terrorism and diverted attention and resources away from securing the American homeland against further assault by an undeterrable Al Qaeda."[229] Thus, even before the first year of the US military's occupation, Iraq had become the Great Terrorist Boomerang.

In January 2005, a CIA report confirmed that the Iraqi conflict had become the world's top breeding ground for terrorists. Robert Hutchings, the chairman of a CIA think tank, declared, "At the moment, Iraq is a magnet for international terrorist activity."[230] CIA analyst David Low warned that the conflict in Iraq was

---

229 Jeffrey Record, "Bounding the Global War on Terrorism," U.S. Army War College, December 2003.

230 Dana Priest, "Iraq New Terror Breeding Ground," *The Washington Post,* January 14, 2005.

providing terrorists with "a training ground, a recruitment ground, the opportunity for enhancing technical skills." The CIA concluded that the Iraqi terrorist trainees would replace "the al-Qaeda membership that was distinguished by having trained in Afghanistan."[231]

In February 2005, then-CIA director Porter Goss told Congress that "Islamic extremists are exploiting the Iraqi conflict to recruit new anti-US jihadists" who "will leave Iraq experienced and focused on acts of urban terrorism."[232]

In June 2005, details of a classified CIA report leaked out that described Iraq as a "terrorist laboratory" and a training ground for Islamic extremists.

In 2006, the government's top intelligence experts and agencies concurred in a National Intelligence Estimate—Trends in Global Terrorism—that the Iraqi conflict was a disaster for the global war on terrorism. The report noted: "The Iraq conflict has become the 'cause celebre' for jihadists, breeding a deep resentment of US involvement in the Muslim world and cultivating supporters for the global jihadist movement . . . The Iraq jihad is shaping a new generation of terrorist leaders and operatives; perceived jihadist success there would inspire more fighters to continue the struggle elsewhere."[233]

According to the US government, the number of terrorist incidents around the world has soared since the US attacked Iraq. Terrorist attacks within Iraq almost doubled between 2005 and 2006, according to the US government. And while the number of US-defined "terrorist incidents" subsided in 2007, it remains far above what prevailed before the commencement of Operation Iraqi Freedom.

Bush and his defenders justify perpetuating the US occupation of Iraq because "we have to fight them over there

231 Ibid.

232 Dana Priest and Josh White, "War Helps Recruit Terrorists, Hill Told," *The Washington Post*, February 17, 2005."

233 "The Iraq Jihad Is Shaping a New Generation of Terrorist Leaders,'" *The Los Angeles Times*, September 27, 2006.

instead of fighting them over here." But it is time to realize that the number of terrorists is elastic and perceived US abuses multiply this pestilence.

The Iraq War is Far More Costly Than Advertised, or The Trillion-Dollar Cakewalk

Americans cannot afford to invade and rebuild foreign nations when the cost of living is skyrocketing at home. We must no longer sacrifice American living standards to allow politicians to pretend to forcibly remake the world.

One of the biggest frauds of the Iraq war was the notion that it would be a cost-free, good-intentions adventure for the American people. Before he invaded Iraq, Bush refused to provide any estimate of the cost of the war. Andrew Natsios, the chief of the US Agency for International Development, announced on April 23, 2003, however glibly, that "the American part of this will be $1.7 billion. We have no plans for any further-on funding for this."[234] Defense Undersecretary Paul Wolfowitz irresponsibly informed Congress that Iraq "can really finance its own reconstruction, and relatively soon."[235]

The war and occupation quickly proved vastly more expensive than advertised. The combined total costs of the Iraq and Afghanistan wars are now forecast to exceed $2 trillion, according to the Congressional Budget Office. According to Nobel laureate economist Joseph Stiglitz, the total cost of the war in Iraq could reach almost $3 trillion.

The Bush administration mortgaged America's economic future to underwrite its adventure in regime change and nation building. Thanks to massive deficit financing, no American has paid an extra dime in taxes to cover the war's cost. Those costs have been dumped on future generations of workers and taxpayers

---

234 Dana Milbank and Robin Wright, "Off the Mark on Cost of War, Reception by Iraqis," *The Washington Post*, March 19, 2004.

235 Ibid.

—most of whom had no vote in the elections that preceded the war's commencement or its perpetuation. The Bush administration has routinely relied on supplemental or emergency legislation to finance the war—thus making it more difficult for Congress to carry out the normal scrutiny of such spending.

The Bush administration made no real attempt to avoid wasteful spending in Iraq. As of 2005, the Department of Defense inspector general's office did not maintain a single auditor in Iraq. Only a small percentage of the funds appropriated for the Iraq effort have been audited. The Government Accountability Office found that at least $7 billion supposed to be used for the Iraq war was completely unaccounted for. Large politically connected companies like Halliburton and KBR have made out like bandits, while soldiers sweated and taxpayers were skewered.

The White House last year specifically exempted US contractors in Iraq from any obligation to report waste, fraud, and abuse to the US government. Other US government contractors must make such reports, but someone in the Bush administration apparently decided that the contractors in Iraq should have a free pass to plunder the till. Rep. Peter Welch (D-VT) complained: "This [exemption] was slipped in at the last minute . . . It's obviously something you can't justify in any way, and there's no answer to why you'd allow this to occur abroad any more than you'd allow it to occur domestically."[236]

Americans need to know the facts: what did the Bush administration know regarding waste and corruption in Iraq, and when did they know it? Those who conspired to defraud American taxpayers deserve to face charges and have their perp walks in front of the cameras—the same way the Justice Department treats alleged corporate wrongdoers.

The costs of the Iraq conflict have also spiraled out of control because the Bush administration chose to give a blank check to the corrupt Iraqi government. Currently there is absolutely no incentive whatsoever for the Iraqi government to assume

236 Josh White, "Mystery Loophole Wouldn't Require Reporting Fraud While Abroad," *The Washington Post*, March 13, 2008.

responsibility for its own economic, political, or security affairs. So long as it has the American military and American taxpayers to prop up the government as its security blanket, the country can live off its "American Express" charge card.

American taxpayers are also getting hammered because the Bush administration is engaging in nation building in an environment where there are more groups tearing things down than working together. Bush was correct in his 2000 presidential campaign when he criticized the Clinton administration's nation building fiascos. Unfortunately, he has poured far more tax dollars into this bottomless pit than Clinton ever did.

The monetary costs are only one part of the total burden the war is inflicting. Most Americans greatly underestimate the costs of the Iraq war on the soldiers. More than four thousand Americans who have been killed in Iraq and the more than thirty thousand who have been officially reported as wounded are only the beginning of the losses. One in five Iraq and Afghanistan veterans suffer from major depression or post traumatic stress disorder, according to an April 2008 report released by the Rand Corporation, the premier government-funded defense think tank. Rand estimated that "300,000 US troops are suffering from major depression or post traumatic stress from serving in the wars in Iraq and Afghanistan, and 320,000 received brain injuries."[237] The suicide rate among Army personnel has almost doubled since before the Iraq war commenced.

American politicians obliged American soldiers to sacrifice their time, their health, and often their lives for an adventure that was never justified by the soldiers' obligation to defend the United States. Yet instead of trying to reduce the impact on soldiers, the Pentagon is busying itself suppressing media coverage of soldiers' funerals at Arlington National Cemetery.

We also must recognize the cost of our invasion of Iraq and the occupation on the Iraqi people themselves. The Iraqis were oppressed by Saddam, but they have been ravaged by the chaos

---

237 "One In Five Iraq and Afghanistan Veterans Suffer from PTSD or Major Depression," Rand Corporation press release, April 17, 2008.

and strife that followed his fall. Estimates of the number of Iraqis who have died by violence since the US invaded ranged from 200,000+ (an Iraqi government study), to 600,000+ (*Lancet*, a respected medical journal), or more. The vast majority of the victims were not killed by the United States or other coalition forces. But the US invasion opened the Pandora's box that unleashed lethal forces that are still scourging that land.

On top of the dead, almost three million Iraqis have become refugees. This is the equivalent of the entire populations of Wyoming, Montana, North Dakota, and South Dakota being forced to flee their homes and often struggling to survive hand-to-mouth. This is one of the least recognized and most tragic results of the US invasion.

Lying the Nation into War: The Need for a Truth Commission

In a memo sent to Congress on March 18, 2003, Bush announced that he was attacking Iraq "to take the necessary actions against international terrorists and terrorist organizations, including those nations, organizations, or persons who planned, authorized, committed, or aided the terrorist attacks that occurred on September 11, 2001."[238] Bush tied Saddam to 9/11 even though confidential briefings he received informed him that no evidence of any link had been found. Encouraging Americans to believe Saddam was behind 9/11, and to see the Iraq war as vengeance for 9/11, allowed Bush to justify an unprovoked attack on a nation that posed no threat to America.

The Bush administration has had more than five years to offer up evidence to support the Saddam–9/11 tie. They have offered nothing except hot air and attacks on the motives of people requesting evidence.

Some of the war's defenders insist that "everybody" believed

---

238 "Text of a Letter from the President to the Speaker of the House of Representatives and the President Pro Tempore of the Senate," White House Office of the Press Secretary, March 19, 2003.

Iraq had WMDs and posed a serious threat before 9/11. But my friend Congressman Ron Paul denounced the rush to war in September 2002: "We're willing to go to war over phantom weapons."[239] Many other experts, here and abroad, declared that the evidence was slim or none that Saddam possessed WMDs capable of posing a threat to the United States.

The lies and deceptions did not end after the invasion began. Instead, this nation has had five years of continual propaganda out of the White House.

The Bush team sometimes acts like it should be a federal crime to doubt the administration's claims. In late 2005, Vice President Cheney proclaimed that it was "dishonest and reprehensible" to suggest that "the President of the United States or any member of his administration purposely misled the American people on pre-war intelligence." Americans were supposed to assume that any political appointee's assertions on Iraq were sacrosanct. Cheney proclaimed that "untruthful charges against the Commander-in-Chief have an insidious effect on the war effort itself."[240] So is it treason for Americans not to forget the cons by which the war was sold?

The American soldiers who fought in Iraq deserve to know the truth about what the White House and the Pentagon leadership knew, and when they knew it. Americans cannot tolerate the perpetual cover-up of the lies about the war without betraying those who were sacrificed because of those lies.

---

239 Jim Bovard, "Ron Paul, the 2002 Szasz Award Winner," November 19, 2007.
Accessed at http://jimbovard.com/blog/2007/11/19/ron-paul-the-2002-szasz-award-winner

240 Dana Milbank, "Opening the Door to Debate, and Then Shutting It," *The Washington Post*, November 22, 2005;

Withdrawal Now

President Bush declared in May 2007 on the question of whether US troops would remain in Iraq: "It's their government's choice. If they were to say, 'Leave,' we would leave."[241] But when the Iraqi government said *leave*, the answer of the Bush administration (on July 8, 2008) was *not so fast*.

The Iraqi government's National Security Adviser, Mowaffak al-Rubaie, announced that the Malaki government is "impatiently waiting" for the complete withdrawal of US troops. Al-Rubaie declared, "We would not accept any memorandum of understanding with [the US] side that has no obvious and specific dates for the foreign troops' withdrawal from Iraq."[242]

The Iraqi government's declaration should bring to an end all efforts to establish a permanent US military presence in Iraq or to prolong the existing massive American military, economic, and diplomatic presence. The Bush administration's expenditure of billions of dollars building up massive long-term bases is one of the great boondoggles of the war.

Before Americans become irate at the Iraqi withdrawal request, they should recognize what the Bush administration was demanding. Bush loudly bragged in 2004 that the Iraqis had sovereignty because of a transfer of signed documents between the Coalition Provisional Authority (CPA) and some Iraqi politicians handpicked by the US government.

But the reality was that the US has long claimed and exercised free sway in Iraq.

The Bush administration, as part of a long-term agreement with the Iraqi government, demanded that US soldiers and US contractors continue to have complete immunity when they kill Iraqis, and that the US military would have the right to attack almost wherever and whenever it pleased. On top of this, the Bush

---

241 The White House Press Conference, May 24, 2007. Accessed at http://www.whitehouse.gov/news/releases/2007/05/20070524.html.

242 Ernesto Londoño and Dan Eggen, "Iraq Wants Withdrawal Timetable In U.S. Pact," *The Washington Post*, July 9, 2008.

administration demanded the right for US forces to continue seizing and detaining Iraqi citizens without charges. (At last count, more than twenty thousand Iraqis were locked up by the US military.)

Obviously, if the Iraqi government were to grant these demands, it would be a mere puppet to the US forces.

Since the Iraqi government has formally demanded a withdrawal date, the longer our troops stay, the greater peril they face. The Iraqi armed forces and police the US military trained and equipped could be used against our own forces. The announcement on July 8, 2008, was the final confirmation that the Iraqi people no longer wish American forces in their country. As early as 2006, polls showed that "64% of Iraqis believe that crime and violent attacks will decrease if the US leaves Iraq within six months, 67% believe that their day-to-day security will increase if the US withdraws and 73% believe that factions in parliament will cooperate more if the US withdraws."[243]

Opponents of withdrawal must explain why the US is obliged to occupy an Arab nation that the president long bragged about liberating. The same people who said we should forcibly impose democracy on Iraq now insist that we should scorn the will of the Iraqi people by keeping our troops there after they are clearly unwanted.

The opponents will seek to lay all the blame on the Iraqi debacle on those who end it. But the war was lost by the people who started it. A Pentagon report in June noted that the post-invasion Iraq failures were due in part because senior leaders chose to "*savor the euphoria* over seemingly easy successes in Afghanistan"[244] (emphasis added). The fact that the world's most advanced military was able to easily rout cadres of ill-equipped and poorly trained personnel, many of whom rode around in the back of pickup trucks with only light weapons, somehow conferred

---

243 Daniel Ellsberg, "Where are Iraq's Pentagon Papers?" *The Los Angeles Times*, June 11, 2006.

244 Josh White, "Army's History of Iraq After Hussein Faults Pentagon," *The Washington Post*, June 29, 2008.

invincibility upon Rumsfeld and crew. This was the caliber of the strategic delusions that led the Bush team to drag America into the Iraqi sinkhole.

Americans need to avoid being lulled by the apparent success of the surge in US troops in Iraq in 2007. Offering the surge's success as a justification for the invasion and occupation misses the point. Of course the surge works in terms of reducing attacks; we'd be in really bad shape if injecting twenty to thirty thousand more troops into a theater of operations didn't reduce violence able to be perpetrated by an enemy! The real question is not whether or not the surge is working, but whether it was appropriate, justified, responsible, or necessary for the United States to have invaded and then occupied Iraq. The answers to each of those questions is no.

The same politicians who misled Americans to support the invasion and the occupation will continue in that vein regarding any withdrawal.

The difficulty of a contriving a clean or politically attractive exit strategy was a huge factor in US government thinking on the Vietnam War from 1964 onwards. Politicians and experts at the highest level of government recognized that victory in Vietnam was very unlikely. But as long as politicians and political appointees lied and denied obvious facts, they could perpetuate their power and prestige. The goal came to be avoiding losing on one's own shift—or at least until after one is reelected. For politicians, postponing admission of failure is a victory.

Vietnam should have taught Americans not to permit politicians to drag out a war merely so they could deny their own mistakes. We must not allow politicians to trade soldiers' blood and American taxpayers' hard-earned dollars for their own poll ratings.

It is no criticism against America's brave fighting men and women to admit that the war and subsequent occupation was a mistake and has been badly mismanaged. It is not soldiers' fault that politicians sent them on a no-win mission. With violence in Iraq currently lower than in the recent past, now is the time to accelerate the turnover of full security authority to the Iraqi government, since only when we leave will they have an incentive to take the tough steps necessary to meet their nation's many challenges—military, economic, and political. So long as Washington dominates Iraq, US forces will remain the target of antagonistic groups, militias, and insurgents.

The surest victory in Iraq is to limit further American losses. And that is within the immediate power of the president, by withdrawing forces ASAP. We must not permit politicians to waffle on withdrawal in the same way they have regarding the reasons for starting the war five years ago.

Conclusion

In the 1960s, liberal politicians would shrug off the spiraling crime and riots spurred in part by Great Society programs by claiming that since they had good intentions, they could not be blamed for the damage.

We are hearing the same thing now from politicians who supported attacking Iraq. It was as if a purported wish to spread freedom and democracy should absolve politicians of all their deceits and mistakes.

One lesson from Iraq is that Americans should not permit politicians, pundits, or other experts to claim vast benefits as a reason for conquering foreign lands, regardless of the purported ideal.

American politicians did American soldiers wrong in Iraq. We cannot resurrect the dead and the sunken losses by perpetuating a wrong-headed operation. To perpetuate the war is merely to allow politicians to continue sacrificing other Americans so they can avoid admitting their mistakes.

IRAN: TALKING IN LIEU
OF BOMBING

I graduated from Community High School, an international school, in Teheran, Iran, in 1966. My family was evacuated to Teheran in September 1965, from Lahore, West Pakistan, where my father was working on a project as a civil engineer. During the year I spent in Teheran, I made many friends among my Iranian classmates. I was struck by the decency and honesty of the Iranian people, who are far more similar to Americans than the inhabitants of many other nations in the Middle East.

I have been saddened to see the saber-rattling and threats of nuclear annihilation that have poured out of Washington in regard to Iran in the last few years, especially during the election year of 2008. Pentagon Deputy Assistant Secretary Debra Cagan reportedly told several British Members of Parliament last September, "I hate all Iranians."[245] Congressman Ron Paul commented in June 2008: "I hear members of Congress saying, If we could only nuke them [Iran]."[246] The Bush administration has reportedly considered using tactical nuclear weapons on underground targets in Iran. British newspapers reported last year that the Pentagon has already compiled a list of thousands of bombing targets.

The Iranian people have done nothing to deserve such wrath by American politicians or policymakers. The Iranian government is problematic in many ways, but that nation's political system is far

---

245 Simon Walters, "I hate all Iranians, US aide tells MPs," *Daily Mail* (UK), 29 September 2007.

246 Steve Watson, "Ron Paul: I Hear Members of Congress Saying 'If We Could Only Nuke Iran'," Infowars.net, July 4, 2008. Accessed at http://intelligence.senate.gov/press/record.cfm?id=298775.

more open to peaceful reform than most regimes in the Middle East.

The Bush administration has consistently shown bad judgment and bad faith on its Iran policy. This is another area in which Congress has failed dismally to perform any effective oversight. Instead, many congressmen have been cheerleaders for carnage.

Despite the fact that most Americans would probably confuse Iraq with Iran on a map (if they could locate either one) and lump them together as Arab countries, the two countries are more dissimilar than alike. For starters, only about 3 percent of Iran's population is Arab, compared to nearly 80 percent in Iraq. Historically, the predominantly Persian Iran and its Arab neighbor to the west have been at odds more than they've enjoyed cordial relations.

Iran is very different from Iraq in any number of ways—size, economic power, political background, political history, religion. And unlike Iraq, the Iranian people have a very strong and tangible basis in participatory government that the people in Iraq did not have, having gone from an artificial British-imposed monarchy in 1958 to a forty-five-year succession of military dictatorships. At the time of the US invasion in 2003, there was no basis whatsoever in the Iraqi society for understanding participatory government. Iran, on the other hand, is a nation that has a very sophisticated economic structure; again, unlike Iraq. It is a nation that is much more homogeneous in terms of its culture and its religious history than Iraq. It is a nation that has a very large number of very strong, very patriotic Iranian-Americans in this country.

Too Proud to Talk

President Woodrow Wilson declared in 1916, "There is such a thing as a nation being too proud to fight." But the Bush administration turned this on its head, becoming a government that is too proud to talk. The Bush team almost always threatens to destroy the people in a foreign nation rather than sit down and have diplomatic exchanges with the country's leaders. John McCain gives every appearance of continuing the swaggering "big stride" characteristic of George W. Bush.

Almost all of the disagreements with the government of Iran over the last five years could have been resolved early on, and still can be.

The Iranian government sent the United States government a secret diplomatic proposal in May 2003 offering to end support for Hezbollah in Lebanon and Hamas in Gaza, make its nuclear program more transparent, and aid in stabilizing Iraq after the US invasion. The offer was parlayed to the US by the Swiss government. The US ambassador to Switzerland, Tim Guldimann, sent a note to Washington along with the Iranian offer (which Iran labeled a "roadmap"): "I got the clear impression that there is a strong will of the (Iranian) regime to tackle the problem with the US now and to try it with this initiative."[247] In return for its concessions, "Tehran asked Washington to end its hostility, to end sanctions, and to disband" a US-aided terrorist group that was attacking Iran, the BBC revealed last year.[248]

Vice President Cheney torpedoed the Iranian offer. Retired colonel Lawrence Wilkerson, who then served as Secretary of State Colin Powell's chief of staff, explained that as soon as the Iranian offer "got to the Vice-President's office, the old mantra of 'We don't talk to evil' . . . reasserted itself." The BBC noted, "Observers say the Iranian offer as outlined nearly four years ago corresponds pretty closely to what Washington is demanding from Tehran now."[249]

I don't know how many American soldiers have died in Iraq because of Cheney's refusal to talk to evil. Perhaps spurring the Iranian offer helped some neoconservatives strut at Washington receptions. The neocons liked to say in 2003, "Wimps go to Baghdad, but real men go to Tehran."

Until July 2008, the Bush administration was adamant it would never even sit down and formally talk with representatives of the Iranian government. Even as our handpicked Prime Minister

---

247 "Washington 'snubbed Iran offer'," BBC News, January 18, 2007.

248 Ibid.

249 Ibid.

Maliki in Iraq talked with Iranian leaders, and even as the Olmert government in Israel talked with the Assad regime in Syria, the Bush administration refuses to engage one of the largest and most important countries in that part of the world. This makes no sense.

I think there is tremendous room yet unexplored, working with the Iranian people, working with our allies and those other countries that are also legitimately concerned about the possibility, remote as it may be, of Iran obtaining a nuclear capacity.

Bogus Warmongering on a False Threat

From 2003 onwards, the Bush administration has been claiming that the Iranians were building a nuclear bomb, and posed a grave and imminent threat to world peace. Last year, the rhetoric heated up to the point that many observers feared the Bush administration was creating a pretext for a preemptive attack.

But Americans learned last December that the administration had been making the same type of false claims on Iran that it made about Iraq prior to attacking that nation. The declassified key findings of the National Intelligence Estimate (NIE)—the key findings of sixteen US government intelligence agencies—revealed: "We judge with high confidence that in the fall of 2003, Tehran halted its nuclear weapons program . . . We assess with moderate confidence Tehran has not restarted its nuclear weapons program as of mid-2007 . . . Tehran's decision to halt its nuclear weapons program suggests it is less determined to develop nuclear weapons than we have been judging since 2005."[250]

The US intelligence agencies confirmed the findings of the International Atomic Energy Agency, which has long reported that there was no evidence the Iranians had an active nuclear weapons program.

Bush was notified of the new NIE findings in August 2007. Instead of cooling his rhetoric, he seemed to ratchet it up, warning

---

250 "Key Judgments From a National Intelligence Estimate on Iran's Nuclear Activity," *The New York Times*, December 4, 2007.

of Iran causing a nuclear holocaust or of starting World War Three —even after being informed that the Iranians were not pursuing a nuclear weapon.

The NIE findings destroyed any justification Bush might have claimed for a preemptive attack on Iran. Yet Bush and some members of Congress continue to talk as if the NIE had actually reached the opposite conclusion of what the report revealed regarding Iran's nuclear weapons efforts. In March 2008, in an interview with US government-controlled Radio Farda (which broadcasts to Iran in Farsi), Bush said the Iranian government "declared they want to have a nuclear weapon to destroy people." The Iranian government has never said it sought a nuclear weapon, and never suggested it would use such weapons to destroy people. (The White House subsequently issued its version of a correction: a spokesman said that Bush "shorthanded his answer" regarding Iran's nuclear policies).[251]

Intentionally Subverting Democracy in Iran?

The Bush administration's indignation with the current government in Iran is especially ironic because they helped put it in power.

In June 2005, Bush denounced the pending Iranian presidential election for ignoring "the basic requirements of democracy." Bush declared that the elections would be "sadly consistent with this oppressive record"[252] of the Iranian government. Iranians were also urged to boycott the election in Farsi-language broadcasts on US-financed television and radio stations.

The Bush administration's efforts contributed to the defeat of Mohammad Khatami, a comparatively moderate reformer, and to the victory of Mahmoud Ahmadinejad, whose strident rhetoric on Israel helped Bush and others paint the Iranian government as

251 Jonathan S. Landay, "Bush erroneously says Iran announced desire for nuclear weapons," McClatchy Newspapers, 20 March 2008.

252 Scott Stearns, "Bush Critical of Iran Elections," *Voice of America*, June 16, 2005.

an imminent peril. But Ahmadinejad is largely a figurehead. The real power in Iran is wielded by Ayatollah Ali Khamenei.

In 2006, the Bush administration announced it was seeking emergency funding from Congress to promote democracy in Iran. Congress gave the State Department $120 million to create a secret democracy program for Iran. The State Department has disclosed almost nothing about how it divvied out the cash (except for revealing that it gave big chunks of money to some large organizations such as Freedom House and the Eurasia Foundation).

Bush's high-profile handouts have devastated Iranian democrats. Last October, Trita Parsi, the president of the National Iranian American Council, and other prominent Iranian-Americans sent members of Congress a letter complaining that the "secret State Department 'democracy promotion' funding has enabled Iranian authorities to label those supporting reforms or engagement with the West as foreign agents and traitors. Recent detentions of Iranian-American scholars, journalists, union leaders, student activists, and others are widely viewed as responses to threats posed by US-funded efforts."[253]

Shirin Ebadi, 2003 Nobel Peace Prize winner, and USC professor Muhammad Sahimi declared in an op-ed last year, "Iranian reformists believe that democracy can't be imported. It must be indigenous. They believe that the best Washington can do for democracy in Iran is to leave them alone. The fact is, no truly nationalist and democratic group will accept such funds."[254]

There is no evidence that Bush administration policymakers or congressional hardliners care about the adverse effect of US democracy aid to Iranian democratic reformers. As long as the Bush administration can claim to be spreading democracy, any victims can be swept under the carpet. (As Iranian human-rights activist Emad Baghi bitterly complained, "We are under pressure

---

253 "Joint Letter to Congress Requesting Scraping of Flawed 'Democracy Funds,'" National Iranian American Council, October 11, 2007.

254 Shirin Ebadi and Muhammad Sahimi, "The follies of Bush's Iran policy," *International Herald Tribune* (Paris), 30 May 2007.

here both from hard-liners in the judiciary and . . . Bush."[255])

It is hard to tell whether the Bush White House is sincere in its efforts to help the Iranian people achieve democracy, or whether some administration officials are setting up Iranian democratic reformers so the regime's repression can prove the government is incorrigible and must be overthrown. When the Iranian government responds to US meddling in the name of democracy with new crackdowns, it makes it easier for Bush to portray the Iranian government as implacable dictators who must be destroyed —for the good of the Iranian people, of course.

Besides, the US lacks credibility in promoting democracy in Iran, considering it was a CIA coup in 1953 that overthrew an elected leader and put the Shah in power. The US supported the Shah's economically beneficial but increasingly repressive policies —which helps explain why some Iranians see the United States as the Great Satan.

Financing Terrorism

At the same time the Bush administration claims it wants to give the gift of democracy to Iran, it is financing terrorist attacks on the Iranian people.

The US government officially designated Mujahedin-e Khalq, an Iranian group known as MEK (the People's Holy Warriors) as a foreign terrorist organization in 1997.[256] MEK earned the odious label by killing US soldiers and civilians and by attacks inside Iran that killed hundreds of people. MEK seeks to overthrow the current Islamic government, as it previously sought to overthrow the Shah. In 2001, the FBI arrested MEK fund-raisers for giving "material support to a terrorist organization." MEK is widely regarded as a Marxist cult organization.

But after Bush announced that Iran was part of the Axis of

255 Karl Vick and David Finkel, "U.S. Push for Democracy Could Backfire Inside Iran," *The Washington Post*, March 13, 2006.

257 http://www.fas.org/irp/news/2001/10/fr100501.html

Evil in his 2002 State of the Union address, the White House decided MEK were really good guys. The US State Department still classifies MEK as terrorists, but the US military protects MEK camps in Iraq, including providing its leaders with chauffeurs, guards, and other perks.

Seymour Hersh revealed in July 2008 in *The New Yorker* that Congress agreed late in 2007 to a $400 million program for covert operations, including military and terrorist attacks, within Iran. The MEK is one of three organizations receiving US funding to carry out subversion and attacks. According to the Iranian government, a terrorist attack earlier this year at a cultural center in Shiraz killed a dozen people and injured two hundred. Hersh also revealed that MEK members have been brought to America and trained in Nevada—an unwise policy, given the MEK's long record of killing innocent people for political purposes.[257]

The Bush administration's infatuation with MEK may be in part because the group tells them what they want to hear.

The Washington Post reported in March 2007 that MEK leaders bragged that "they are a main source of intelligence" on Iran for the Bush administration. Mohammad Mohaddessin, MEK's chairman, declared, "All the important things that are talked about [regarding Iran's nuclear ambitions] are things revealed by us."[258] The MEK has been accused of fabricating evidence—which could explain why its allegations were completely debunked by the National Intelligence Estimate revelations in late 2007. Are the White House and Pentagon giving their blessings and protection to MEK while MEK gins up evidence to justify a US preemptive attack on Iran?

As a former CIA official, I am distressed to see the apparent corruption of the administration's data on Iran. We appear to be seeing a replay of the Iraq debacle, starting with the administration

---

257 Terry Gross, "Journalist Seymour Hersh on the administration's covert plan to induce turmoil in Iran," National Public Radio, *Fresh Air*, 30 June 2008.

258 Ernesto Londo and Saad allzzi, "Iraq Intensifies Efforts to Expel Iranian Group," *The Washington Post*, March 14, 2007.

choosing to rely on extremist, fringe expatriates with a grudge, a bad record, and a hidden agenda. The US government was profoundly deceived by the Iraqi National Congress and Ahmed Chalabi before the invasion of Iraq. Numerous professionals in the CIA warned the White House that the expatriate Iraqis were untrustworthy, but their concerns were buried. The White House—especially Vice President Dick Cheney—became intensely involved in the intelligence process, significantly biasing the analyses. America cannot afford a repeat of this deck-stacking charade.

Bush's bankrolling of the MEK and other Iranian terrorist groups' attacks on civilians makes a mockery of everything he has claimed the United States stands for since 9/11. How can the president of the United States tell everyone in the world that "you're either with us or against us in the fight against terror," when the US government is bankrolling and arming a premier terrorist group?

The Folly of Attacking Iran

Our own intelligence services tell us Iran is not actively working to build a nuclear bomb and is many years away from having nuclear weapons capability. There is no imminent threat, and *only* a truly imminent, credible, and significant threat can ever justify preventative action. The tragedy in Iraq demonstrates the counterproductive consequences of initiating war without any compelling justification.

Almost no reasonable person alleges that Iran poses any direct threat to the security of the United States. There is no Iranian naval force that could seize Manhattan, nor any army of Iranian paratroopers waiting to descend upon Baltimore. There is no Iranian army that could surge across the St. Lawrence Seaway. Instead, the case against Iran is based almost entirely upon distant hypotheticals—and on the notion that the United States needs to totally dominate the Middle East.

The lack of a direct threat has not deterred the Bush

administration from continually seeking to spark a conflict with the Iranian government. *The New Yorker* reported in July 2008 that "United States Special Operations Forces have been conducting cross-border operations from southern Iraq, with Presidential authorization, since last year. These have included seizing members of Al Quds, the commando arm of the Iranian Revolutionary Guard, and taking them to Iraq for interrogation, and the pursuit of 'high-value targets' in the President's war on terror, who may be captured or killed."[259] The US government has not refuted the charges, and other sources corroborate similar US efforts.

The potential consequences of war with Iran include attacks on our troops stationed in Iraq, threats to the Gulf oil trade, terrorist attacks around the world, subversion of friendly Arab and Muslim governments, destruction of the democracy movement within Iran, and enduring hostility towards America throughout much of the world. Defense Secretary Gates told a group of Democratic senators last year that if the US launches a preemptive attack on Iran, "We'll create generations of jihadists, and our grandchildren will be battling our enemies here in America."[260]

Geographically, Iran presents a much more complex set of logistical concerns for the US military than did Iraq. Iran has significantly longer land and maritime borders than does Iraq. Iran borders three bodies of water—the Caspian Sea, the Persian Gulf, and the Gulf of Oman; Iraq possesses but a tiny sliver of a sea coast. Iran's much larger landmass and population base, including potential armed forces strength of fifteen to thirty million, and its more homogenous citizenry, work to complicate military planning considerably. On top of that, much of Iran is mountainous—the type of terrain from which it is easy to launch a guerilla resistance against an occupying force.

The economic muscle Iran wields, while weakened by corruption and inefficiency (as in Iraq), far exceeds that of its Arab

---

259 Seymour Hersh, "Annals of National Security: Preparing the Battlefield," *The New Yorker*, July 7, 2008.

260 Ibid.

neighbor—more than $600 billion compared to Iraq's anemic $88 billion. Iran's international trade, like Iraq's, is predominantly based on petroleum exports, and is about twice Iraq's. However, Iran's list of trading partners is much more diverse than Iraq's, which relies on exports to a single country—the United States—for nearly half its exports. Many US allies, including Japan and Germany, are major trading partners with Iran. China figures just as significantly in Tehran's international trade. Further complicating the picture is the fact that recent intelligence establishes that China is supplying military arms and equipment to Iran.

While many in the United States delight in ridiculing Iranian president Ahmadinejad, such practice can beguile leaders into potentially serious miscalculations about the support the leadership in Tehran enjoys—and which the regime would enjoy if the US were to attack or to be perceived as attacking through surrogates.

It is vital to quell the simplistic blustering by the White House and by other political leaders in both parties, often designed to prove each will be tougher on Iran than the others. Also helpful would be putting a lid on unnecessary and repetitive insults and threats directed at the Ahmadinejad administration—a pastime that simply strengthens the regime in Tehran and does nothing to build support for any legitimate efforts to weaken the regime.

Positive steps could include strengthening economic and political pressure on Iran, and increased efforts to quietly but actively build on the deep base of political understanding that already exists among a large segment of the Iranian population (and including the more than one million Iranian-Americans).

The primary reason that the US would attack Iran at this point is to support Israel and to perpetuate that country's monopoly of nuclear weapons in the Middle East. Israel doesn't need our help in defending itself from a third-tier military nation that has not invaded a foreign nation in over a century. Israel possesses more than two hundred nuclear weapons—more than enough to defend its own turf from a nonnuclear challenger.

Unfortunately, the friends of Israel may stampede Congress

to support policies that lead to a shooting war with Iran. House Concurrent Resolution 362, which currently has 220 sponsors in the House and 50 in the Senate, demands that the president take action "imposing stringent inspection requirements on all persons, vehicles, ships, planes, trains, and cargo entering or departing Iran; and prohibiting the international movement of all Iranian officials not involved in negotiating the suspension of Iran's nuclear program."[261] This is a demand for the United States military to impose a *de facto* blockade on Iran—an unmistakable act of war.

The United States government should make it clear to the world that it is not giving any other nation a green light to attack Iran. The Pentagon warned in early July that the Israeli government may launch air strikes against Iranian targets. It would be almost impossible for the Israelis to attack Iran without passing through Iraqi air space, which is controlled by the US military. This would almost certainly drag the US into a broader Israeli-Iran conflict. Joint Chiefs of Staff Chairman Adm. Mike Mullen returned from Israel in July and was asked how concerned he was about an Israeli unilateral strike on Iran. Mullen declared, "My strong preference, here, is to handle all of this diplomatically . . . as opposed to any kind of strike occurring. This is a very unstable part of the world. And I don't need it to be more unstable."[262]

We should also recognize that attacking Iran would destroy whatever movement for democracy currently exists in that country. Foreign attacks usually make nations more authoritarian in their response—both to the aggressors and their own citizens.

Unfortunately, it is not clear if the laptop bombardiers in the White House will stoop to listen to real military experts.

This is not a time for Americans to blindly support the White House. Under our Constitution, it is not up to the president to immerse the nation in a foreign war at his own whim. The Bush administration has already made far too many false assertions on Iran to deserve knee-jerk trust if an incident occurs that provides

---

261 Accessible at http://thomas.loc.gov/home/gpoxmlc110/hc362_ih.xml

262 Jonathan Karl, "Pentagon Warns Against Israeli Attack on Iran," ABC News, 2 July 2008.

the red carpet for a massive attack by the US military. Americans —including the media—trusted Bush before the start of the Iraq war. Our soldiers, their families, and American taxpayers will be paying for that folly for a long time.

We must make sure people in our government understand the very clear, fundamentally important differences between Iran and Iraq, and to understand that if one superficially believes that simply engaging in a preemptive military strike or a strike based on some manufactured happening or activity, the consequences would be extremely dire for everybody involved.

We need an Iran policy that respects the lives of American soldiers, and that keeps the broader, strategic, and long-term interest of the US in the world in mind—not the egos of American politicians.

ABSOLUTE POWER OVER THE EDGE: TORTURE AND HABEAS CORPUS

Nowhere are my differences with the current rulers in Washington more stark than on the questions of *habeas corpus*, warrantless surveillance (discussed in chapter 10). The issues of *habeas corpus* abuse and of illicit use of torture illustrate how far wrong America has gone in the last seven years.

Locking Up and Throwing Away the Key

Some 793 years ago in Runnymede, England, a very unhappy King John was forced by a group of barons to sign a document called the Magna Carta. Despite the passage of so many centuries since that June day, and notwithstanding the fact that no one save a devoted cartographer could find the "meadow that is called Runnymede" on a modern map, the notion of a Great Charter, clearly establishing rights of individuals and limiting the power of the governing authority, remains a central underpinning of Western civilization. These ideas also form the very basis of our own representative democracy; that is, until the administration of George W. Bush.

While many provisions in the Magna Carta dealt with parochial interests of barons that have little relevance today, such is not the case with paragraph 39: "No free man shall be seized or imprisoned, or stripped of his rights or possessions, or outlawed or exiled, or deprived of his standing in any other way, nor will we proceed with force against him, or send others to do so, except by the lawful judgment of his equals or by the law of the land." The eloquence, relevance, and importance of these words ring as loudly today as they did nearly eight hundred years ago.

This paragraph, reciting the inherent right of each person in a free society to be protected against incarceration or deprivation except by rule of law, was well known and clearly understood by our Founding Fathers as an underpinning of civilized society. The "Great Writ" of *habeas corpus*—whereby a person has a fundamental right to be brought before a court to determine the lawfulness of his or her detention or deprivation—is a vital element of liberty growing out of this paragraph in the Magna Carta. Its importance to the fledgling republic occupied many pages of debate and court decisions in those early years that defined our nation to the world as the "beacon of liberty." The Great Writ was considered a core element in the foundation of our republic.

So important was the writ of *habeas corpus* deemed by the Constitution's drafters that Article I expressly forbids the "Privilege of the Writ of Habeas Corpus" from being even temporarily suspended. Only if our country is invaded or faced with overt rebellion could the Congress move to suspend—not eliminate—the right of every person to be brought before a court if the government seeks to detain or otherwise imperil his or her freedom. The president is not granted that power at all. President Lincoln attempted to suspend the writ of *habeas corpus*, a move later determined by the Supreme Court to have been unconstitutional.

But times have changed. In 2007, Attorney General Alberto Gonzales told a Senate committee that "the Constitution doesn't say, 'Every individual in the United States or every citizen is hereby granted or assured the right to habeas.' It doesn't say that. It simply says the right of habeas corpus shall not be suspended . . ."[263]

In effect, Gonzales was telling the American people, *don't worry so much about* habeas corpus *because you don't really have that right under our Constitution anyway.* The Bush administration's chief law enforcement officer was treating one of

263 Bob Egelko, "Gonzales says the Constitution doesn't guarantee habeas corpus," *San Francisco Chronicle*, January 24, 2007.

the most sacred passages of the Constitution as if were a mere technicality, something that could be erased, perhaps, simply by Justice Department appointees writing another confidential memo to the White House. Gonzales's words stunned many Americans of all political stripes.

Sadly, Gonzales was simply verbalizing the Bush administration's tacit policy since 9/11.

Bush formally suspended *habeas corpus* on November 13, 2001, when he issued an order establishing military tribunals for the trial and potential execution of any person Bush has labeled an "enemy combatant." Bush dictated that people classified as enemy combatants "shall not be privileged to seek any remedy . . . directly or indirectly . . . in any court of the United States."[264] President Bush thereby effectively entitled himself to unlimited, unchecked power over anyone in the world that he accused of being a terrorist or terrorist supporter.

Bush defined an enemy combatant as a person whom the president has reason to believe is a current or former member of Al Qaeda, or someone who "has engaged in, aided or abetted, or conspired to commit, acts of international terrorism, or acts in preparation therefore, that have caused, threaten to cause, or have as their aim to cause, injury or adverse effects on the United States, its citizens, national security, foreign policy, or economy."[265]

Bush's order was not limited to terrorists who committed war crimes. Instead, it could sweep in people *suspected* of threatening to cause adverse effects on the US economy via alleged terrorist conspiracies—a potentially very expansive category. A Justice Department lawyer later told a federal judge that even a "little old lady in Switzerland" who sent a contribution to an Afghan orphanage could be seized as an enemy combatant if, unbeknownst to her, some of her donation was passed on to Al Qaeda.

---

264 The White House, "President Issues Military Order," Office of the Press Secretary, November 13, 2001. Accessed at http://www.whitehouse.gov/news/releases/2001/11/20011113-27.html.

265 "Military Order—Detention, Treatment, and Trial of Certain Non-Citizens in the War Against Terrorism," White House Office of the Press Secretary, November 13, 2001.

A few days after Bush issued his decree, I was the only Republican to join thirty-eight Democratic members of Congress in signing a letter to the president condemning his action. I was confounded in part because Bush's action was unnecessary. In every single case in modern history in which we have had to deal with acts of terrorism committed on our soil, our court system has proven itself fully adequate to address them.

As I explained on CNN's *Crossfire* on November 20, 2001, "What we are talking about here is suspending the rules of habeas corpus, suspending rules of trial by jury, suspending a whole range of civil liberties for crimes committed in this country, and that is something that we should not do lightly. It's a massive suspension of civil liberties in a way that has never been done before in our country. It is very, very serious."

Many of my Republican colleagues shrugged off concerns about the edict, since they claimed it would only apply to foreigners. But as I noted at the time, Bush's order could apply to people in the United States, since the Bill of Rights applies to all persons lawfully here in this country. I warned that Bush's action will likely set precedents that will come back to haunt us terribly. I was disappointed that so many of my conservative colleagues had forgotten all they seemed to learn during the Clinton years about the danger of arbitrary power. As Alexander Hamilton warned in the Federalist Papers, "The practice of arbitrary imprisonments, in all ages, is the favorite and most formidable instruments of tyranny."

Some of my concerns were vindicated in June 2002, when the government announced that Jose Padilla, an American citizen, had been arrested in Chicago, labeled an enemy combatant, and was being held in a military brig. The government continually changed its story on Padilla—he was supposedly on his way to set off a "dirty" nuclear device in a big city—and finally transferred him out of the military tribunal system into a real courtroom after years of tormenting him. A Florida jury—which was prevented from learning of allegations of Padilla's torture—convicted him on the equivalent of a terrorist *misdemeanor* last year.

The suspension of habeas corpus is the *de facto* ticket to absolute power. This has come out clearly time and again regarding the detainees held on American-controlled territory at the Guantanamo military base in Cuba. In a 2003 case over whether the detainees could be permitted to raise any challenge in a federal court, the Justice Department argued that US courts would have no right to interfere even if the Pentagon was summarily executing the detainees.

And, like everything else, this is not a power that is limited to foreigners in faraway lands. Steven Bradbury, head of the Justice Department's Office of Legal Counsel, told a closed session of the Senate Intelligence Committee in 2006 that Bush could order killings of suspected terrorists within the United States. And, as anyone who has followed the news the last few years knows, the Bush team has a long record of falsely accusing people of being terrorists.

In June 2006, the Supreme Court struck down Bush's system of military tribunals as unconstitutional. The Court also declared that the administration was dead wrong in claiming that the Geneva Conventions did not apply to detainees in the war on terror. The Court proclaimed, "The executive is bound to comply with the Rule of Law that prevails in this jurisdiction."[266]

The Bush administration responded by railroading the Military Commissions Act (MCA) through Congress just before the 2006 congressional elections. The MCA largely rubber-stamped the system of military tribunals the Supreme Court had just condemned. The MCA empowered the US president to designate anyone on earth as an enemy combatant and to keep that person locked up as long as the US government pleased, nullifying the *habeas corpus* provision of the Constitution and "turning back the clock 800 years," as Sen. Arlen Specter (R-PA) said (he voted for the bill anyway). While only foreigners can be tried before military tribunals, Americans accused of being enemy combatants can be detained indefinitely without charges and without appeal. Even though the Pentagon has effectively admitted that many of

---

266 Charles Lane, "High Court Rejects Detainee Tribunals," *The Washington Post*, June 30, 2006.

the people detained at Guantanamo were wrongfully seized and held, the MCA presumes that the president of the United States is both omniscient and always fair.

Unfortunately, this nation's leaders made little or no effort to educate the American people about the core constitutional principle that the government cannot be trusted to lock someone up and throw away the key while denying him a trial. Instead, this issue was demagogued shamelessly and repeatedly.

After the Military Commission Act was enacted, the National Republican Senatorial Committee denounced incumbent Democrats who voted against suspending *habeas corpus* for having "sided with trial lawyers and terrorists." After Bush signed the bill, a Republican National Committee press release was headlined, "Democrats Would Let Terrorists Free." Any failure to bow to the president's absolute power supposedly put all Americans in grave peril.

In June 2008, the Supreme Court, in the case of *Boumediene vs. Bush*, struck down the Military Commissions Act's tribunal regime as a violation of *habeas corpus*. The court declared, "The Framers viewed freedom from unlawful restraint as a fundamental precept of liberty, and they understood the writ of habeas corpus as a vital instrument to secure that freedom."[267] The court stressed the "Framers' inherent distrust of government power"—a welcome reminder in the post 9/11 time of blind submission to whatever Washington thinks is best. The court reminded Americans: "The laws and Constitution are designed to survive, and remain in force, in extraordinary times. Liberty and security can be reconciled; and in our system, they are reconciled within the framework of law."

This was one of the soundest and most important decisions the Court has made in a long time. It was a victory for all Americans more than any particular litigant, since it affirmed the duty of the executive branch to obey the law. The government's most fundamental duty is to respect and defend our liberties, and

---

267 Cornell University Law School, "Boumediene v. Bush," 476 F. 3d 981, reversed and remanded, Supreme Court Collection, June 12, 2008. Accessed at http://www.law.cornell.edu/supct/html/06-1195.ZO.html.

the executive branch must be held accountable for every new power that it acquires over the American people. It was a relief to see the Court quashing what clearly was one of the most breathtaking extensions of federal law enforcement power in our nation's history.

Unfortunately, the battle over *habeas corpus*—and the rule of law, generally—is far from finished. Much of the Washington political establishment will seek to find ways around the Court's decision, the same way it evaded the restraints the court sought to impose in its 2006 decision. For instance, Attorney General Michael Mukasey proposed in July 2008 that Congress allow the administration to evade the Supreme Court's ruling by formally declaring war against Al Qaeda.

Toture: Barbarism Doesn't Pay

As a teenager, I loved to read comic books. Superman comics were my favorite. Among the many challenges the Man of Steel faced (and always vanquished) was Bizarro World. In Bizarro World, everything was the opposite of that which prevailed in our world. Up was down, clean was dirty, black was white, good was bad . . . you get the picture.

Events of the past few years remind me more and more of Bizarro World, except now it is not a comic-book world; it is the real world. The effect of witnessing a federal government operating according to Bizarro World standards instead of those enshrined in our Constitution and legal system is truly frightening.

Nowhere is this Bizarro World standard clearer than in the contortions the Bush administration has followed regarding torture. Administration officials won't even discuss torture, preferring instead to talk about "enhanced interrogation techniques." Federal officials like the latter term because it is not defined in federal or international law ("enhanced interrogation" being essentially a made-up term), and therefore activities falling within its ambit are not—and cannot be—illegal.

The torture scandal resulted from the same notion of

absolute power that resulted in suspending *habeas corpus*. But the torture scandal provides far more graphic evidence of what happens when government unleashes itself.

The road to the torture scandal was paved by legal scams that continue to imperil Americans. In early 2002, Bush issued a ruling to prevent the War Crimes Act from applying to actions taken by US officials against Al Qaeda and the Taliban. The War Crimes Act, passed by Congress in 1996, applied to all Americans and defined war crimes in part as acts that would be "grave breaches" of the Geneva Conventions on the treatment of prisoners. Then-White House counsel Alberto Gonzales advised President Bush: "The nature of the new war places a high premium on other factors, such as the ability to quickly obtain information from captured terrorists and their sponsors in order to avoid further atrocities against American civilians. In my judgment, this new paradigm renders obsolete Geneva's strict limitations on questioning of enemy prisoners and renders quaint some of its provisions."[268] Bush decreed that the Al Qaeda and Taliban forces did not have protection under the Geneva Conventions.

Justice Department lawyers busied themselves creating legal pretexts for the president to ignore the federal Anti-Torture Act and the Geneva Conventions. A secret 2002 memo written by Justice Department official John Yoo proclaimed that "the President enjoys complete discretion in the exercise of his Commander-in-Chief authority and in conducting operations against hostile forces . . . we will not read a criminal statute as infringing on the President's ultimate authority in these areas."[269] Mr. Yoo has also opined, in another secret memo written in late 2001, that when the US military engages in domestic operations, it is not subject to the restraint of the Fourth Amendment. Alberto Gonzales has publicly declared that Bush had a "commander-in-chief override." Thus, the statute book no longer applied to the nation's Supreme Leader.

---

268 John Barry, Michael Hirsh and Michael Isikoff, "The Roots of Torture," *Newsweek*, May 24, 2004.

269 "Standards of Conduct for Interrogation under 18 U.S.C. §§ 23402340A" Department of Justice Office of Legal Counsel, August 1, 2002.

The torture memo effectively gave US interrogators a license to kill. The memo declared that the "necessity defense" could pre-absolve such fatalities because "the harm inflicted by necessity may include intentional homicide, so long as the harm avoided is greater (i.e., preventing more deaths) . . . Any harm that might occur during an interrogation would pale to insignificance compared to the harm avoided by preventing such an attack, which could take hundreds or thousands of lives."[270]

A confidential Pentagon memo on interrogation guidelines also stressed that "the necessity defense can justify the intentional killing of one person to save two others." And the memo— approved by the Pentagon's top lawyers—assured interrogators: "Sometimes the greater good for society will be accomplished by violating the literal language of the criminal law."[271] In other words, the end justifies the means.

In late 2002, the US interrogators at Guantanamo were given a special class on a chart showing "coercive management techniques," including semi-starvation, exploitation of wounds, sleep deprivation, prolonged constraint, and exposure. The chart specified that one goal of such methods was that it "reduces prisoner to 'animal level' concerns." The chart was lifted verbatim from a 1950s post-Korean War study entitled "Communist Attempts to Elicit False Confessions from Air Force Prisoners of War." The CIA also relied on Soviet, Egyptian, and Saudi intelligence models for devising their interrogation methods. Interrogation systems designed to compel victims to sign false confessions somehow provided the model for protecting America in the Age of Terror. The interrogators were not told that the model they were given consisted of methods the US government denounced as war crimes during and after the Korean war.

The same Supreme Court decision that struck down the military tribunal system also invalidated Bush's interrogation

---

270 Ibid.

271 Wayne R. LaFave and Austin W. Scott, Jr., *Substantive Criminal Law* § 5.4, at 629 (2d ed. 1986).

regime, since it declared that the detainees had rights that the US government must respect under the Geneva Conventions.

The Military Commissions Act responded by redefining torture, stating it must include a "substantial risk of death, extreme physical pain, a burn or physical disfigurement of a serious nature, not to include cuts, abrasions or bruises; or significant loss or impairment of the function of a bodily member, organ or mental faculty."[272] As political science professor Darius Rejali noted, "The new US legislation absurdly disqualifies as torture not just the enhanced interrogation techniques used by the CIA, but the vast majority of techniques used by torturers worldwide."[273]

The MCA pretty much allowed the president to do as he pleased. Yale law professor Jack Balkin wrote, "The President has created a new regime in which he is a law unto himself on issues of prisoner interrogations. He decides whether he has violated the laws, and he decides whether to prosecute the people he in turn urges to break the law."[274]

Perhaps the most shocking aspect of the Military Commission Act was its rubber-stamp for using coerced confessions in judicial proceedings. Evidence gained via coercion is admissible as long as a military judge deigns that the methods used did not, in his view, rise to the level of torture. But there was no reason to assume that the Pentagon's military commissions would use a more credible definition of torture than that employed by the Justice Department or the White House. This was clear in one of the first cases decided by the Guantanamo tribunals—that of Australian David Hicks. Hicks was sexually assaulted, isolated in the dark for more than two hundred days, forcibly kept awake for long periods, and psychologically tormented. Yet his "confession" was sufficient for the court the Pentagon created to judge him.

---

272 Darius Rejali, "How Torture Begets More Torture," *Slate*, October 27, 2006.

273 Ibid.

274 Jack Balkin, "Rights Against Torture—Without Remedies," *Balkinization*, October 17, 2006. Accessed at http://balkin.blogspot.com/2006/10/rights-against-torture-without.html

In October 2007, Americans learned that the Justice Department produced a secret legal opinion in 2005 permitting CIA interrogators to use combined effects on detainees, including head slapping, simulated drownings ("waterboarding"), frigid temperatures, manacling people for many hours in stress positions, and blasting them with loud music to assure sleep deprivation. *The New York Times*, which published the leaked memo, labeled it "expansive endorsement of the harshest interrogation techniques ever used by the Central Intelligence Agency."[275] The memo signaled that the Bush administration explicitly rejected the definition of torture that had been used by the US government for the prior century.

Torturing individuals by our government is not only morally repugnant—or at least it used to be—but is unlawful. However, perhaps like his predecessor Bill Clinton, who justified any of his actions that required explanation by reciting that, "it all depends on what the meaning of 'is' is," President Bush apparently believes torture is not torture if you simply modify the word with a benign adjective. Thus the Award for Creative Sophistry goes to the Bush administration for justifying the practice of waterboarding, in which a prisoner is drowned but just not to the point of death, by calling it simulated drowning.

Waterboarding as an interrogation technique thats has been employed for centuries as a tool with which to elicit information from prisoners. The fact that the technique often achieves the desired result even as it leaves no obvious, lasting physical evidence accounts for much of its popularity by practitioners, from the time of the Spanish Inquisition to Nazi Germany. Waterboarding causes excruciating physical pain as the immobilized victim's lungs fill with water. At the same time, the process inflicts profound psychological pain by creating the very real impression in the victim's mind that he faces imminent death by drowning. Waterboarding is, in essence, a torturer's best friend: easy, quick, and nonevidentiary. It had always been considered

---

275 Scott Shane, David Johnston, and James Risen, "Secret U.S. Endorsement of Severe Interrogation," *The New York Times*, October 4, 2007.

torture by civilized governments such as ours—until, of course, the administration of George W. Bush.

The fundamental value of waterboarding to an interrogator lies in the pain it inflicts and the fear of death by drowning it engenders. Why else would it be used? However, in typical Bizarro World fashion, the Bush administration refuses to concede that the technique even exists as torture. Although experts (and common sense) tell us that if not stopped in time, waterboarding will cause the death of a person subjected to it, the administration delights in referring to it as simulated drowning. The fact is, there is nothing simulated about the process of drowning by waterboarding and there is nothing simulated about the pain it causes. Waterboarding is just drowning that stops short of death (unless, of course, a mistake is made during its infliction).

Understandably, some of the US government interrogators were concerned that waterboarding might come to a bad ending for the victim. CIA counterterrorism lawyer Jonathan Fredman told Guantanamo interrogators in 2002, that "if the detainee dies, you're doing it wrong." But Fredman assured his audience that torture "is basically subject to perception."[276] And it was clear that the Bush administration was determined to see no torture.

In February 2008, White House spokesman Tony Fratto announced that the Justice Department had reviewed waterboarding and "made a determination that [waterboarding] under specific circumstances and with safeguards was lawful." Fratto said that the CIA was not currently waterboarding but that "we're not going to be able to speculate on what might be the case in the future."[277] The *Los Angeles Times* noted, "The White House position on the issue is in some ways consistent with its long-standing efforts to expand executive power and resist attempts by

276 Joby Warrick, "CIA Played Larger Role in Advising Pentagon," *The Washington Post*, June 18, 2008.

277 Greg Miller, "Waterboarding is Legal, White House Says," *The Los Angeles Times*, February 7, 2008.

Congress to rein in the president's authority."[278]

At that time, in early 2008, the Senate was on the verge of voting for legislation to prohibit waterboarding. Bush responded by explaining: "The reason I'm vetoing the bill—first of all, we have said that whatever we do . . . will be legal."[279] But it is legal only in the sense that the opponents of Bush's policies did not have enough votes to override his veto and compel him to obey the law.

Bush and other top officials have vehemently denied for years that the US government is using torture. ABC News revealed in April that Vice President Cheney and other top Bush administration officials would sit at the White House and decide exactly how Muslim detainees would be tortured. ABC noted: "The high-level discussions about these 'enhanced interrogation techniques' were so detailed . . . some of the interrogation sessions were almost choreographed—down to the number of times CIA agents could use a specific tactic." Even Attorney General John Ashcroft had qualms about the meetings, reportedly warning, "History will not judge this kindly."[280]

When Bush was asked about the ABC report, he said the top officials' involvement was not so startling. He explained: "I'm aware our national security team met on this issue. And I approved." Bush burnished his get-out-of-jail-free card: "We had legal opinions that enabled us to do it."[281] As long as Bush's appointees rubber-stamp the president commands, there is rule of law—at least in the view of the president and his apologists.

Aside from being illegal and immoral, torture doesn't work. That is why the FBI vigorously opposes such methods in its own interrogation. The Judicial Advocate Generals of the service branches vigorously opposed the "extreme interrogation methods"

---

278 Greg Miller, "Waterboarding is legal, White House says," *The Los Angeles Times*, February 7, 2008.

279 "Bush to veto Senate ban on waterboarding," Agence France Presse, February 14, 2008.

280 Scott Horton, "History Will Not Judge This Kindly," Harpers.org, April 9, 2008.

281 Jan Crawford Greenburg, "Bush Aware of Advisers' Interrogation Talks," ABC News, April 11, 2008.

championed by the White House and its political appointees. The dispute over interrogation policy was between lawyers and political hacks sitting around in the White House and the Pentagon —and the officers who have seen combat and who know that they are exposing American soldiers to the same methods that the US government sanctions.

Torture is sometimes justified by its proponents who say it saves lives by providing the surest way to get the evidence of a ticking time bomb. In fact, there are no good, verified examples of that from American experience. However, it was torture that produced evidence that spurred the American public to support Bush's rush to war against Iraq. The smoking gun linking Al Qaeda to Saddam Hussein came from an Al Qaeda operative captured in Afghanistan, Iban al Shakh Al Libby. Thousands of American soldiers died in part because of the exploitation of this false confession to justify attacking Iraq.

Torture continues costing American lives. In June, former Navy general counsel Alberto Mora told a Senate committee: "There are serving US flag-rank officers who maintain that the first and second identifiable causes of US combat deaths in Iraq—as judged by their effectiveness in recruiting insurgent fighters into combat—are, respectively the symbols of Abu Ghraib and Guantanamo."[282] After the fall of Saddam, the conflict in Iraq became a battle for the hearts and minds of the Iraqi people; US use of torture made a bad situation far worse.

Army Major General Antonio Taguba led one of the first investigations into US interrogation abuses at Abu Ghraib. As punishment for telling the truth about US government actions, however, the Pentagon forced Taguba to retire. Taguba recently declared, "There is no longer any doubt as to whether the current administration has committed war crimes. The only question that remains to be answered is whether those who ordered the use of torture will be held to account."[283]

---

282 Ibid.

283 Warren Stroebel, "General who probed Abu Ghraib says Bush officials committed war crimes," McClatchy News Service, June 19, 2008.

The use of torture will come back to haunt the United States in ways this administration apparently either doesn't realize or simply doesn't care about. This is not something of which we as Americans should be proud. While the extreme sophistry and word-gamesmanship practiced to a fine art by this administration might make a high school debating coach proud, it does great disservice to the notion that we exist in a society in which there are rules and norms of behavior with clarity and definitiveness and in which government agents as well as the citizenry are held to standards of behavior.

Conclusion

Absolute power imperils not only its direct victims, but all the citizens living under the government's sway. As Lord Acton warned more than a century ago, "power tends to corrupt and absolute power corrupts absolutely." Unless this nation speedily returns to its constitutional roots, the post-9/11 power grabs will reap a growing toll of our rights, liberties, and lives. As the Supreme Court declared in 1866, "No doctrine, involving more pernicious consequences, was ever invented by the wit of man than that any of [the Constitution's] provisions can be suspended during any of the great exigencies of government."[284]

---

284 "Hearing on the Treatment of Detainees in U.S. Custody," Senate Committee on Armed Services, Statement of Alberto J. Mora, June 17, 2008. Accessed at http://armed-services.senate.gov/statemnt/2008/June/Mora%2006-17-08.pdf.

FORWARD TO FREEDOM

Americans need to be coldly realistic with themselves about where this nation is going. Many conservatives were outraged at Bill Clinton's abuses, and many liberals have been indignant about George W. Bush's abuses.

But we must recognize that both major parties are trampling the law and grossly abusing government power when they get their hands on the controls. Americans cannot complacently assume that further chipping away of their freedom will happen at a pace sufficiently gradual to allow countersteps to be taken. With fear of terror supplanting common sense as the prevailing formulation for public policy in America in this first decade of the twenty-first century, and with neither of the two status quo parties serving as a counterbalance to the other, the erosion of freedom in American and the corresponding explosive growth in government power has reached the point at which it will soon become virtually impossible to reverse.

It is time for Americans to throw out the Robber Barons of Freedom ruling Washington.

The Libertarian Party is the only party that respects freedom across the board. Both the Republican and Democratic parties talk of freedom and of respect for the Constitution, but in fact, neither party consistently stands up for the freedoms they claim to cherish. A majority of Democrats in the Congress voted with the Bush administration to retroactively legalize its illegal surveillance of Americans' phone calls and e-mails.

Freedom is not something we should permit politicians to shave and splice and cut to their heart's content. Freedom is freedom—whether economic freedom or freedom to live the peaceful lifestyle of one's choice. Only the Libertarian Party stands for, and will deliver, that promise.

Break the Special Interest Stranglehold

We need to shatter the special interest stranglehold on Washington. The lobbyists have far more control over the details of legislation and the making of policy than do average Americans. Here are a few of the lobbies that must be shown the door way out of the corridors of power in the nation's capitol:

The banker/mortgage lobby: Fannie Mae, Freddie Mac, and other financial institutions have Congress at their beck and call. Politicians receive millions from the same institutions to which they later give billions of dollars in bailouts. The problem has only gotten worse since the Bush administration and the Federal Reserve began bailing out Wall Street entities and mortgage institutions in order to prop up stock and housing prices. The mortgage giants, the banks, and the Federal Reserve are conspiring not only against average American workers, but also against the value of the dollar, since they profit when tidal waves of new currency are cranked out to benefit political favorites.

The military contractor lobby: In his 1961 farewell address, President Dwight Eisenhower warned, "We must guard against the acquisition of unwarranted influence . . . by the military-industrial complex . . . We must never let the weight of this combination endanger our liberties or democratic processes."[285] Now some of the most powerful companies in the world are busily bankrolling politicians who seem to favor perpetual American warring abroad across the globe and, concurrently, pervasive surveillance of Americans and Americans' financial privacy domestically. We can no longer sacrifice either taxpayers or soldiers to underwrite this collusion.

The farm lobby: This lobby has been insuring that Washington sacrifices American taxpayers to farmers since the 1930s. Our farm policy has not made any sense for almost a century, and it is time for government to get out of the business of manipulating agricultural markets. The ethanol lobby has significantly compounded the damage from bad farm policies, resulting in rising domestic gas prices and soaring international

---

285 http://www.eisenhower.archives.gov/speeches/farewell_address.html

food prices. We owe it both to ourselves and to people around the world to end this mischief.

The American Association of Retired Persons: The AARP is an eight hundred–pound gorilla blocking any effort to liberate young Americans from onerous Social Security taxes. AARP wraps itself in a do-gooder image, but it is determined to continue sacrificing everyone to its members and government aid recipients.

Lobbies pushing for the US to meddle abroad are draining America's resources. There are coalitions of non-governmental organizations always willing to scoop up US government handouts to the United Nations. American banks who made foolish loans abroad vigorously advocate US government support for the World Bank and International Monetary Fund, which bail out deadbeat borrowers and enable them to repay the bankers. The American Israel Public Affairs Committee (AIPAC) is championing a US military attack on Iran to eliminate any distant threat the Iranian government might pose. Across the board, Americans must learn to be far more wary of groups pushing foreign agendas that will bleed American taxpayers or American soldiers.

Government employee lobbies have worked tirelessly to insure that Americans have no escape from government monopolies and government services. The teachers' unions, especially the National Education Association (NEA), fight tirelessly to prevent parents from having real choices for their children's education. We cannot expect the government to serve the people when government workers' organizations insure that taxpayers are sent to the back of the bus.

The Democratic Party and the Republican Party are perhaps the two largest unrecognized special interests in our nation's capital. The two parties have conspired both in Washington and in state capitols across the country to make sure Americans do not have a chance to vote for real change. Ballot access laws require third parties to spend much, if not most, of their resources each election getting on the ballot—which is an automatic privilege for the two major status quo parties.

Federal election laws and regulations are full of arcane

provisions that do nothing except impede Americans' ability to choose honest leaders who will respect the Constitution. The two parties worked together to enact the McCain-Feingold Bipartisan Campaign Reform Act of 2002. This act purports to clean up government but, in reality, it simply further entrenches incumbents and the two-party monopoly. Many congressmen, working in cahoots with state legislatures who gerrymander congressional districts, have practically guaranteed lifetime jobs. The McCain-Feingold act effectively bans most "issue advertisements" by private organizations on radio and television in the sixty days before a general election (there is a narrow loophole for Section 527 Committees). Congress created a new category—electioneering communication—and pretended that it had to forcibly intervene to protect voters against practically any communication that might make people think badly of their rulers. Justice Antonin Scalia, in a noble dissent to the Supreme Court 2003 decision upholding the law, bluntly warned that the McCain-Feingold law "cuts to the heart of what the First Amendment is meant to protect: the right to criticize the government."[286] It is not a fair election if politicians can both use people's tax dollars to pay for their own campaign promotions and also invoke federal law to stick a sock in critics' mouths.

We cannot trust the two parties that got us into this mess to magnanimously provide Americans with escape from the hole they dug. The two parties are unfit to fix the problems with the current political system. Only an outsider and an outside political party can do the job.

A free society must allow free political competition—not a system in which the two major parties are always rigging the rules and sharing the spoils.

---

286 http://www.supremecourtus.gov/opinions/03pdf/02–1674.pdf.

Immediate Action Required to Rescue Rights and Liberties

There is a solution. Following are my proposals for returning the United States to a Constitution-abiding state:

1. Impose an immediate freeze on federal discretionary spending (and then begin the process of *reducing* spending in upcoming fiscal year budgets). This will draw the line in the sand proving that the US Treasury will no longer be the plaything of Washington lobbies and special interests. Also, slash the budget of the White House itself by at least 10 percent to start. There are too many hangers-on in the West Wing and the East Wing. The example for time change and reduced government spending needs to start at the epicenter of government profligacy.

2. Appoint a commission to report on wasteful government— not just fraud, waste, and abuse in government, but wasteful government programs and agencies. The experts will judge federal programs by the standards of the Constitution. For each dubious program, they must ask: Is there constitutional authority for the expenditure, regulation, or agency? If the program has a constitutional basis, is that activity best conducted by the national government, or by states and localities? Assuming the program is constitutional and best provided at the federal level, is the specific initiative cost-effective? Any program that cannot answer affirmatively to these questions should find itself on the chopping block.

3. Appoint a Freedom Commission to find and expose government policies that violate the Constitution and unjustifiably violate the freedom and privacy of American citizens. It is vital that Americans learn how far government power has already stretched.

4. Immediately cease unconstitutional federal operations. From the warrantless wiretaps of Americans' phone calls by the National Security Agency to the wrongful seizures of innocent Americans' property by the Internal Revenue

Service. Executive orders must be issued to stop such abuses. The *habeas corpus* guarantees the Bush administration suspended in late 2001 must be restored, and torture must no longer be an instrument of government policy or action. The United States must once again honor its commitment to respect the Geneva Conventions.

5. Any legislation that clearly violates the Constitution must be vetoed. Congress in recent decades has routinely passed bills that obviously trampled the First Amendment guarantee of freedom of speech, the Fourth Amendment guarantee against warrantless unreasonable searches, and the Fifth Amendment protection of property rights. A president must honor his oath to uphold and protect the Constitution and guarantee that any such legislation will be struck dead as if it was hit by lightning in the Oval Office.

Opening the Books for Liberty

To make sure the statute book once again becomes the law of the land, the files and books on the actions of the past presidents must be opened. Presidential power has been stretched beyond reasonable limits in part because presidents assumed their successors would conceal their actions, the same way they shielded the actions of their predecessor.

It was President Jimmy Carter who first talked of the ideal of "government in the sunshine." However, in the subsequent almost thirty years since his term ended, there has been very little sunshine curative in Washington.

For decades, politicians and pundits have scorned those who did not trust Washington. Some criticisms of the federal government are simply wrong or misguided, and some of the conspiracy allegations are almost comical.

The best way to restore trust in government is to open the files and let the American people know what the government has done. For example, Americans must be allowed to learn what the government really did at Waco in 1993; what happened in the

White House and other agencies as part of the Clinton scandals in the mid-1990s; the real facts behind the "Pardongate" machinations in Clinton's final days. Americans must be privy to what happened behind closed doors in the Bush administration—from ginning up evidence to attack Iraq; to the directives to telecommunications companies to unlawfully reveal information on and access to communications of their customers; to working in cahoots with state education bureaucrats to fix test scores to create No Child Left Behind Act success stories. Americans must learn which congressmen and White House aides pulled the strings at the Internal Revenue Service to target specific individuals and nonprofit organizations for audits. Freedom of speech is a mirage if politicians can "send in the Revenuers" to punish their critics. We cannot put government back on a leash if we don't know what the government is doing and has done.

Of course, we must not reveal information that would directly threaten or undermine our national security. But previous presidents have used this pretext as a catchall to wrongfully deny American citizens vast amounts of information.

Protecting Americans Instead of Ruling the World

Before we seek to bring liberty to Baghdad, Pyongyang, or Tehran, we must once again guarantee and maintain it here at home. Before we engage in preemptive warfare abroad, we have to ensure that constant war will not strip us of our freedom at home. It is far more important for Americans to enjoy their God-given rights and liberties at home than for American politicians to swagger abroad.

In the short term, it is vital that the American people make it clear that they will not tolerate their government starting new wars. In August 2008, for example, some officials in the Bush administration seemed to be chomping at the bit to militarily confront Russia over Russia's response to the government of Georgia's unprovoked attack on separatist areas adjoining the Russia border. The US military is already stretched almost to the breaking point. If politicians drag us into another war (whether in

Georgia, Iran, or elsewhere), it is likely they will bring back military conscription to compel millions of young Americans to risk their lives.

We must abandon the notion of perpetual war against all potential terrorists everywhere. Instead, we must take action against those who have attacked the United States or are poised to do so. The first line of defense is sound foreign intelligence: gathering, analysis, dissemination, and use. There are indeed those individuals and entities who want to do us harm. But it is folly to assume that all so-called radicals and extremists pose deadly perils to America. The fact that some group dislikes the United States does not oblige us to track it down and kill its members. Sound intelligence and an emphasis on defense in our national defense strategy will result in a safer America, and an America once again respected by our friends and adversaries alike.

Forward to Freedom

American citizens themselves must return to the forgotten wisdom of their forefathers. Americans need a better attitude towards Washington. For too many decades, Americans have been taught to either view presidents as saviors or benign, rich parents. Neither one of these attitudes are fit for free citizens.

Americans must remember that rights are not something a generous government spoons out to a grateful people. Instead, rights existed before the government was created and they are inalienable, as Thomas Jefferson recognized in the Declaration of Independence.

We must recognize that we are all Americans first—not Republicans or Democrats. America can no longer afford (if it ever could at all) to place allegiance to party above principle. Our first loyalty must be to the Constitution—not to the standard-bearer of one of the two parties that are busy undermining the Constitution.

It is time to end the two-party monopoly that has dragged America down for too many decades. It is time for courageous political action to roll back political control of Americans' lives. It is time for the Libertarian solution.

Index

Printed in the United States
128595LV00005B/2/P